The Dark Wood of Hell
Romanesque capital from Autun.
Cathedral Museum, Autun, France

Front cover by Lillian Seddon Lozano©
after a panel representing the *Creation
and Fall of Adam and Eve*.
Cathedral of Modena, Italy

CARNAL KNOWLEDGE

Essays on the Flesh, Sex and Sexuality in Hispanic Letters and Film

Pamela Bacarisse, editor

Ediciones Tres Ríos
Pittsburgh

In memoriam: MANUEL PUIG, 1932-1990

CONTENTS

Preface 9

Symposium: Sex and Sexuality in Hispanic Film and Letters (Pittsburgh, April 1991). Original Program 13

Introduction 17
PAMELA BACARISSE
University of Pittsburgh

"What Does Cannibalism Speak? Jean de Léry and the Tupinamba Lesson" 23
SARA CASTRO-KLAREN
Johns Hopkins University

"La retórica de los celos: *Dom Casmurro*" 43
ALFRED MacADAM
Barnard College/Columbia University

"Will the Story Tell? Unamuno's *San Manuel Bueno, mártir*" ... 55
PAMELA BACARISSE
University of Pittsburgh

"Dalí's Oedipal Version: 'The Great Masturbator'" 73
JAVIER HERRERO
University of Virginia

"Contextos y sextextos en Octavio Paz" 83
PETER EARLE
University of Pennsylvania

"Buñuel and *Tristana*: Who Is Doing What To Whom" 91
PETER W. EVANS
University of Newcastle upon Tyne

CONTENTS

"La periferia del deseo: Julián Casal y el pederasta urbano" 99
ÓSCAR MONTERO
Lehman College, CUNY

"More Notes on the Presentation of Sexuality in the Modern Spanish American Novel" 113
DONALD L. SHAW
University of Virginia

"Escritura erótica: Cristina Peri Rossi y Tununa Mercado" 129
GABRIELA MORA
Rutgers University

"Desde afuera: asco y placer en la literatura latinoamericana" 141
ALICIA BORINSKY
Boston University

"Homosexual Desire in Goytisolo's *Señas de identidad*" 151
PAUL JULIAN SMITH
Cambridge University

"Back to the Suture: Patriarchal Discourse and Susana Thénon's *Ova completa*" 163
BERNARD McGUIRK
University of Nottingham

"La vanguardia a partir de sus exclusiones" 183
GEORGE YÚDICE
Hunter College, CUNY

"Staging the Pre-scription of Gender: Manuel Puig's *La traición de Rita Hayworth*" 199
SHARON MAGNARELLI
Albertus Magnus College

Interview with Manuel Puig (Rio de Janeiro, 10 August 1987) 217
PAMELA BACARISSE
University of Pittsburgh

Preface

An invitation to a group of friends from England, Spain, the United States and Latin America to take part in a two-day Symposium on Sex and Sexuality in Hispanic Film and Letters which would take place at the University of Pittsburgh in April of 1991 produced two surprises. The first, which could not have been more agreeable and which perhaps should not have surprised me, given the eternal fascination of the topic I had suggested, was their positive and enthusiastic response. Great efforts were made to fit the Symposium into busy schedules, and several of the contributors were prepared to travel very long distances, some even crossing the Atlantic, in order to be present. The guests of honor, the novelists Manuel Puig and Gustavo Sainz and the film director José Luis Borau, also accepted with alacrity.

The shocking and untimely death of Manuel Puig in July of 1990 came not only as a personal loss but also threatened to cast a pall over the whole event. Ultimately it was felt that the least we could do —indeed, all we could do— was to remember him with great affection, recall his previous visit to Pittsburgh and dedicate the Symposium to his memory. It is with an increasing awareness of how much he meant to me that now, three years after his death, I also dedicate this volume to him and, since it is so relevant to its theme, I have decided to incorporate in it a previously unpublished conversation we had in Rio de Janeiro in the summer of 1987.

My original intention for this volume had been to reproduce verbatim all the papers that were presented at the Symposium, but I have gradually discovered that it is not possible to do so. Many people wished to have the opportunity to revise, elaborate on, or even rehash, their original lectures: examples are Sara Castro-Klaren's "What does Cannibalism Speak? Jean de Léry and the Tupinamba" and Gabriela Mora's "Escritura erótica: Cristina Peri Rossi y Tununa Mercado", both of which have been considerably modified since their 1991 presentation. Then, for various reasons, the texts of some of the talks that contributed so much to the success of the occasion could not be used again. For instance, to my great regret, copyright problems prevent the reprinting of the ground-breaking paper, "El carnaval palatino de 'Sem'", given by Lee Fontanella (then of the University of Texas, now of Worcester Polytechnic Institute, Massachusetts), in which he showed and discussed the scabrous watercolors by the Bécquer brothers which form part of a collection he had discovered in the Madrid *Biblioteca Nacional*. And now, because of the amount of time that has passed since the Symposium took place, several of the papers have appeared elsewhere, but the versions in this collection have been amended and revised: these include Sharon Magnarelli's "Staging the Pre-scription of Gender: Manuel Puig's *La traición de Rita Hayworth*" and Alfred MacAdam's "La retórica de los celos: *Don Casmurro*". Finally, two of the articles —as well as the Puig interview— are entirely new: one is George Yúdice's "La vanguardia a partir de sus exclusiones", which replaces his beguilingly entitled paper, "Tacky Love Scenes", given at the Symposium; the other is my own piece on Unamuno's *San Manuel Bueno, mártir*, in which I consider what Gabriela Mora calls the enigma of female desire.

The other unexpected element of the Symposium was the orientation of the papers. Although I had hoped that these would cover all periods and more than one genre, I suspected that most emphasis would be placed on the openness with regard to sex and the newfound comprehension of sexuality that are manifest in post-Franco Spain and postmodern Latin America, and that there would be a strong tendency towards the consideration of contemporary works, authors and filmmakers. In fact, what emerged was evidence of contemporary critical approaches to the work of many different periods, stretching from the Columbus "Carta de Jamaica" (1503) to the most recent and explicit examples of narrative fiction and poetry. If there is any unity in this admittedly disparate collection, it is precisely because of the utilization of new critical visions that have been illuminated by the lifting of taboos and by the loosening of the stranglehold of *bienséance*.

I should like to record here my sincere gratitude to all those who worked so hard towards the success of the Symposium and the production of this collection of essays. In the first place, the Symposium could not have taken place without generous financial contributions from the University of Pittsburgh Center for International Studies, the Center for Latin American Studies, the University Honors College, the Cultural Studies Program, the Department of Film Studies and, of course, the Department of Hispanic Languages and Literatures. All of these were acknowledged, if not thanked, in the printed program of the event, but only now can the invaluable help of two later contributors also be recorded: these are the West European Studies Program and the College of Arts and Sciences.

Many other people made invaluable contributions and I should like to thank Connie Tomko, Sandi Mathews and Yolanda Castellano of the Department of Hispanic Languages and Literatures for all their efforts; Andrew McDuffie and Paul Mosey, who recorded and filmed the event; Bill Judson, Geralyn Huxley and Carol Sullivan of the Film and Video Section of The Carnegie Museum who solved all the problems that attended the showing of the José Luis Borau films; Ashley Jackson, of the University of Oregon, who provided a video cassette of Buñuel's *Tristana* when this had seemed to be unobtainable; Marta Perezpayá of The Arenas Group, Los Angeles, who was so helpful in locating and supplying copies of the Borau movies; and my colleagues Antonio Cornejo-Polar, Keith McDuffie and Carmen Rabell of the Department of Hispanic Languages and Literatures, and Patrizia Lombardo, Director of the Cultural Studies Program, who organized and chaired the various sessions. I should also like to acknowledge the willing and cheerful assistance of so many of our graduate students —in particular Michelle Ortuño and Samuel Gordon, who introduced the Plenary Lectures— and to reiterate my gratitude to all those who made the journey to Pittsburgh to participate in a memorable two days.

The existence of this book is in no small part due to the efficiency and skill of Erika Braga and Lillian Seddon Lozano of the *Instituto Internacional de Literatura Iberoamericana*, University of Pittsburgh, and I am deeply indebted to them both. But above all I want to record my appreciation of the calm, generous and unstinting support of Keith McDuffie, former Chair of the Department of Hispanic Languages and Literatures of the University of Pittsburgh, who has the gift of finding solutions for all problems.

PAMELA BACARISSE
Department of Hispanic Languages and Literatures
University of Pittsburgh

SYMPOSIUM:
SEX AND SEXUALITY IN HISPANIC FILM AND LETTERS

University of Pittsburgh
April 27, 28, 1991

In memory of Manuel Puig (1932-1990)

ORIGINAL PROGRAM

Films shown previously at The Carnegie Museum

    Furtivos (José Luis Borau, 1975)

    Mi querida señorita (produced by José Luis Borau, directed by Jaime de Armiñán, 1972)

Sessions

Chair: Keith McDuffie	*Chair: Antonio Cornejo-Polar*
"Contextos y sextextos en Octavio Paz"	"El cuerpo de la antropofagía: dentro del Doctor Chanca, Léry y *Como era gostoso o meu francês*
Peter Earle (University of Pennsylvania)	Sara Castro-Klaren (Johns Hopkins University)
"Dalí's 'The Great Masturbator': Subversion and Unreality"	"Paternalismo y supresión de la sexualidad en la literatura puertorriqueña contemporánea"
Javier Herrero (University of Virginia)	Juan Gelpí (Tulane University)

"Desde afuera: asco y placer en la literatura latinoamericana"	"Abierta y problemática sexualidad en *Solitario de amor* de Cristina Peri Rossi"
Alicia Borinsky (Boston University)	Gabriela Mora (Rutgers University)
Chair: Keith McDuffie	*Chair: Pamela Bacarisse*
"Homosexual Desire in Goytisolo's Trilogy of Treason"	"Machado de Assis and the Esthetics of Jealousy"
Paul Julian Smith (University of London)	Alfred MacAdam (Barnard College/Columbia University)
"Tacky Love Scenes"	"El carnaval palatino de 'Sem'"
George Yúdice (Hunter College, CUNY)	Lee Fontanella (University of Texas at Austin)

Plenary Lecture

   Chair: Michelle Ortuño   "El cine español actual"
                                                  José Luis Borau

Film

   Río abajo (José Luis Borau, 1984)

Chair: Patrizia Lombardo	*Chair: Pamela Bacarisse*
"Pre-scribing Gender in Puig's *La traición de Rita Hayworth*"	"Pre-Post-Eros: on Reading Love Poetry before and after Theory"
Sharon Magnarelli (Albertus Magnus College)	Bernard McGuirk (University of Nottingham)

"Reading the Closet: Gay and Lesbian Figurations in Latin American Literature"

Sylvia Molloy
(New York University)

"More Notes on Sexuality in Contemporary Latin American Fiction"

Donald L. Shaw
(University of Virginia)

"Peripheral Desires: Julián del Casal and the Urban Pederast"

Óscar Montero
(Lehman College, CUNY)

"Buñuel and *Tristana*: Who's Doing What to Whom?"

Peter W. Evans
(University of Newcastle upon Tyne)

Round Table

Chair: Carmen Rabell

José Luis Borau, Alicia Borinsky, Gustavo Sainz, Donald L. Shaw, George Yúdice

Plenary Lecture

Chair: Samuel Gordon

"Transgresión y complacencia en las representaciones eróticas de la literatura mexicana"

Gustavo Sainz

Film

Tata mía (José Luis Borau, 1986)

INTRODUCTION

If there is one single thing that both contemporary Hispanic writing and current literary analysis of Hispanic works can confidently be said to have acquired —something positive, that is, as opposed to the cloudy, discomfiting and uncomfortable ambivalence of a postmodern world into which criticism, at least, has (understandably, though unjustifiably) been reluctant to venture— it is uninhibited curiosity regarding corners of human existence and motivation hitherto considered taboo, especially those concerned with sex and sexuality.

This cannot fail to produce a vision that is much more broadly based (though less assured) and, it has to be said, eminently more sensible than those which resulted from the study of a limited set of externals: visible social and political structures and behaviour (without considering psychological foundations), social *mores* and tyrannical religious precepts. However, there is also a risk of critical descent to a cold, clinical level of investigation which, I suggest, is misleading. It is also almost certainly counterproductive if a profounder understanding is a basic critical goal. If, for example, and as Manuel Puig claimed in our 1987 discussion (219), it is true, or even partly true, that sexual oppression is the root of all other types of oppression, it scarcely needs underlining that this must be the result of a force that is irresistibly powerful, one that can change lives, destroy people, cement relationships, dictate the nature of individual personalities and give rise to complex power structures, social hierarchies and religious morphologies. It can lead to amazing behaviour, to mendacity, duplicity and cruelty, which will then be justified or rationalized in non-sexual terms.

The impact of the sex drive and of sexuality has always been overwhelming, and it is as pointless and fatuous a practice to indulge in the passionless demystification process that the present anything-goes acceptability of the subject encourages as it previously was to overlook it at the various levels of life and society represented in literature and film. However strongly Manuel Puig might have argued that there is, or should be, nothing special about sex ("just an activity of the vegetative [?] life [...] like eating and sleeping [...], devoid of moral meaning", 219), I would argue that it is *not* merely one of several areas still waiting to be explored. Furthermore, as far as Puig was concerned, this opinion was a typical symptom of his ambivalence, since for him the opposite was also true.[1] This point is made implicitly in the present collection of essays by Gabriela Mora (132), who points out that although eroticism —unlike pornography— is at last beginning to be judged natural and healthy in the contexts of Hispanic literature and Hispanic literary criticism —even now it is rare to come across it as a central narrative/poetic or investigative theme. There is, we are currently supposed to think, little real excitement in the sexual: it is no longer *verboten* but a serious, and intellectually respectable, service topic. It should not have been ignored for so long, in spite of the social and religious strictures in Spain and Latin America, but, for heaven's sake, it cannot be thought the be-all-and-end-all of a basis for analysis or criticism or even of a fictional or poetic text or a film. It is fashionable for even flamboyantly postmodern critics to point out that pornography is "boring", for example (though no-one, as far as I know —and Gabriela Mora also elaborates on this point— has yet set up any ground rules for the disposition of the exaggeration and repetition that comprise it, far less dictated that its powers of titillation should or must follow rules of literary/stylistic *bienséance*). Indeed, what was left unsaid, often being indicated merely by asterisks, in nineteenth century novels and what was implied in the reactions of their exegetes, may have been more accurately mimetic, revealing and exciting than the current critical assumption that there is no more interest in human sexuality than, say, in pigeon fancying. They are both, after all, stimulating and life-enhancing elements of everyday life.

My task in introducing a group of essays that, inevitably, are heterogeneous and individualistically focused is not without problems. The principal difficulty arises when an attempt is made to link them in a fruitful way, to underline what it is they may have in common, even though they deal with texts from different periods and different countries, written in different languages (like the articles themselves), or even with different *genres*: Peter Evans writes about the cinema;

---

[1] I have drawn attention to Manuel Puig's ambivalence elsewhere, attempting to demonstrate that, among its other implications, it suggests postmodern uncertainty. It is worth repeating, though, that the confused ideology that can be gleaned from his novels and plays is very different from the clearcut, but possibly ephemeral, views he often expressed in interviews. His approach to these, though entirely serious, was self-conscious and analytical. Before we recorded the interview included here (in English because it was intended for the British newspaper, *The Guardian*), he said he wanted to try out a new theory that had just occurred to him. It is hard to avoid the suspicion that this consoling theory served to reconcile two mutually incompatible concepts in his mind: that of (homosexual) promiscuity and that of single-minded, romantic fidelity.

INTRODUCTION

Sara Castro-Klaren is stimulated by a Columbus letter; Bernard McGuirk deals with contemporary Argentine poetry and Peter Earle with establishing a poetics of a poetic *corpus*, while Javier Herrero's field of interest is constituted by two paintings by Salvador Dalí. Alfred MacAdam, Paul Julian Smith, Sharon Magnarelli and Alicia Borinsky concentrate on various aspects of the novel; George Yúdice and Donald Shaw on what is revealed by literary historiography and Óscar Montero on the relationship between a life, a reputation and a social context. Gabriela Mora reflects on an unusual contemporary novel[2] and a collection of odd pieces (essays, poetic prose and short stories); I myself am concerned with a *novella* that, in spite of its relatively recent appearance, has become a kind of classic within the canon of Spanish literature and which I felt was a good example of a text whose sexual implications have been largely ignored. *Can* all these be connected in some way? It is a particularly daunting task given the different levels of criticism involved. There is the philosophical approach, for example —Alfred MacAdam's essay on Machado de Assis, the concept of jealousy and the question of the author's intentions, rhetoric and, ultimately, his classification —versus (or side by side with) an exercise in deconstruction— Bernard McGuirk's detailed Derridean dissection of Susana Thénon's language. Then we have Peter Evans' Freudian interpretation of *Tristana*, which might be judged a strange bedfellow (if this expression may be permitted) for Óscar Montero's reconstruction of the gay scene in *fin-de-siècle* Havana and present-day New York.

Of course, the establishment of (possibly imagined) unity is an arbitrarily chosen and perhaps unnecessary aim. In a postmodern age, no editor should feel embarrassed by the discovery that an anthology of invited essays appears to contain few common elements, even though everyone is exercised by the same given topic. However, in the case of *Carnal Knowledge*, it is my contention that in fact there is much that links one piece to the next, and that these linking threads are of significance in the history of Hispanic writing and criticism.

The, for me, principal link is actually constituted by the incontrovertible fact that for very many of these commentators the sexual element, or the role of sexuality, is indeed the central theme of their investigation —not just *one* motivating force, but *the* motivating force, *the* foundation of action, attitude and language.[3] Under the general heading of *desengaño* —a sophisticated, twentieth century, post-Freudian version of this phenomenon— we are beginning to discover that things are not what they seem (perhaps this awareness could be seen as the

---

[2] "Unusual" in its emphasis on sex as a central theme.
[3] Needless to say, I would exempt Alfred MacAdam's article on *Dom Casmurro* from this generalization; indeed, he argues that the text is not a study of sexual jealousy and its lamentable outcome, but that it is, rather, a satirist's collection of rhetorical techniques.

second characteristic that these textual/sexual analyses may share) —and that underneath, the apparently unrelated force is sexual. At the risk of being accused of reductionism, I contend that what lies beneath the surface is desire, which, without the predicate of an immutable, achievable, once-and-for-all object, is the life force, a pivot of power, a handy —indeed, unavoidable— survival kit.

The phenomenon can be located in what would hitherto have been judged the strangest places. Until recently few have connected the sociopolitical element of the discovery/conquest/investigation of the New World with the eternally relevant pressures of the carnal and its ramifications. Yet that is precisely what Sara Castro-Klaren does in an article of, in my view, great brilliance. Of course she is not alone in having seen through the establishment, colonialist view of the events of the 15th and 16th centuries and their protagonists' reactions to these, but her emphasis on the threatening carnal and sexual incomprehensibility of the Other innovatively highlights (male) human registers that were —but, more importantly, *are*— "forgotten, repressed or momentarily disallowed" (24). Of course the natives are exploited. Of course females are abused. Of course the Indians are cannibals. Everyone knows that. What we are only beginning to understand is how our own sexuality causes us to *produce* (to borrow Sara Castro-Klaren's term) the truth of the Other and how relevant this perception is to the analysis of world history. In this case it obliges us to reconsider the whole period and its communal psychology. It might be argued that if sexual motivation is all-important, then things are at least explicable, and therefore might not be judged as bad as all that. In fact, it is depressing to conclude that the atemporal universality of the motivation of the 16th century "masters of the codes" (27) indicates that they were worse.

Obviously, the combination of a newfound critical emphasis on desire as an autonomous and fundamental power and a revisionist awareness of the deceptive, even wilfully deceitful, nature of some traditional analysis cannot fail to lead to the discovery and uncovering of areas that were previously not merely taboo but also —and this, of course, was partly because they were taboo— uncomprehended.[4] It would be arrogant to claim that criticism has made dramatic progress in these

---

Nevertheless, my own piece on *San Manuel Bueno, mártir* should be included: although the ontological theme is textually present, it is only by referring to the narrator's sexual motivation that this can be adequately illuminated.

[4] In Peter Earle's essay on the *sextextos* of Octavio Paz, he laments the absence of the word "love" in the title of the original Pittsburgh Symposium. In spite of the difference between the make-up of the papers given on that occasion and the essays included in this volume, this is still the case. The reason is that the subject of love has never been taboo. Even in mediaeval condemnations of *loco amor*, its peculiarities were explicitly described and the topic was universally aired. Our approach may have changed, but when we consider love we are not examining a vital topic for what amounts to the first time.

ancient, but novel, contexts, but it is important to point out that it would be even more foolhardy to suggest that any clarification of the topics that may have been achieved is therapeutic. In the same way that greater understanding of the motives of the *conquistadores* and explorers of the 16th century is less than consoling (other than on an intellectual level), so any exploration of desire and its manifestations and ramifications may, I suggest, be judged pure research. The present collection, in spite of its brevity, deals with a vast number of subjects: homosexuality, incest, masturbation, *jouissance*, pornography, exhibitionism, voyeurism, sodomy and prostitution. The concepts of cannibalism, of castration, of the *femme fatale*, and of female pleasure. What appears to be —but perhaps isn't— the object of desire (a kind of *méconnaissance*), emotions related to sexuality that might be classified as diseases, the idea of creating identity around sexuality, the link between sex(uality) and society (particularly its political aspect and political systems). Hierarchies, marginalization and even nationhood. Theatricality, morality and the practice of confession, punishment, gender models and the role of women. And on top of all this, there is reference to the theories of Freud, Lacan, Kristeva, Hocquenghem, Weeks, Deleuze, Guattari and Foucault, among others. It is incontrovertible that virtually none of this would have been discussed with such frankness, or indeed percipience, fifty years ago,[5] and the consideration of the sex drive as the principal motor in human life indubitably constitutes a major shift in critical emphasis —perhaps one of the most important shifts in Hispanic critical history. But this sensible "answer" to questions that could not even be asked until fairly recently actually resolves very little, perhaps nothing. Human sexuality may well be the profoundest of mysteries, and, like all worthwhile mysteries, it is a provocative, exciting, beguiling and engaging topic. But —and this is its most marvellous aspect— it is ultimately inexplicable. Thus we have the best of both worlds: combined with the *jouissance* of intellectual investigation and discussion (with the possible bonus of at least some social improvement as obfuscation is lessened) we can go on contemplating, and being thrilled by, the ineffable.

---

[5] Peninsular Hispanic criticism has always been particularly prudish and shortsighted. No-one who was in the field at that time will ever forget the shock/horror that greeted Schonberg's 1956 revelations of García Lorca's homosexuality. And, when editing a journal more than twenty years ago, I personally recall a learned assessor's paroxysms of outrage in the face of an article submitted by a young graduate student that dealt with transvestism and gender roles in Lope de Vega.

What does Cannibalism Speak? Jean de Léry and the Tupinamba Lesson

SARA CASTRO-KLAREN

In December of 1503 Columbus wrote of his disastrous year in Jamaica. The European mariner chronicled his desperate exploration of the greater Caribbean in what is known today as the "Carta de Jamaica". This text constitutes his account of his fourth and last voyage to this continent. In this last attempt to locate the ever elusive gold of his desire Columbus spent roughly two years (1502-1504). He battled the fury of tropical storms, the sheer enormity of the world he had accidentally encountered and the immense challenge that the unforeseen difference of this world posed for him and his fellow travelers. Not only was Columbus lost, in as much as his portolano and mystical cartography[1] proved insufficient, but he was ill and exhausted. The public persona of the mariner gives way, in this text of 1503, to a man who freely writes of his private physical and spiritual suffering in the face of the unearthly obstacles blocking his way to Hangchow or Quinsay. It is indeed hard to resist sharing Columbus' point of view when he tells the story of his calamities:

> Así a gatas me llegué a Jamaica ... De allí navegué a tierra firme, donde me salió el viento y corriente terrible al opósito: Combatí con ellos setenta días ... en todo este tiempo no encontré puerto ... ni me dejó tormenta del cielo, agua y trombones y relámpagos de continuo que parecía el fin del mundo ... La gente deseaba la muerte y yo con fiebre.[2]

Here Columbus has indeed reached the outer limits of his endurance. He and his men have finally accepted the idea that they are lost. And they are lost because the

---

[1] Margarita Zamora provides a thorough discussion of Columbus' use of the technology of portolano sailing charts and his gradual shift to the mystical maps which at the time of the Crusades placed Jerusalem at the center of the "earth" in "Inventing the Discovery: Map/Journey/Text", lecture given at the Johns Hopkins University, Baltimore (1 April 1992).
[2] Martín Fernández de Navarrete, editor, *Viajes de Colón* (Mexico City: Porrúa, 1986), 292-294.

storehouse of knowledge which had thus far sustained them in search of their desire has simply been exhausted. Nothing makes sense now. Neither the idea of Cathay, nor the supposition of Atlantis, nor the lost memories of a Biblical paradise seems verifiable. At this moment of exhaustion death is wished for as the only possible escape from a world which evades and resists interpretation —cartographic, nautical, mystical, economic, etc. At this point the space of the letter should have been overtaken by a silence corresponding to Columbus' retreat from the Caribbean. However, the letter, like the voyage, proceeds. Further discursivity is made possible by reaching into existing, but forgotten, repressed or momentarily disallowed, registers. These paths of meaning making will be brought forth to articulate the no-sense of present experience.

The death scene quoted above will be subsequently reinscribed by means of a process of substitution in which the waters of the Caribbean storm are changed into the fire and blood of a Dantesque hell. It is as if Columbus, having passed through death, found himself already in hell, in another world. The earlier placid waters of Jamaica thus become a "sea of boiling blood". The sky itself burns like a blacksmith's furnace. "Ardió como forno" (294) writes the Mediterranean explorer, aware, no doubt, of the etymological common root shared by the Spanish "infierno" and the Italian "forno".

As could be expected, Columbus' descent into hell is not unmotivated. Christ presides at the center of the metaphor. Descent into the underworld is a mere teleological preamble. Reporting himself spent and feverish, with no greater desire than to survive the night, sore and moaning from pain and fatigue, the body and soul in hell hear a compassionate voice ("voz piadosa"). This voice redirects the mariner's scriptural context from the earthly concerns of cartography to the holy Hebrew scriptures. There, the voice assures him, he will find the necessary knowledge to survive the night and to interpret the resisting reality of diurnal objects and events. In Columbus' dream, the voice reminds him of God's compassion for Moses and David when they found their faith and resolve small and weak. Further, the Captain of the expedition is reprimanded into remembering that the Indies were promised to him by God himself (295). Stirred to emulate Moses leading the Jewish people out of slavery in Egypt and David's defeat of Goliath, the Columbian discursive enterprise reaches further and further into registers which portray the opposing other as demoniacal evil or monstrously inhuman. This is the opening which the compassionate voice clears as the starting point for further discursivity.

As he passes through and out of hell he is led from silence into speech. The dream sequence fades out and the subject returns to the "real" world. Overnight, order and sense become possible again. The weather also changes. The hellish storm turns into a fair breeze and Columbus sets sail for "home" again: "Volví a mi camino" (266).

The allegorical structure of the Jamaica letter which allows Columbus to report events of consciousness in juxtaposition with events in the journey holds throughout the entire text. Immediately after having found his way and feeling restored to power in Jamaica, he continues his report to his masters by introducing a commonplace scene in Europe's recent experience of conquest and expansion. He suggests an image of himself as if he were a great lord receiving the opulent gifts of his very rich and newly-conquered vassals. But the Jamaica "court scene" turns out to be quite different. In fact, it is so different that the court scene on which it is modeled is effaced in light of the gift given to Columbus. In complete reversal, Columbus opens the scene by *returning* a rare, and yet common, native gift. It appears that the local chief has sent him two "women". Irate and offended, the Admiral denounces and rejects the gift on the grounds that he suspects those two females of being whores. The naïve reader could think that certifiable virginity could make the gift acceptable and thus dispel the implicit violence of the rejection. But such an assumption would be a misreading of Columbus and of the place women occupy in this constellation of signs. Columbus adds that the ages of the "women" are seven and eleven. At that juncture he writes that he suspects the girls/gift of witchcraft. This last charge stands as his essential reason for rejecting the gift.

This sequence of scenes —hellish storm, fever, voices, return to land, native gift— represents the compressed narrative of nine months (September 1502-June 1503) of wandering in the Caribbean. Both the nature of the series and the conflation of time and experience into this strange series allow the reader to examine the terms of displacement by which the original inhabitants of the area —Tainos, Caribs, Arawak— and, by extension, all the native inhabitants of his hemisphere were constructed into creatures whose ferocity and lasciviousness bordered on what Europe had already elaborated as the bestial other.

In the otherwise incongruous contiguity of these scenes from Jamaica we can read the logic of an Imaginary by which Columbus, the Queen, the Pope *et al* choose to believe the visions of anthropophagy rather than the ocular report and logic of Las Casas. Not only was it desirably necessary, at the time, to weigh the truth value on the side of the unconfirmed "sightings" of anthropophagy among the Caribs in order to justify enslavement and dispossession, as Peter Hulme has shown in *Colonial Encounters*,[3] but as late as 1556, when Jean de Léry sailed for Brazil, the register of

---

[3] See Carl Ortwin Sauer, *The Early Spanish Main* (Berkeley: University of California Press, 1966). Also see Peter Hulme, *Colonial Encounters. Europe and the Native Caribbean, 1492-1797* (London & New York: Methuen, 1986), especially Chapter 1. In this regard Kirkpatrick Sale writes that the bestialization of the native Caribbean "was not only a cynical device-of-empire to denigrate the Indian into Savage Beast [but also] it was, in a still deeper sense, a response to the unresolved burden of guilt that was an inherent part of the cast-from-Eden mythology of Christianity". See Kirkpatrick Sale, *The Conquest of Paradise. Christopher Columbus and the Columbian Legacy* (New York: Knopf, 1990), 203.

the "monstrous", activated and disseminated by Gonzalo Fernández de Oviedo's *Sumario*,[4] continued to motivate the "observations" made upon the Tupinamba in the bay of Guanabara. In this analysis of the little whores in the Columbus letter from Jamaica and the flesh-devouring beauties in Léry's *History of a Voyage to the Land of Brazil Otherwise Called America* (1578),[5] I shall show how anthropophagy and the orgies observed among the Caribs and the Tupi speak, as they construct the "savage", of the dark night of the soul of the subject. In the face of the other as part of the Real, the subject displays hidden and repressed registers of a hegemonic discourse which by the very virtue of its hegemony —true unless proven false— produces the truth of the other. Because in these texts anthropophagy is consistently depicted in conjunction with excessive or boundless female appetites —sexual, alimentary and bellicose— one can argue that in the construction of the Amerindian as savage and as the transgressor of norms newly embraced by European consciousness, the Amerindian "orgy" ascends, like the moon, as the sign of a resuscitating female principle long put to rest by the symbolic order of European identity.

* * *

As we return to the scene in which a righteous and restored Columbus rejects the Indian gift, we can point to the series of transgressions that flow from the polluting presence of the two girls. Columbus uses the arrival of the two girls to build his gesture into a scene of temptation overcome. He, unlike Adam, will not fall from God-given order by accepting a poisonous (sexual) gift. The naked girls are offered as gifts to

---

[4] Gonzalo Fernández de Oviedo (1478-1557), *Sumario de la natural historia de las Indias* (1526). See also the expanded version, *Historia natural y general de las Indias* (1526-1549). Oviedo has been much praised for writing as an eye-witness. This was his own contention to truth. However, when it came to seeing the inhabitants of this hemisphere, Oviedo turns out to be one of the blindest of men. Though he accepted the notion that the Indians had souls, he nevertheless felt that their souls —not being Christian— were ugly, and that such ugliness was reflected in their countenances. Oviedo is indeed the architect of the ugly and the repellent "savage". Anderson Imbert's summary of Oviedo still holds: "Y la fealdad de las almas se convertía en fealdad de los cuerpos. Es decir, que la inferioridad espiritual, de origen histórico, se convertía en inferioridad material, de origen étnico ... Entretanto los indios deben pagar su idolatría ... Son hombres viciosos, supersticiosos, ingratos, falsos, perezosos y estúpidos ... Ellos son culpables de su propia destrucción". Enrique Anderson Imbert, *Historia de la literatura hispanoamericana*, 2 vols. (Mexico City: Fondo de Cultura Económica, 1954), I, 29.

[5] Jean de Léry, *Histoire d'un Voyage fait en la terre du Brésil autrement dite Amérique* (Geneva, 1578). I will be quoting from *History of a Voyage to the Land of Brazil, Otherwise Called America*, translated by Janet Whatley (Berkeley: University of California Press, 1990).

gratify the well-known sexual appetites of the Caribbean explorers. The nakedness of the girls' bodies is made even more enticing, and thus transgressive, by the gold that they wear. These two pleasures had been taken freely since the earliest days of contact. What is different about this occasion is both the age of the girls and the deliberate formality of the occasion. Accepting publicly, as the case would have been in a true court *there*, in Europe, the gift of sexual intercourse with the girls, would turn Columbus and his men into rapists. The mariner rejects the gift, without regard for the girls and in full regard of an official denial of the truth of their raiding of local men (slaves) and women (sexual objects).

Instead of investing his feeling with pity for the girls, he projects upon them horrifying powers. He does not write that the older one must have been eleven. He writers that the older of the two old women ("la más vieja") must have been eleven. With this slip the two girls are transformed into two overdecorated old whores, who, in keeping with the unstable status of prostitution, conceal bewitching powders. Here, the feared figure of the European witch displaces the faint image of the two girls. The terror of the girls, as they are brought to ship and face all those strange, filthy and bearded men, is pushed under by the subject's own terror of the transaction being proposed by the gift from the local chief. What the reader is given to feel is the fear of a righteous man called Columbus who truly believes that he and his men have been bewitched by an evil so great and so resourceful as to masquerade in the guise of their own two most powerful objects of desire: gold and female bodies. It is not Europe which transgresses with the land or possessions of the Indians. It is they who transgress by daring to assume that gifts, that is women, can be exchanged, as if there were a symmetry between invaders and locals. Columbus rejects the idea, for the gold, the land or the women can be, as they have already been, taken wherever found. Accepting the gift would confer upon the local chief a status which Columbus and the generalized colonial discourse which he inaugurates seek to deny.[6] Only the subject of colonial discourse can initiate exchanges. The locals' role is to remain passive, to be read, that is to say to be produced by the needs of the master of the codes.

---

[6] Peter Hulme, in *Colonial Encounters*, defines colonial discourse as "an ensemble of linguistically-based practices unified by their common deployment in the management of colonial relationships, an ensemble that could combine the most formulaic and bureaucratic of official documents ... with the most non-fictional and unprepossessing of Romantic novels ... Colonial discourse is the presumption that during the colonial period large parts of the non-European world were *produced* for Europe through a discourse that imbricated sets of question and assumptions, methods of procedure and analysis, and kinds of writing and imagery, normally separated out into the areas of military strategy, political order, social reform, imaginative literature, personal memoir and so on" (2).

As we read the encoding of colonial discourse it is apparent that the gift of the girls acquires a fuller context if we find the series where it belongs. The girls are inscribed in a series of noxious, polluting and poisonous contacts. In a chain worthy of Herodotus and his elaboration of the Greek city as subject and the surrounding wilderness as object,[7] Columbus places next to the scene of the girls-witches two other equally strange and seemingly discontinuous scenes: American fauna and anthropophagi. It is as if the memory of the girls precipitated the writing of the two other encounters with that which is not *imago*. All three instances are framed within the gnostic uncertainty that envelops the entire letter, itself the point of insertion for the teratologic archive.[8]

On the one hand Columbus quotes from his men's belief that they are lost because they have been bewitched. On the other hand, he laments not having appropriate interpreters who might facilitate his unraveling of the secrets of this unknown world. He feels literally tongued-tied ("por falta de lengua") but he does not give up trying to read the profound heterogeneity facing him. In order to do so he projects upon the Caribbean the very status that he feared has enveloped them: bewitchment or enchantment. However, in rendering the location and its peoples readable to the logic of bewitchment, in a reversal of the subject-object relation and position, it is he who casts the spell upon them.[9] Having descended into the pre-linguistic stage of the Imaginary—"without language"—Columbus recovers into the Symbolic Order and

---

[7] Again, Peter Hulme writes that "the discourse of savagery had in fact changed little since Herodotus' investigation of Greece's 'barbarian' neighbors". This discourse was hegemonic in the sense that it "provided a popular vocabulary for constituting otherness and was not dependent on *textual* reproduction" (21). See in Herodotus' *History*, the Fourth Book, entitled "Melpomene". It deals with his investigation of the wandering Scythians. Of the Issedonians Herodotus writes that: "When a man dies, all the near relatives bring sheep to the house; which are sacrificed, and their flesh cut into pieces, while at the same time the dead body undergoes the same treatment. The two sorts of flesh are afterwards mixed together, and the whole is served up at a banquet". See *The History of Herodotus*, translated by George Rawlinson, in Robert Maynard Hutchins, editor, *Great Books of the Western World* 6 (London: Encyclopaedia Britannica, 1952), 128.

[8] I use "archive" here in the sense developed by Michel Foucault in *The Archaeology of Knowledge* (New York: Pantheon, 1972). "The archive is that which, at the very root of the statement-event, and in that which embodies it, defines at the outset *the system of enunciability* .... It is that which defines the mode of occurrence of the statement thing; it is the *system of its functioning*" (129).

[9] Fredric Jameson, in "Imaginary and Symbolic in Lacan: Marxism, Psychoanalytic Criticism and the Problem of the Subject", in *Literature and Psychoanalysis: The Question of Reading Otherwise*, Yale French Studies 55/56 (1977), frees the psychoanalytical model from its dependence on the family and its ideology of individualism. He finds the basis for such a model

inaugurates one of the most lasting events in ideological representation: the elaboration of the aboriginal peoples into "savages" whose telling mark is anthropophagy.[10] If, as Fredric Jameson has argued, ideology can be redefined as "the representation of the Imaginary relationships of individuals to their Real conditions of existence" (Jameson 394), the question we now ask is: what indeed does cannibalism speak?

The secret of the Columbian spell can be reached and unraveled when attention is paid to the elaboration, often in the margins, of the female side of anthropophagy. The gravity of the feminine appears even more clearly in the Jean de Léry rendition of the Tupinamba war-religion-feast complex. The female-anthropophagy relation is distilled in the widely-circulated and powerfully-illustrated *Great Voyages* (1590-1634) of Théodore de Bry.[11]

* * *

in Lacan's conception of the three orders or registers of experience: the Imaginary, the Symbolic and the Real. "According to Lacanian epistemology, indeed, acts of consciousness, experiences of the mature subject, necessarily imply a structural coordination between the Imaginary, the Symbolic and the Real .... The notion of the Real is the most problematic of the three since it can never be experienced immediately, but only by way of the mediation of the other two" (350-351). What is meant by the Imaginary is a kind of pre-verbal register whose logic is visual and precedes the symbolic stage in the psyche (352). It is associated with the mirror stage. The Imaginary in the mature subject is buried under the rationality of everyday life and under the exercise of the Symbolic Order. The Imaginary is thus already a state of alienation. Further, the Symbolic Order restructures the Imaginary by introducing a third term —the Real— into the infinite regression of duality of the latter's mirror images. The Real is History itself, but History is not an effect of the signifier, it is rather a text-to-be-(re)constructed (384-85). Further, if ideology is redefined as the representation of the Imaginary relationships of individuals to their Real conditions of existence, ideology becomes the place of insertion of the subject in the realms of the Symbolic and the Real (394).

[10] "Ideological representation can thus be described as a narrative by which the individual subject invents a 'lived' relationship with collective systems which otherwise by definition exclude him in so far as she or he is born into a pre-existent social form and a pre-existing language" (Jameson 394).

[11] Théodore de Bry, *Histoire de l'Amérique (...) en treize parties* (Frankfurt, 1590-1634). For a recent reproduction of de Bry's texts and illustrations of the *Grands Voyages* see Michèle Duchet, editor, *L'Amérique de Théodore de Bry. Une Collection de voyages protestants du XVIe siècle. Quatre Études d'iconographie* (Paris: Éditions du Centre Nationale de la Recherche Scientifique, 1987).

In order to appreciate completely the mechanisms of contiguity and metonymy which attend the female definition of anthropophagy, it is necessary to quote the Columbian text as fully as possible.

> En Cariay... me enviaron dos muchachas muy ataviadas la más vieja no sería de once años y la otra de siete, ambas con tanta desenvoltura que no serían mas unas putas; traían polvos de hechizos escondidos .... las envié luego a tierra: allí vide una sepultura en el monte, grande como una casa y labrada, y el cuerpo descubierto y mirando en ella. De otras artes me dijeron y más excelentes. Animalias menudas y grandes hay artas y muy diversas de las nuestras ... Un ballestero había herido una animalia, que se parece a un gato paul, salvo que es mucho más grande y el rostro de hombre: teníale atravesado con una saéta desde los pechos a la cola, y porque era feroz le hubo de cortar un brazo y una pierna... Algunos se les puso que andábamos enfechizados, que hoy en día están en ello. Otra gente fallé que comían hombres: la deformidad de sus gestos lo dice (297-98).

The scenes of Cariay place side by side four instances in which culturally decontextualized bodies appear in increasing degrees of isolation, fragmentation and disjunction. The frame of the naked concubines/girls is followed by the sighting of a sepulchre with a buried —not buried— naked body "staring in it". Eros and Thanatos animate these two images, which in turn are followed by the frame of the "gato-paul". Distinct from all the other images, the "gato-paul" condenses the time and action of a previous struggle between one of his men and the cat with the human face. What we see in the arrested frame is a fabulous beast on its hind legs, traversed by a shaft and bearing the marks of a mutilated arm and leg. All these naked bodies, eroticized, demonized and mutilated, come to rest in the "deformity of the faces of the people who eat men".[12]

---

[12] Dr. Chanca accompanied Columbus on his second voyage out. His "report" on the Caris' anthropophagy is the first detailed writing on the subject and it has always been included in the ensemble of texts disseminated under the title *Viajes de Colón*. Chancas' Imaginary owes much to the hegemonic Herodotan "savage". The ethnography and history of cannibalism remains a difficult and controversial subject. Recent scholarship has contributed much to clarification of its practices in cultural systems all over the globe and across time. In *Flesh and Blood: A History of the Cannibal Complex* (New York: Stein and Day, 1975), Reay Tannahill offers ample data on different cannibalistic practices and beliefs in different regions and periods. Especially relevant for this discussion is her chapter on Near Eastern food offerings of human sacrifice and the re-symbolization of the Hebrew covenant into the Christian Eucharist. In his *The Man-Eating Myth* (New York: Oxford University Press, 1979), W. Arens writes that: "excluding survival conditions, I have been unable to uncover adequate documentation of cannibalism as a custom in any form for any society. Rumors, suspicions,

The transformation of the beautiful bodies and docile nature of the first voyage, which began to change with the assessment of the need to have slaves, was certified by Dr. Chanca's report. With the letter from Jamaica the cannibal complex appears fully wrought. What has forged it, as is plain to see in the passage quoted above, is not observation but rather the inner eye of a mind turned upon itself and onto its own logic. There it finds the practice of fitting new material into old schemes. Writing a "new" world entails, as Nietzsche put it in *The Will to Power*, "making equal what is new".[13]

The process of equating what is unequal, in order to produce —paradoxically— a difference, is correlative to what happens in Lacan's mirror stage of the psyche's formation. The child looks in the mirror and sees not himself but another, an "other" who alienates him from him-self. The alienated self identity of the mirror stage ("I" [am] good —"You" [are] bad)[14] requires a careful selection of terms if it is going to be posited as the metaphor for colonial encounters.

Both the Caribs and Tainos were obviously perceived as unequal to the self and to the expected Oriental other. The problem was then how to erase those two differences and yet produce an equality of difference. Within this insurmountable paradox the term that could speak that difference of equality was anthropophagy. It was not new. Its place in discourse, its power, the contours of its origin, the anxieties of its position, had been drawn in Europe's practices and imagination long before Dr. Chanca or Léry crossed the ocean blue. Regarding the antiquity and the power of the idea of anthropophagy, the assertion made by W. Arens in *The Man-Eating Myth* (1979) is pertinent here. To this day, he writes, "for layman and scholar alike the idea of cannibalism exists prior to and thus independent of the evidence" (22).[15]

---

fears and accusations abound, but no satisfactory first hand accounts ... The sustaining ethnography is lacking" (21). I find Arens' general case to hold in spite of the fact that Marshall Sahlins and Peggy Reeves Sanday claim that he may have overstated his case. A distinction between anthropophagy as a dietary custom and anthropophagy as a religious ritual is specially pertinent here. See Marshall Sahlins, "Cannibalism: An Exchange, *New York Review of Books* 26, 4 (1979), 45-47. Also see Peggy Reeves Sanday, *Divine Hunger. Cannibalism as a Cultural System* (Cambridge: Cambridge University Press, 1986).
[13] Friedrich Nietzsche, *The Will to Power*, translated by Walter Kaufmann and R. J. Hollingdale (New York: Viking Books, 1968), 227.
[14] Jameson has shown how the mirror stage of Lacan marks also a fundamental gap between the subject and his own self-*imago* which will never be bridged. The subject faces his alienated image. The primordial rivalry of the mirror becomes the stage for the ethical positioning in which good is identified with the self and bad with the rival. See Jameson 352-55.
[15] Arens' questioning of the uncritical reports of cannibalism have a special bearing on how the Caris and the Tupi were elaborated by European writing. On Tupi ethnography Arens offers the following comment: "(Collins 1973) chooses to illustrate an economic lesson on

What matters then is that from the earliest moment in his writing Columbus made a place for the teratological difference.[16] In his letter of 1493 to Rafael Sánchez, Columbus reports not having seen monsters, excepting for the island of the Caris, where he has not as yet been, but where he is told one can find the most ferocious people. "Éstas se alimentan de carne humana" (227). It is in this sentence that the key substitution takes place. One absence has been filled with another. What is monstrous and excessive about the yet-to-be-seen Caris is that they are naked and yet they are ferocious. Their ferocity, not coming from weapons, can only be attributed to a transgression of *the* prohibition. They live ("se alimentan") by eating human flesh. Léry's own admiration for the Tupi's dexterity in warfare and extreme valor in battle relies fully on this substitution. In the French version the fit becomes clearer. An unavoidable linkage of cause and effect is marked. The Tupi are ferocious warriors because they eat human flesh and they eat human flesh because (despite appearances) they are ferocious warriors who wage war in order to eat human flesh rather than conquer other people's lands or possessions. Léry, always the measured and careful observer, completes the figure of the naked warrior's irrationality when he writes that: "They fight with such fury that a madman could do no worse".[17]

The divide between the "I"/"You" alienation of the mirror stage is no longer circumscribed to things visible ("El gesto de su cara lo dice"). Like madness, it springs from within. It leaves its trace on the countenance of their face, that is to say race. This alienating difference will be pushed past the edge of language with the position ascribed to the Tupi women by Léry's lesson on the translation of Tupi into French.

* * *

distributive systems by describing how the parts of an enemy captive are allocated during a cannibalistic feast among the never-to-be-forgotten Tupinamba. The writer uses the present tense to relate the event even though the case is taken from another anthropologist's essay composed some thirty years earlier (Métraux 1948), which relied upon Staden's sixteenth-century reminiscences" (175-76). For the people in Columbus' reports Peter Hulme states that there simply is no evidence that they "ate people" (41).

[16] The intertextuality of the monstrous and the marvelous in Columbus and other producers of colonial discourse has been amply studied with regard to its medieval sources and its impact upon the Renaissance. For an up-to-date discussion see Chapters 1 and 2 in Peter Hulme's *Colonial Encounters* and Stephen Greenblatt, *Marvelous Possessions. The Wonder of the New World*, (Chicago: Chicago University Press, 1991).

[17] See Jean de Léry (118). In Chapter 14, Léry praises "our savages". He compares them favorably with the best of English bowmen. "Our savages will have sent a dozen [arrows] before the English have loosed six" (114). It is not to be forgotten that Lévi-Strauss in *Tristes Tropiques* (1961) calls Léry the father of modern ethnography, as indeed he is still regarded.

Hayden White has shown in *Tropics of Discourse* (1978) that the early description of the Amerindian, originally interpreted as a projection of Edenic innocence, in fact contained all the elements of a nightmare. "For the description contains no less than five references to violations of taboos regarded as inviolable by Europeans of that age: nakedness, community property, lawlessness, sexual promiscuity and cannibalism".[18] However, White's proposition collapses time, the time which accounts for the transformation of the Edenic scene into the scenes of orgiastic anthropophagy. What transposes Paradise into Hell is the need to punish as the justification for conquest, in correlation with the idea of a universally fallen humanity[19] condemned to pain and work without joy.

In spite of Léry's elegant organization and logical arrangement of his treatise on the Tupi, his description of anthropophagy follows rather closely the *topoi* of Dr. Chanca:

> Esta gente saltea en las otras islas, que traen las mujeres que pueden haber, en especial mozas y hermosas ... las cuales tienen para su servicio y para ser mancebas ... que los hijos que en ellas han se los comen, que solamente crían los que han en sus mujeres naturales. Los hombres ... llévanselos a sus casas para hacer carnicerías ... Los que han muerto luego se los comen. Dicen que la carne de hombre es tan buena que no hay tal cosa en el mundo ... Los mochachos que cautivan córtanlos el miembro y sírvense de ellos hasta que son hombres y después cuando hacen fiesta mátanlos e cómenselos" (235).

The series of sexual transgressions intertwined with the gastrosophy of human flesh overwhelms even the Herodotan registers. Not even the mention of Sodom and Gomorrah seems ample enough to encompass the notion of making war on peaceful people in order to raid them, raise them, rape them and eat them. The pleasure principle is totally out of control in Dr. Chanca's scene. The unremitting mixture of death and Eros brings on the revulsion associated with defilement which Julia Kristeva has called the abject. Orgiastic anthropophagy here has passed beyond the limits of the other. It is no longer an object, an otherness ceaselessly fleeing a systemic quest of desire. It is abject because it cannot be a correlation of the subject. "The abject has only one quality of the object—that of being opposed to I ... What is abject is radically excluded and draws me toward the place where meaning collapses."[20] Moreover, like the abject,

---

[18] Hayden White, *Tropics of Discourse. Essays in Cultural Criticism* (Baltimore: Johns Hopkins University Press, 1978), 187.
[19] See Peter Hulme (41).
[20] See Julia Kristeva, *Powers of Horror. An Essay on Abjection*, translated by Leon S. Roudiez (New York: Columbia University Press, 1982), 1-2.

this scene of Dr. Chanca "is a challenge to established thought. It lies there. It emanates from an exorbitant outside or inside. Ejected from the scope of the possible, the tolerable, the thinkable" (1).

The discursive fact that the Catholic Dr. Chanca inaugurated in 1493 articulates, some seventy years later, the Calvinist's classic discourse on self and other overtaken by the polluting powers of the abject. This hypothesis places the production of the other beyond de Certeau's ground-breaking study on the "writing of the other" in *Voyage to the Land of Brazil*.

In "Etnografía o el espacio del otro: Léry",[21] de Certeau states that ethnography organizes four fundamental notions which constitute the "other", or primitive man: orality, spatiality, alterity and the unconscious. Modern historiography in turn deploys the corresponding four oppositions: writing, temporality, identity and consciousness. The ethnographic position, drawn of course from the example of Léry's writing of the Tupi, assumes a parity between orality and the unconscious. According to de Certeau, "el lenguage oral espera, para hablar, que una escritura lo recorra y sepa lo que dice" (226). If that is the case, even if there had been adequate interpreters for Columbus, informants for Dr. Chanca and more Tupi lessons for Léry, the essentially monologic situation attendant upon the colonizing gesture would nevertheless deeply mark the text. In fact, one can go even further than de Certeau and say that Léry's writing of the Tupi is less a production of the man in the Brazilian forest than an ideological representation as Jameson would have it. It is in the representation of the Tupi as exotic, as a borderline humanity, as an ensemble of indigestible practices (pun intended), that the writing subject deployed by Léry constitutes itself as history or consciousness. Self-conscious writing, temporality and identity mark a text which, as the title already has it, tells the story of Léry's experience in radical alterity.

Three months of precarious exile (October 1557-January 1558) among the Tupi, away from the inimical French Catholic settlers in the bay of Guanabara, arrested and traversed by twenty years in a France bled and scorched by religious wars, are transformed into a text that surreptitiously and yet obviously deals with the hottest issue of the day: the transubstantiation of bread and wine into the flesh and blood of the only son of God. Anthropophagy among the Tupi is the substitute construct for theophagy among the Christians. The representation of the Tupi as orgiastic cannibals enables Léry, the survivor of at least three major famines (Guanabara in 1557, the return voyage in 1558 and Sancerre in 1573), in which civilized men were allowed to eat human flesh, to collect his thoughts on the great prohibitions. He collects them, he reinscribes them as memory of the journey to "over there" and projects upon them the

---

[21] Michel de Certeau, *La escritura de la historia*, translated by Jorge López Moctezuma (Mexico City: Universidad Iberoamericana, 1985), 225.

business of the other "over here". The unspeakable status of incest, offerings of the flesh of the firstborn, sex outside a guilt complex, cannot and do not therefore fall within the realm of the subject. As Kristeva puts it, abjection transforms the "anxiety of the borderline subject into the site of the Other" (54).

The translation metaphor used by de Certeau is thus not quite accurate. And the proof of its insufficiency is not only the overdrawn opposition between the oral and the written but is also internal to the text itself. The progression outlined by de Certeau from exteriority (geography, fauna and flora) to interiority (disease and death) meets an insurmountable wall with the spectacle of the *boucan* and the placid/ecstatic joy of eating human flesh. The whole progression of meaning laid out in the chapter previous to the one on cannibalism collapses at the scene of the feast. Léry admits that in spite of the great pleasures and even ecstasy that he has experienced among the otherwise bucolic and wise Tupi, their food proclivity disqualifies them as future citizens of civilization. For the Calvinist minister proselytizing in the tropics, this is a new item that is added to his list of prohibitions. Therefore, what seems evident is that Lery's "literary product", the treasure that he brings back from his voyage, falls short of producing a discourse that holds and understands a world. Rather it produces an unbreachable separation between the subject and the other (the abject).[22]

Positing the abject as the outcome of Léry's lesson would also lead us to question the argument that holds that as the ethnographer's analytical powers grow, he is able to render the alterity of the "savage" he constructs into assimilable categories. De Certeau is correct in stating that the theological reason with which Léry left France is transformed as he faces the other. It becomes the initiating point for a new science ("saber"). However, if that very science is founded on the opposition between the "savage" as unconscious and the subject as the consciousness that "knows" the savage, and is by definition distinct from the "savage", then the ethnographer's discourse cannot be said to become "un lugar de *verdad* puesto que en él se produce *el discurso que comprende a un mundo*" (245). Such truth will always be partial and it will belong to the realm of the subject and his Imaginary.

---

[22] De Certeau's notion that Léry's text entails a translation of the "original language in which it is said" can hold only if we accept a pre-Derridean distinction between oral and written language. In his polemic with Lévi-Strauss over the "writing lesson" learned by the Nambikwara (*Tristes Tropiques*), Derrida shows that if the Nambikwara forbid and make secret the use of proper names, there is an originary writing within language. "From the moment that the proper name is erased in a system, there is writing. There is a subject from the moment that this obliteration of the proper is produced. That is to say from the first appearing of the proper and from the first dawn of language. This proposition is universal". Jacques Derrida, *Of Grammatology*, translated by Gayatri Spivak (Baltimore: Johns Hopkins University Press, 1974), 108.

It is only by bringing in the concept of the abject and its connection to the mother's body that a totalizing reading of Léry's text on his voyage and on the Tupi —a text which unconsciously merges ecstasy and horror— may be possible. Reading *History of a Voyage to the Land of Brazil* without regard to the binding thread of anthropophagy is to misread its central import, for it was the eating of human flesh that resonated most loudly in the European imagination of the time. For example, charges of incest and anthropophagy leveled against Aztecs and Incas eventually made regicide tolerable to the mind of worried European monarchs. The newly-coined word for an old phantasm, cannibalism, caught on like wildfire. Montaigne glossed and explored the image of anthropophagy in America in his classic "On Cannibals" (1580). Théodore de Bry illustrated the European voyages around the world, together with his views on the differences between Catholic and Protestant encounters with the "savages", by relying on the nudity of the new peoples. He filled his pages with sumptuous women gorging themselves on plump legs and arms which, though cooked, managed to retain the look afforded by the most perfect preservation. These same women are depicted boiling entrails and brains and passing out the broth and the meats to their beautiful, naked and very rotund little children.

* * *

The description of Tupi material and social culture is placed in the *History of a Voyage* between two extended scenes of eating human flesh.[23] Though in the time of the fable the scenes are only three months away from each other, it is precisely the body of the text which establishes their burning connection. As the book opens, Léry starts by recalling the Calvinist dispute with the Catholic Villegagnon. The scandal of Villegagnon's beliefs regarding the Mass and the Eucharist is denounced by Léry by quoting "word for word" (36) from the speeches and prayers of the Catholic settler.

> Jesus Christ son of God, living, eternal and consubstantial to His living image by which all things are made ... Thee our Lord, who, moved by time immense and inexpressible charity offered thy self to God the Father ... for our purification ... Finally, desiring to graft onto Thine own body that of all his posterity, nourishing their souls with Thy flesh and Thy Blood, Thou has been willing to suffer death, so

---

[23] In "L'automne des cannibales ou les outils de la conquête", Frank Lestrignant recognizes that Léry's rendition of cannibalism is "rêvé plutôt que vu, fantasmé bien plus qu'observé, comportant cet instrument de fracture indiscutiblement européenne". In *L'Amérique de Théodore de Bry. Une Collection de voyages protestants du XVIe siècle. Quatre Études d'iconographie*, 79.

that as a member of Thy Body they may be nourished in Thee and that they please God Thy Father, offering Thy death in payment for their offenses as if it were their own body ... Thou hast willed and obtained from Thy Father that Thy justice be ascribed to believers, who by their eating of Thy flesh and blood, Thou hast made one with Thee and transformed into Thee (40).

For clarification Léry adds that Villegagnon's people wanted to eat the flesh and blood of Jesus Christ "grossly rather than spiritually ... They wanted to chew and swallow it raw" (41).[24]

The evocation of the sacrifice of a willing victim in Villegagnon's prayer is distantly and, perhaps distortedly but unmistakably, marked in the warrior sacrifice at the Tupi feast.[25] The Tupi captive, like Christ himself, knows the rules and their outcome. He obeys them. While alive he does what is expected of him. He lives a "normal" life among his captors. He enjoys his new wives. He fathers children. He complies with all the rituals on the day of his death. On the eve he enjoys himself dancing, singing, drinking *cahuin* (the wine of a last supper). Here in the tropical forest, the Law of the Father, cruel as it may be, organizes, *by mixing*, a world of peace and war, of pleasure and pain, of inside and outside, of relatives and enemies. Though the Tupi victims are not the "first-born" offerings to any God,[26] the reason that articulates the recurrent raiding, killing and eating of human flesh is vengeance, a motif familiar enough and well naturalized in Europe. With vengeance as the motive for anthropophagy, the Tupi eating of flesh still has the appearance of an order which if not divinely prescribed is at least humanly possible.

However, the readability of Léry's scene of anthropophagy in terms of a primeval covenant of blood between God and his people [27] begins to recede as the Calvinist

---

[24] For further discussion on Villegagnon, see Frank Lestrignant, "Calviniste et Cannibales: Les écrits protestants sur le Brésil français (1555-1560)", *Bulletin de la Société de l'Histoire du Protestantisme Français* 1-2 (1980), 9-26, 167-192.

[25] In his chapter on "The Go-Between", Stephen Greenblatt discusses the blocked recognition of the similarities between the Aztec and Christian cults of human sacrifice (132-138).

[26] For a discussion of the Near Eastern traditions of the sacrifice of the first-born son see Chapter I in *Flesh and Blood*. Tannahill writes that the "biblical narrative is a tangled web of historical fact and mythological fantasy and that it takes an industrious theologian indeed to disentangle it into its component strands, but sacrifice of the first-born and the first fruit both have a place in it" (25). Also see this chapter for the blood covenant between God and His people (29).

[27] Tannahill shows that the "Passover was originally a Near-Eastern spring festival on which the immigrant Jews grafted historical meaning" (25). Moreover, the Bible was not written down until human sacrifice had ceased. By the beginning of the first millennium B.C. "human sacrifice had been commuted into animal sacrifice. This changed is signalled in the story of

"quotes" from the speech of the Tupinamba warrior about to become food. The sacrificial offering of the first-born on which Villegagnon's speech turned now appears to mark a difference with the "reason" for the consumption of human flesh in Brazil. As the Tupi warrior speaks it becomes clear that neither the offering of a first-born to God nor the eating of the God's flesh in atonement motivates the Tupi custom. As the Tupi speech stands in Léry's text, the logic of Tupi anthropophagy disconnects consumption of human flesh from religious belief. Divine hunger as a cultural system does not seem possible here,[28] for the Tupi of Léry are said to lack the concept of a unitary God. Thus anthropophagy among them is a purely secular affair. It appears to be the result of, the excuse or the reason for, a never-ending cycle of revenge and feasting.

Léry's chapter on Tupinamba warfare and cannibalism tells the story of how the Tupi talk themselves into going to war in order to capture prisoners so that they may eat them right after battle in a great feast. Often they save some of the male prisoners. These men are treated very well, a "fact" that erases the difference between captivity and freedom. They are given many wives and everyone enjoys the situation. One day, for no particular calendric reason, a decision is made to feast on this man's body. He complies by making his ritually defiant speech. He reminds those about to eat him that he has in the past eaten of the flesh of their relatives and that his relatives will avenge him by eating of the flesh of those who today eat of his flesh.

As Léry goes on to tell of the feast, this Godless eating of human flesh moves along two different lines of symbolic formation. On the one hand, Tupi cannibalism is set in close parallel to the Catholic Eucharist so as to suggest similarities, but it is also far enough away to efface these. On the other, Tupi cannibalism blurs the lines that separate the key opposition in Léry's cultural system between self and other. Léry's

---

Abraham's sacrifice of his son Isaac" (25-26). "Sharing a sacrifice with the Gods was occasionally advisable, eating people for revenge was understandable, eating them for food was on the whole uncalled for. What brought Jews into absolute conflict with this view was their newly adopted belief that a man still needed his body after death" (31). Offering no theological or anthropological reason, Tannahill nevertheless asserts that "whatever the reason, Christianity adopted into its most sacred ritual an act of pure cannibalism or an unequivocal God-eating on the most primitive level" (60).

[28] Ritual cannibalism, as in the case of human sacrifice among the Aztecs, is now understood to be a "ritual intimately connected both with the constructs by which the origin and continuity of life are understood and assured from one generation to the next and with the way in which that understanding is used to control the vital forces necessary for the reproduction of society". Peggy Reeves Sanday amply demonstrates this view in her *Divine Hunger. Cannibalism as a Cultural System* (1986).

dream of cannibalism, like the abject,[29] blurs the distinction between us and them, between relatives and enemies, between parent and child, between "I" and rival, between life and death, between soul and body, between pleasure and pain. The way the Tupi warrior (as constructed by Léry) puts it, cannibalism conflates all living things into one gigantic food chain. The secular modernity of such a view of the interfacing of culture and nature is simply unthinkable to Léry's Calvinist consciousness for the religious wars in which he is caught up (the St. Bartholomew's Day Massacre, 1572) have everything invested in a cultural system that insists on cuts, separations, distinctions and opposition.

Nowhere is the convergence of symmetry and asymmetry with the rites of the Eucharist more revealing than in the story of the feast itself. It is the dominant participation of the women at the ritual which produces the eclipse of the original term of the comparison. The female activity erases the symmetry between the eating of the flesh of the "lamb of God" and the eating of the flesh of the enemy-lover-father, the flesh of one's flesh.

Before and after the transition of the warrior's body from object of sexual pleasure to object of feeding pleasure, he is consigned to the care of the women (as a dead body ordinarily would be among Christians). But these women are the very women who have enjoyed him in the hammock and who bore him children. These wives and mothers now cut him up, separate his flesh into soft and hard tissues good for boiling or roasting. They cook, distribute and enjoy the flesh and juices of the cooked meats. Léry punctuates the whole banquet with a richness of detail that his future illustrators, aware of European structural culinary rules, will not miss.[30]

The "old women", those past reproductive age, mainly but signficantly stick to the body fluids (débris and excretions), which roll down the poles of the *boucan* where the more substantial pieces roast while conserving their perfect living shapes. In an ecstasy of delight the "old women", breasts sagging and teeth missing, look at the men and say: "Iguató".

---

[29] Julia Kristeva links the appearance of the abject to the lapse of the unitary bent of the sign, itself built on the outside/inside dynamics of the subject. "Thus when Lacan posits the Name of the Father as the keystone to all sign, meaning and discourse, he points to the *necessary* condition of one and only one process of the signifying unit, albeit a constitutive one: the process of condensing one heterogeneous set with another, releasing the one into the other and ensuring its unitary bent" (53-54).

[30] For a fascinating study of the European gastronomic logic which organizes de Bry's illustrations of Léry's cannibalism, see Bernadette Bucher, *Icon and Conquest. A Structural Analysis of the Illustrations of de Bry's Great Voyages*, translated by Basia Miller Gulati (Chicago: Chicago University Press, 1981).

The women's lust for sex and meat in Léry's text fades out of the biblical register of anxieties about sacrificial lambs and brings to the fore the archaic but very much alive Greek myth of the devouring mother. The myth is preserved in *The Bacchae* of Euripides.[31] In fact the symmetries at the base of the sacred in both orgies correspond to the non-representable, as Kristeva has called it. The Bacchants, who have followed Dionysus from Asia, lust for blood in their lyrics. They long for the "delight of devouring raw meat" (Euripides xiv). Like the Tupi women they are pitiless in the face of tragedy, for once inside the circle of the ritual they hunt and devour (bestially) their very sons. Nussbaum believes that *The Bacchae* explores the threatened difference between gods, humans and beasts without being able to offer a clearcut separation. Dionysus, who can take the shape of snake though he is divine, in ecstasy, and not unlike the Tupi warrior, celebrates his oneness with nature. Thus cannibalism in the tropics inverts the sacrificial relation of the first-born to God the father by showing the mother devouring the father and/or the son in the sheer ecstasy of a primordial oneness, which is of course intolerable to the subject. The Tupi, like the Bacchants, provoke the horror of the abject, the desire to exclude and deny its existence as part of the dynamic of the subject with the other. Thus Léry will report that the Tupi are not fit for conversion, not fit to enter as humans into the global order being created by the age of exploration.

Conclusion

Léry's cannibalism starts by articulating the prohibitions upon human sacrifice inherent in the rites of the Eucharist. The initial thrust of *History of a Voyage to the Land of Brazil* is to deploy Tupi anthropophagy as a slanting critique of the declaration of the Fourth Lateran Council (1215) on the consubstantiality of the bread and wine with the body and flesh of the divinity. Léry's text aims to denounce the idea that "the body and blood of Christ are truly contained under the appearance of bread and wine in the sacrament at the altar" (Tannahill 56) unless one lapses into cannibalism, and thus into savagery. However, as his discourse unfolds, and it has to account for the religion of the Tupi which under the Christian claims to a single God and a single true religion must appear as no-religion, his symmetry breaks. The irrupting asymmetry is reinforced by the polluting presence of women at the center of all activities and relations in Tupi society. But the ecstatic eating of the male body in conjunction with the full participation of naked women is what inscribes the scenes of cannibalism into the area of the abject, for as Kristeva has argued, the abject is an other without a name.

---

[31] *The Bacchae of Euripides*. A new version by C.K. Williams. With an Introduction by Martha Nussbaum (New York: The Noonday Press, 1990).

It is the feminine as "an unnameable other" which lines the incest taboo, and which, along with the prohibition of murder, constitutes the double basis of the sacred (58). This feminine is "most secret and invisible, non-representable, oriented towards spaces of unstable identity" (58) and it is accessible only in poetic language or primitive man's personification of opposing states of feeling (61). Having come face to face with what his culture has made unnameable, Léry must close his essay on the (his) other turned abject by directly quoting a word that resists translation and is spoken by the ecstatic women: "Iguató".

La retórica de los celos: *Dom Casmurro*

ALFRED MacADAM

No hay escritor que no haya sido tentado por el tema de los celos. Machado de Assis no fue una excepción, y su novela satírica *Dom Casmurro* (1899)[1] parece derivada directamente de *Othello*: el capítulo 62 se titula "Uma ponta de Iago"; hay citas directas de Shakespeare en el capítulo 72; y el capítulo 135 contiene referencias a la ópera de Verdi (de 1887). Es decir, Machado no deja dudas sobre las afiliaciones literarias de su texto. *Othello* examina los celos y *Dom Casmurro* también, pero la manera en que Machado redefine los celos para sus propios propósitos es la dimensión más sutil de este texto ambiguo, dimensión que sólo podemos captar viendo sus técnicas retóricas. Ésta es también la mejor manera de aclarar la relación entre el autor brasileño y la tradición literaria europea que él rechaza.

Dom Casmurro es el producto de la madurez machadiana. Nacido en 1839, Machado tiene sesenta años cuando la obra aparece, la tercera de la serie deslumbrante que empieza en 1880 con las *Memórias Póstumas de Brás Cubas* y que sigue con *Quincas Borba* (1886-1891). *Brás Cubas*, con sus innovaciones tipográficas y narratológicas —sus juegos a lo *Tristram Shandy*, su narrador muerto— podría ser el fin de una carrera y no su comienzo. ¿Qué tipo de libro escribiría Machado después de *Brás Cubas*? Abandona la pirotécnica, tanto la visual como la estructural, y se dedica a estudiar los humores, tomando la palabra en su sentido renacentista. Los protagonistas de estas tres novelas son locos: Brás Cubas sufre de una especie de impotencia existencialista; Rubião, en *Quincas Borba*, es lo que el siglo dieciocho inglés habría llamado un *entusiasta*, o sea, un obsesionado o monomaníaco; y Bento Santiago en *Dom Casmurro* tiene la enfermedad de los celos.

Donde Flaubert, como señala Victor Brombert, teje sus ficciones alrededor del tema del *ennui*,[2] Machado teje las suyas (al menos en estos tres ejemplos) alrededor

---

[1] Joaquim-Maria Machado de Assis, *Dom Casmurro* (1899). *Obra Completa* 1 (Río de Janeiro: José Aguilar, 1962).
[2] Victor Brombert, *The Novels of Flaubert: A Study of Themes and Techniques* (Princeton: Princeton University Press, 1966).

del concepto general de locura. Pero lo que salta a la vista es la diferencia enorme entre sus respectivos métodos de realización. Flaubert desarrolla el drama del *ennui* en una realidad que él percibe por medio de los sentidos (o, en el caso de *Salammbô*, por medio de una mezcla de turismo e investigación libresca), que luego recrea, mientras que Machado subordina la representación realista a una recreación alegórica de cómo un monomaníaco vería su mundo.

Ni Frédéric Moreau ni Emma Bovary habla en su propia voz, pero los dos locos más interesantes de Machado, Brás Cubas y Bento Santiago, son narradores confesionales. La narrativa en primera persona le permite a Machado excluir la realidad del texto. Si Cervantes utiliza la tercera persona en el *Quijote* y en las *Novelas ejemplares* para evitar la perspectiva limitada de la picaresca episódica, podemos imaginar a Machado recurriendo a los narradores en primera persona para prohibir la intromisión del mundo real, personificado por el narrador omnisciente decimonónico, en sus ficciones.

Para entender a Bento Santiago, tenemos que entender los celos —emoción, según Rousseau, tan antigua como el mismo amor:

> Jóvenes de ambos sexos viven en chozas vecinas, el trato fugaz exigido por la Naturaleza pronto lleva a otros tratos no menos dulces y, como resultado de visitas mutuas, más permanentes .... Mientras más se ven, más el no verse resulta insoportable. Un sentimiento cariñoso y dulce entra en el alma que con el menor obstáculo se transforma en un frenesí impetuoso; los celos nacen con el amor; triunfa la Discordia, y la pasión más mansa recibe sacrificios de sangre humana.[3]

Con muy pocos cambios, el retrato de Rousseau del nacimiento simultáneo del amor y los celos en el *Discurso sobre los orígenes de la desigualdad* (1755) sería una descripción del *Dom Casmurro* de Machado de Assis, en particular de la vida temprana de Bento y Capitolina (su futura esposa), que viven "en chozas vecinas", y que se enamoran cuando todavía son adolescentes. Capitu (su apodo) hasta experimenta, según Bento, el "frenesí impetuoso" que menciona Rousseau, cuando se entera de que la madre de Bento propone cumplir con un voto sagrado y hacer de Bento un cura. Pero por supuesto, son los celos de Bento los que "reciben sacrificios de sangre humana".

El pasaje de Rousseau tiene más que una relevancia superficial a la novela satírica de Machado. Rousseau describe una sociedad que nunca vio y que inventa como una ficción filosófica, parte de su acusación alegórica contra la sociedad contemporánea. Arrastrado por el lenguaje y por lo que Rousseau llama irónicamente la "perfectibilité"

---

[3] Jean-Jacques Rousseau, *The First and Second Discourses together with the Replies to Critics and Essay on the Origin of Languages*, editado y traducido por Victor Gourevitch (New York: Harper & Row, 1986), 175.

hacia la sociedad civil donde estimamos y anhelamos irrealidades —palabras como "belleza" o "verdad" por ejemplo— vivimos en un mundo artificial que literalmente nos enferma. Consciente de que un retorno a las etapas tempranas (y felices) de la sociedad humana es imposible, Rousseau tácitamente sugiere que reescribamos la ficción —es decir, que cambiemos nuestra sociedad, la ficción en que vivimos, para hacerla tal vez menos letal. Este concepto es relevante también al discurso de Bento Santiago, una re-invención del pasado, una ficción que toma el lugar de la experiencia real.

El pasaje de Rousseau también contiene temas importantes para nuestra lectura de *Dom Casmurro*: los celos (el tema más obvio del libro), el amor, y el lenguaje como vehículo destructivo. Durante décadas, hemos —y el estudio de Helen Caldwell *The Brazilian Othello of Machado de Assis: A Study of "Dom Casmurro"* es un ejemplo excelente[4]— leído la novela de Machado como un estudio de los celos. Esta lectura de Machado preparó el camino para infinitas especulaciones sobre los pecados capitales (especialmente la *invidia*), la ciencia de la *melancolía*, desde la *Anatomía de la melancolía* (1621) de Robert Burton[5] hasta los estudios proto-sicoanalíticos decimonónicos, sin mencionar algunas tentativas de transformar a Machado en un precursor de Proust.

Algunos lectores de *Dom Casmurro* prefieren ver el texto como una novela sicológica e intentan ubicar a Machado en la tradición del Realismo. Este proyecto ve en el Realismo un valor, y define a los Realistas como buenos y a los no-Realistas como inferiores, de manera que estos críticos se ven obligados a salvar a Machado de ser clasificado como escritor fantástico. Dejando aparte la buena voluntad de estos críticos, es un misterio, porque debemos tomar una declaración como la siguiente como una *apologia* socio-moralista para una obra de arte:

> Lo que pretenden hacer las novelas de Machado no es, en esencia, distinto de lo que muchas novelas del siglo XIX (y del XVII, del XVIII, y del XX) tratan de hacer, es decir, de darnos una visión de la sociedad a que pertenece el novelista.[6]

---

[4] Helen Caldwell, *The Brazilian Othello of Machado de Assis: A Study of "Dom Casmurro"* (Berkeley y Los Angeles: University of California Press, 1960).

[5] Robert Burton, *The Anatomy of Melancholy*, editado por Floyd Dell y Paul Jordan Smith (New York: Tudor, 1941).

[6] John Gledson, *The Deceptive Realism of Machado de Assis: A Dissenting Interpretation of "Dom Casmurro"* (Liverpool: Francis Cairns, 1984), 2 (traducción mía). En su *Machado de Assis: Ficção e História*, traducido por Sônia Coutinho (Río de Janeiro: Paz e Terra, 1986), Gledson declara:
> Não existe nada muito original em destacar o interesse de Machado pela sociedade, história e política brasileiras: é coisa do passado remoto (ou deveria sê-lo) criticá-lo por não refletir a realidade local. Mas, aos poucos, ao longo dos anos, um ponto de vista contrário foi surgindo,

Si *Dom Casmurro* es "una visión de la sociedad" a que pertenecía Machado de Assis, es una visión tan oblicua que resulta obtusa. O, para decirlo con las palabras de Roberto Schwarz:

> Entre 1880 y 1906, Machado escribió cinco novelas y docenas de cuentos que hicieron de él un gran escritor. Es una obra donde Brasil está retratado con profundidad. Sin embargo, es un hecho que estos libros no son la representación directa de ninguna de las grandes corrientes ideológicas que se agitaban en ese momento. No son adeptos de la filosofía determinista ... no son republicanos ... y no se someten a la escuela literaria del naturalismo triunfante. Y, lo que es peor, tratan de todos estos temas ... siempre con ironía ... Con el pasar de los años, esta distancia aparece como la expresión misma de su superioridad, de la afinidad profunda de Machado con el proceso brasileño.[7]

Dejando aparte las relaciones entre Machado y el Realismo literario o entre Machado y el siglo XIX brasileño, y enfocando el tema central de *Dom Casmurro*, es imposible no concluir que la autodefensa de Bento Santiago no es un ejemplo de celos. Es decir, Bento sufre de celos, hasta puede personificar los celos, pero su discurso, el cuerpo de esta novela satírica, no tiene nada que ver con los celos. Es una tentativa verbal, o sea retórica, de convencernos de algo: de la traición de Capitu, de que su hijo Ezequiel es en realidad el hijo del mejor amigo de Bento, Escobar.

Si tomamos el texto como la encarnación verbal del alma celosa de Bento —si lo tomamos, entonces, como el vehículo que utilizan los celos para expresarse— tenemos que verlo como una calumnia, "una acusación ignorada por la persona acusada, acusación hecha contra una persona ausente, creída por la otra, sin que haya nadie que la contradiga".[8] Esta definición es la que da Luciano de Samosata en su ensayo sobre la calumnia, el mismo ensayo que contiene la famosa "Calumnia de Apeles", pintada por Botticelli en el siglo XV. He aquí el pasaje específico de "Sobre la calumnia". El pintor Apeles fue denunciado como traidor al tirano Ptolomeo por un pintor rival, Antifilo, pero había sobrevivido la denuncia:

---

o de que a própria sutileza e a profundidade como que ele espera as condições locais, brasileiras, são essenciais para sua grandeza e originalidade como escritor. Desde que, com muita satisfação, situo-me nesta tradição, acredito que seja útil indicar a minha posição dentro dela (22-23).
Admiro las contribuciones del Profesor Gledson a los estudios machadianos; estoy en desacuerdo con sus conclusiones sobre las intenciones estéticas de Machado.

[7] Roberto Schwarz, Introducción, *Quincas Borba*, por Machado de Assis (Caracas: Biblioteca Ayacucho, 1979), xxxi.

[8] Lucian, "On Calumny", *The Works of Lucian* 2, traducido por Thomas Francklin (Londres: T. Cadell, 1780), 363. Aquí la traducción es mía.

Apeles, que durante mucho tiempo recordaba el peligro en que había estado, se vengó contra la calumnia hecha contra él por medio de un cuadro que describiré: A la mano derecha, hay un hombre sentado cuyos oídos son casi tan grandes como los de Midas que alarga su mano hacia la figura de la Calumnia, que aparece en la distancia acercándose a este hombre; con él están dos mujeres, que, imagino, representan la Ignorancia y la Suspicacia. Desde el otro lado se acerca la figure de la Calumnia en la forma de una mujer, extremadamente bella pero al parecer acalorada y enardecida, como si estuviera llena de ira y resentimiento; ella lleva en la mano izquierda una antorcha encendida, y con su mano derecha arrastra por el pelo a un joven, que levanta sus ojos al cielo, como pidiendo a los dioses ser testigos de su inocencia. Delante de la Calumnia hay una figura pálida y fea, con ojos agudos, demacrada, como un hombre comido por una enfermedad, que fácilmente vemos como una representación de la Envidia; y detrás de la Calumnia hay dos mujeres que parecen estar ocupadas en vestirla, adornarla, y ayudarla; una de ellas, según me informó mi intérprete, es la Traición, y la otra la Decepción: a cierta distancia, al fondo del cuadro, hay una mujer vestida de luto, andrajosa, que, nos dijeron, representaba la Penitencia; mientras entornaba los ojos, se sonrojaba y lloraba, atisbando la Verdad, que se acercaba a ella.[9]

Inmediatamente después de este ejemplo brillante de écfrasis, o descripción, Luciano (un poco formalista, al parecer) compara la calumnia con un drama en que hay tres actores principales: "el que acusa, el contra quien se hace la acusación, y el ante quien se hace la acusación".[10] En el caso de *Dom Casmurro*, diríamos, provisionalmente, que estas tres figuras corresponden a Bento Santiago, a su esposa Capitu, y al lector.

Para Luciano, la calumnia resulta de la ignorancia, como vemos en este pasaje que también parece describir la acción de *Dom Casmurro*:[11]

> La ignorancia es el demonio que llena la escena trágica; sus efectos, con respecto a todo, son espantosos: pero, sobre todo, cuando la consideramos la causa de la calumnia y del falso testimonio contra nuestros amigos y conocidos, la razón por la ruina de familias enteras, por la destrucción de ciudades, por la locura de padres

---

[9] *Ibid.*
[10] *Ibid.*, 365.
[11] Bento Santiago alude a Luciano en el capítulo 64: "[A noite] declarou-me que os sonhos já não pertencem à sua jurisdição. Quando eles moravam na ilha que Luciano lhes deu, onde ela tinha o seu palácio, e donde os fazia sair com as suas caras de vária feição, dar-me-ia explicações possíveis." La noche le dice a Bento que los Estados Unidos y Europa están luchando sobre la isla de los sueños. Es entonces que se da cuenta de que en realidad la noche está hablando de las Filipinas; se acuerda de que detesta la política, y se acuesta.

contra hijos e de hijos contra padres, hermano contra hermano, y marido contra esposa: casas enteras se han llevado a la confusión y se han roto amistades a causa del testimonio falso del mal hablar. (12)

Pero es muy difícil ver la ignorancia como el motivo principal de la calumnia, como sugiere David Cast en su *The Calumny of Apelles: A Study in the Humanist Tradition* [La calumnia de Apeles: un estudio en la tradición humanista]:

> La calumnia es como la envidia, y en la alegoría de la Apeles fue la Envidia del que llevó a la Calumnia hacia el Rey ... si podemos ver la ignorancia como una deficiencia de inteligencia, la envidia, en el lenguaje de los humanistas, es un fracaso de nuestra humanidad, una distorsión de lo que todas las relaciones humanas en sus mejores momentos pueden ser. Además, la envidia es una emoción frustrante, puesto que la persona envidiosa no recibe satisfacción de sus sentimientos de envidia.[12]

A menos que Luciano quiera decir con ignorancia algo como el acto de cegarse voluntariamente cuando *ignoramos* algo, entonces estamos casi obligados a estar de acuerdo con David Cast y conectar la envidia con la calumnia. También aquí notamos que una metáfora tomada de la visión es esencial. La envidia o *invidia* deriva de *invidere*, mirar oblicuamente, de *videre*, ver. Sólo cuando separamos los celos de la envidia introducimos un elemento no conectado a la visión: los celos derivan de celo (*zelus*), que combina el deseo ardiente con la indignación. No nos sorprende entonces que la imagen de Apeles de la Calumnia, "una mujer, extremadamente bella pero al parecer acalorada e enardecida, como si estuviera llena de ira y resentimiento ... en la mano izquierda una antorcha encendida", esté imbuida de tanto calor.

"Ira y resentimiento" son, sin embargo, problemáticos; después de todo, ¿por qué está enojada la Calumnia, por qué debe sentir resentimiento, cuando es ella quien hace la acusación? ¿Está loca, está fingiendo, o de veras cree lo que está diciendo? Si cree lo que dice, el punto de Luciano sobre la ignorancia tiene sentido. En todo caso, el melodrama de la alegoría de Apeles es importante porque nos recuerda el aspecto teatral de la novela de Machado: Bento el abogado está defendiéndose en una corte mental, y la ambigüedad de su discurso refleja su naturaleza: ¿es un actor, es decir, un hipócrita, que no cree lo que dice, lo cree de veras, o está loco?[13]

---

[12] "On Calumny", 363. Traducción mía.

[13] Conviene evocar la distinción que establece Wayne C. Booth entre los narradores "seguros" [*reliable*] e "inseguros" [*unreliable*]. Los lectores se acordarán de lo que dice Booth, tan importante para entender a Bento Santiago:
> Si hablamos de punto de vista para averiguar qué relación éste tiene con efectos literarios, entonces las cualidades morales e intelectuales del narrador son más importantes para nuestra valorización

Tradicionalmente se han considerado los celos una especie de locura, y Robert Burton los trata como tal en *La anatomía de la melancolía* de 1621:

> Valescus de Taranta, Aelian Montaltus, Felix Platerus, Guianerius, señalan a la Envidia como una causa de Melancolía, otros dicen que la Envidia es un síntoma de la Melancolía; porque las personas melancólicas, con estas pasiones y perturbaciones de la mente reaccionan tan fuertemente a la Envidia. Pero yo creo que por la amplitud que tiene y su prepotencia sobre síntomas comunes, debemos considerarla como una Especie aparte, por su grandeza y eminencia, por ser una pasión tan furiosa, y casi tan grande como el Amor mismo, como cree Benedetto Varchi. No hay amor sin su parte de celos; el que no siente celos no ama [*qui non zelat, non amat*].[14]

En el siglo pasado, Anthony Trollope trata los celos en su novela, *He Knew He Was Right* [Sabía que tenía razón] (1868-69), que trata el tema de acuerdo con las últimas teorías médicas —el estudio de Jean Esquirol *Des Maladies mentales* (1838, traducción al inglés, 1845), por ejemplo. Los resultados físicos son fascinantes: Trollope publica una obra enorme en dos tomos, mientras que el tomo único de Machado es notablemente delgado.

Trollope documenta con todos los detalles la desintegración mental y física de Louis Trevelyan, el hombre "que sabía que tenía razón" del título, desde el día en que el virus de los celos lo ataca hasta la hora de su muerte, cuando, para dejarlo morir en paz, su esposa confiesa una infidelidad que nunca tuvo lugar. Louis Trevelyan es joven, de unos veintiséis o siete años cuando la novela comienza (su esposa tiene sólo cuatro años menos), rico (tiene ingresos particulares de 3.000 libras esterlinas al año), inteligente (notas sobresalientes de estudiante en Cambridge), y sensible (había "publicado un volumen de poemas"). Como Brás Cubas y Bento Santiago, o como el Frédéric Moreau de Flaubert, Trevelyan se escapa de la lucha por la vida, la búsqueda de dinero, tan central a la novela del siglo XIX, pero sucumbe a su locura. Muere, por así decirlo, un suicidio —se suicida por medio de los celos.

Para Trollope, Trevelyan es un caso patológico además de un personaje rodeado de un mundo en que la gente lucha, trabaja, se enamora y, de vez en cuando, vive feliz. Machado de Assis rechaza este programa totalmente. Hay un sentimiento de totalidad en la obra de Trollope, una amplitud que le permite al autor estudiar los orígenes de

---

que el hecho de referirse al narrador como "yo" o "él," o si está privilegiado o limitado. Si se descubre que el narrador es "inseguro", o mentiroso, entonces el efecto total de la obra que no cuenta se transforma.
Wayne C. Booth, *The Rhetoric of Fiction*, 2ª edición (Chicago: University of Chicago Press, 1983), 158. Traducción mía.

[14] Robert Burton, *op. cit.*, 821. Traducción mía.

los periódicos baratos en Inglaterra, la carrera de un periodista, los detectives privados, las relaciones anglo-americanas, el feminismo americano, y también hacer que sus personajes tomen viajes a Italia. Trollope considera todos estos temas importantes para su narración porque él quiere recrear en su novela al menos la apariencia de un mundo. Machado de Assis no tiene ningún interés en este tipo de proyecto literario. Los personajes de Machado (o de Bento, el narrador) viajan, pero la narrativa se queda en un lugar. Ese lugar es el escenario (o corte) que Bento construye mentalmente mientras forja su historia. El proceso de crear un espacio narrativo empieza antes de que Bento tenga la idea de escribir este libro, en el día en que decide reconstruir la casa en que nació en otra parte de Río de Janeiro. Dice:

> O meu fim evidente era atar as duas pontas da vida, e restaurar na velhice a adolescência. Pois, senhor, não consegui recompor o que foi nem o que fui. Em tudo, se o rosto é igual, a fisionomia é diferente (808).

Su nueva "casa vieja" no puede ser la original; es un simulacro fuera de contexto. No hay ninguna Capitu viviendo al lado. De la misma manera, su reconstrucción de su vida no es sino una fabricación tejida de mentiras.

La razón que da para empezar este proyecto es flaubertiana: el *ennui*. Llevando una vida monótona, de repente siente la necesidad de escribir un libro: rechaza varios temas —derecho, filosofía, política, hasta una "historia de los suburbios" que sería el complemento a las memorias secas sobre Río que dejó el padre Luis Gonçalvez dos Santos. En aquel momento de duda, dice Bento que los bustos pintados en las paredes del salón facsímil de Nerón, Augusto, Masinisa, y César (todos culpables de crímenes contra parientes, incluyendo el homicidio y el incesto) le instan a narrar el pasado. Pero, se pregunta:

> Talvez a narração me desse a ilusão, e as sombras viessem perpassar ligeiras, como ao poeta ... do *Fausto*: "Aí vindes outra vez, inquietas sombras?" (809).

Lo que quiere hacer en realidad es silenciar aquellas "inquietas sombras", y absorber sus voces en su propia voz. Si, como dice Michael Holquist sobre el concepto del dialogismo en Bakhtin:

> Las estrategias manifiestas que utiliza la novela para ilustrar y desplegar las complejidades de las relaciones —sociales, históricas, personales, discursivas, textuales— son su esencia. La heteroglosia es una pluralidad de relaciones, no sólo o meramente una cacafonía de voces diferentes,[15]

---

[15] Michael Holquist, *Dialogism: Bakhtin and his World* (Londres: Routledge, 1990), 89. Traducción mía.

entonces lo que surge de la apropiación hegemónica por Bento de otras voces es que este libro no es, desde el punto de vista del dialogismo, una novela.

Nosotros los lectores estamos en la silla del juez, la misma silla en la écfrasis de Luciano reservada para el rey que se parece a Midas; es decir, nosotros vamos a acompañar a Bento en su narrativa autobiográfica, revivir su vida tal como él la cuenta, y, si tiene éxito retóricamente, llegar a las mismas conclusiones a que llega él. Seremos Bento. Pero si miramos con cuidado, veremos que Bento es todas las figuras en la descripción de Luciano: él es, ciertamente, el rey, "todo oídos" y listo para escuchar a la Calumnia; él es la Calumnia, enarbolando su antorcha encendida —no la antorcha de la verdad sino la antorcha deslumbrante de la retórica, que dejará ciego al lector. La inocencia no puede sobrevivir en una corte donde el juez está flanqueado por la Ignorancia y la Suspicacia, y donde la Envidia presenta la Calumnia, cuyas criadas son la Traición y la Decepción.

Vemos esto en el capítulo 110, "Rasgos da Infância", donde Bento evoca la niñez de su hijo Ezequiel, con la intención de mostrar hasta qué punto el hijo es como la madre, Capitu, y como Escobar, su mejor amigo. Como su madre, el muchacho es calculador (rasgo admirado por Escobar), como ella es codicioso, y como ella (Bento, enojado, señala este rasgo en el capítulo 73), él admira los hombres a caballo. Esta admiración de Ezequiel por los hombres a caballo lleva a su padre a comprarle unos soldados de plomo y grabados militares; mirando un cuadro en que un soldado tiene su espada enarbolada, Ezequiel pregunta:

> "Mas, papai, porque é que êle não deixa cair a espada de uma vez?"
> "Meu filho, é porque é pintado."
> "Mas então por que é que êle se pintou?"
> Ri-me do engano e expliquei-lhe que não era o soldado que se tinha pintado no papel, mas o gravador ... as curiosidades de Capitu, em suma (914).

El soldado de dos dimensiones no es real, pero el muchacho no sabe separar el arte de la vida. Bento sí sabe la diferencia, que él explica, tanto a nosotros como a su hijo. En seguida cuenta una anécdota que no parece relacionada al caso sobre cómo Ezequiel quiere mirar mientras un gato come un ratón. Bento hace un ruido y espanta el gato, y Ezequiel queda frustrado. El punto es que todo en la narrativa de Bento tiene sólo dos dimensiones, como en los grabados de Ezequiel. El arte de Bento consiste en hacernos ver tres dimensiones. El único gato en esta historia es él: destroza a su esposa y su hijo, aprovechándose de nuestra credulidad.

Bento mismo recuerda haber sido víctima de una ilusión óptica en el capítulo 7, donde describe los retratos de sus padres, que él ha colgado en la casa-facsímil precisamente donde habían colgado en la casa de su niñez:

> A pintura escureceu muito, mas ainda dá idéia de ambos. Não me lembra nada dêle, a não ser vagamente que era alto e usava cabeleira grande; o retrato mostra uns olhos redondos, que me acompanham para todos os lados, efeito da pintura que me assombrava em pequeno (814).

Invidia bizquea en las alegorías tradicionales; la mirada directa del padre pintado da miedo al muchacho. El punto es que dentro del discurso de Bento, el texto que leemos, las representaciones de dos dimensiones tienen tanta realidad que las que fingen tener tres. El miedo de Bento de los ojos de su padre y el error de Ezequiel cuando mira al soldado pintado los define como padre e hijo, precisamente la relación que Bento no quiere que nosotros veamos.[16] Él está ciego —ignorante, según Luciano— y espera que nosotros estemos igualmente ciegos.

El discurso de los celos es la Calumnia, que sólo puede tener éxito cuando su víctima está ausente. Pero, como señala René Girard, "Los celos y la envidia implican una tercera presencia: objeto, sujeto, y una tercera persona contra quien se dirigen los celos o la envidia".[17] La *apologia pro vita sua* de Bento es una calumnia contra Capitu, que, junto con Ezequiel y Escobar, se transforma en la persona inocente arrastrada ante el rey en la alegoría de Apeles. Pero ¿dónde está la tercera persona de Girard? Si Bento tiene el papel de la Calumnia y el del Rey, y Capitu es la Inocencia, hay un espacio vacío. Es cierto que el lector está presente en la figura del Rey como el público de la diatriba de Bento, pero el mediador de Girard, el que dicta todo deseo, está ausente. No ausente, sólo invisible; presente como el cuadro en dos dimensiones cuyos ojos siguen al muchacho Bento por todas partes y que posee completamente la madre de Bento.

A Machado de Assis no le interesa narrar el progreso de la enfermedad llamada celos. Su preocupación es el comportamiento verbal, y en sus dos novelas principales, *Brás Cubas* y *Dom Casmurro*, se concentra enteramente en los mundos que sus

---

[16] Los más intrépidos verán en este pasaje algo que les recuerde la meditación sobre los celos en *Glas* de Jacques Derrida:

> But the Nemesis is not only, for the Greeks, distributive justice and *nomos* (share, portion), it is also resentment before injustice, then envy, jealousy, also shame and punishment. This whole chain of significations binds together the law and jealousy or resentment, and in the same stroke [*du même coup*] a certain Greek, a certain Jew, and a certain Kant. Each time the question is of a divinity whose justice is unjust, vengeful, finite, negative, cruel, castrating, fearful. The figure of a father who would not want what he gives birth to to resemble him.

Jacques Derrida, *Glas*, traducido por John P. Leavey Jr. y Richard Rand (Lincoln: University of Nebraska Press, 1986), 213. Como abogado, como padre, como Dios falso (creador de su propio texto), Bento personifica el monstruoso Padre-Dios de Derrida.

[17] René Girard, *Deceit, Desire, and the Novel: Self and Other in Literary Structure*, traducido por Yvonne Freccero (Baltimore: Johns Hopkins University Press, 1969), 12. Aquí la traducción es mía.

personajes crean del lenguaje. Él sabe que el espacio en que trabaja tiene sólo dos dimensiones y sabe también que sus lectores sucumbirán a la tentación de verlo como un mundo con tres dimensiones. Ésta es, tal vez, la más grande de las ironías machadianas: decirle al lector repetidas veces que sus ficciones son alegóricas con la certidumbre de que estos lectores, acostumbrados a las novelas que produce Trollope en *He Knew He Was Right*, las leerán mal. Siempre flirteando con la mimesis, Machado pertenece sin embargo a una tradición literaria más antigua; es un satírico, no un novelista.

Will the Story Tell? Unamuno's *San Manuel Bueno, mártir*

PAMELA BACARISSE

> No debe importarnos tanto lo que uno quiera decir
> como lo que diga sin querer ...
> *San Manuel Bueno, mártir*

There is no doubt that the eponymous protagonist's "lucha cardíaca" for the *mentira vital* of faith is crucial to Unamuno's *San Manuel Bueno, mártir* (1933). Even those convinced that this struggle exists only in the imagination of the narrator, Ángela Carballino (her "knowledge" of the charismatic priest's inability to believe stems entirely from an unsubstantiated conversation she once had with her brother, Lázaro), cannot ignore it.[1] It is undeniable, too, that the *novella* reflects the ontological malaise that was to haunt its author after the crisis year of 1897: to a greater or lesser degree the obsessive, fearful doubts that accompanied his feeling that he was "al borde de la nada" coloured everything written after that date, from an unsuccessful play, *La venda* (1899), to his better-known works. So it is that despite much divergence of opinion about Unamuno's own faith and the extent to which his ontological concerns are manifest in don Manuel,[2] critical interpretations

---

[1] C. A. Longhurst points out that there is no hard evidence for her accusation and sees the basis of the text as "insinuation and supposition" (C.A.Longhurst, *San Manuel Bueno, mártir; and La novela de don Sandalio, jugador de ajedrez* [Manchester and Dover NH: Manchester University Press, 1984]). Reed Anderson refers to don Manuel's "oblique" confession of a "trágico secreto" and adds that since he never explains his anguish, the reader, as well as Lázaro and Angela, is obliged to speculate (Reed Anderson, "The Narrative Voice in Unamuno's *San Manuel Bueno, mártir*", *Hispanófila* L [January 1974], 67-76). It seems to me that the time lapse betweem the production of the *discours* and the *histoire* itself also adds to the reader's confusion and discomfiture.

[2] As is well known, in 1957 he was condemned by the *Santo Oficio* for being an unbeliever, and both *Del sentimiento trágico de la vida* and *La agonía del cristianismo* were placed on the Index. As for the fundamental message of the *novella*, Carlos Blanco Aguinaga sees as hopeful the likely predominance of an intrahistoric, popular memory of don Manuel over Angela's suspect recollections, whereas David G. Turner claims that the text is "a gentle revelation of profound despair". See Carlos Blanco Aguinaga, "Sobre la complejidad de *San Manuel Bueno, mártir*", *Nueva Revista de Filología Hispánica* XV (1961), 569-88; and David G.Turner, *Unamuno's Webs of Fatality* (London: Tamesis, 1974).

will inevitably emphasize spirituality; this is evident even in those cases where the author's own claim that the *novella* is a study of "el pavoroso problema de la personalidad" is acknowledged.[3]

Indeed, if the spiritual question is considered separately, it may not even be essential for the reader/critic to decide whether don Manuel's ontological discomfort was invented by Angela or not. A dedicated humanitarian incapable of accepting the existence of salvation and an afterlife can be considered autonomously as the "tragic embodiment of a modern ethos [the humanistic ideal of supreme virtue] still longing for the old securities",[4] an approach that is particularly seductive given Unamuno's explicit equation of the novel form with philosophical and theological expression (II: 45). Moreover, with textual emphasis on the "enigma de la fe",[5] first considerations of the *novella* will amost certainly be based on what it apparently means to say.

Pace Díaz-Peterson, who claims that *San Manuel Bueno, mártir* is "fácil de explicar",[6] it is ambiguous to an extraordinary degree and it suggests perplexing questions that exclusive concentration on spirituality —an approach best exemplified by Gregorio Marañón's view that it contains no flesh and blood characters, only "almas que pasan sin vestimenta humana" (II: 47)— signally fails to illuminate. However, there is an avenue of investigation which may help in the location of the work's "implied author" —not in the personal sense of that term as originally coined by Wayne Booth, but with recourse to Seymour Chatman's redefinition of it as "the agency within the narrative fiction itself which guides any reading of it", and which constitutes "the locus of the work's *intent*" rather than the author's intention.[7] My purpose is not to deny the presence of a spiritual dilemma in the text in question but to consider those psychosexual factors that might reveal the nature of Chatman's elusive "agency". Perhaps it should be added, though, that it may in the end be impossible to define this: *San Manuel Bueno, mártir* is literature, and as such is unlikely to be susceptible to simplistically clearcut analysis.

---

[3] See Miguel de Unamuno, *Obras completas* (Madrid: Escelicer, 1966), XVI: 575. Future references to *San Manuel Bueno, mártir* will be to this edition and the pagination will be given in parentheses in the text.

[4] Martin Nozick, *Miguel de Unamuno* (New York: Twayne Publishers, 1971), 161.

[5] H. Lijerón Alberdi, *Unamuno y la novela existencialista* (La Paz: Editorial Los Amigos del Libro, 1970), 208.

[6] Rosendo Díaz-Peterson, *Las novelas de Unamuno* (Potomac MD: Scripta Humanistica, 1987), 78.

[7] Seymour Chatman, *Coming to Terms. The Rhetoric of Narrative in Fiction and Film* (Ithaca and London: Cornell University Press, 1990), 74. As an alternative, Chatman suggests "text implication", "text instance", "text design", or even "text intent" (86).

It is my contention that it is human sexuality that presents itself as the most promising area of investigation in *San Manuel Bueno, mártir*. It is a source of surprise to me that so many of the puzzling elements that emanate from the narrator's psyche have been ignored by critics and that others have been explained away within a religious/ontological critical framework. Of those that have been disregarded, a number have so *little* explicit connection with spirituality that they seem to cry out for a psychoanalytic reading. As for the rest, many unconvincing interpretations can be accounted for by critical determination to oblige everything to contribute in a direct way to the composition of a spiritual testament.

In fact, the majority of the anomalous and apparently extraneous textual details form a kind of pattern. They can be classified under three intimately connected headings that reflect the psyche of men and women "de carne y hueso" but they would be gratuitous in any treatment of "almas sin vestimenta humana".

The first is constituted by references to the role —and, in particular, to the absence— of the father, a topic which is introduced at the very beginning of the *novella*, where there is a strange and gratuitous repetition —"mi verdadero padre espiritual, el padre de mi espíritu, del mío"— when Ángela first mentions don Manuel (1129). Then we learn that, like Unamuno himself (and also like a villager who has committed suicide), Ángela was the child of a "forastero" (1129); although the autobiographical nature of this detail seems to provide sufficient motivation for its inclusion,[8] it is difficult to avoid the suspicion that there may be another reason for its presence. It is also thought-provoking that even when the death of Ángela's father was still a relatively recent event, her mother never spoke of him (1129). Don Manuel's own father is, of course, not mentioned, and we discover that the priest's calling was partly determined by his desire to be a surrogate father to his widowed sister's children ("de servirles de padre", 1130). Then, in two intercalated episodes, we find that a visiting puppet-master/*payaso* is not present when his wife dies in childbirth and we learn, too, that don Manuel once acted in a highly unorthodox manner because of his determination to provide an illegitimate child with a substitute father. The ultimate and most striking absence, which all the others echo, is indicated by the repeated quotation of Christ's anguished cry of "My God, my God, why hast Thou forsaken me?" from the cross,[9]

---

[8] Another link between Unamuno's father, who died when the author was six years of age, and Ángela's is that both are said to have brought books from elsewhere —in the author's case, from Mexico— to the family home.

[9] This is itself a repetition of words from the 22nd Psalm (i): "Dios mío, Dios mío ¿por qué me has dejado?" where, in spite of lamenting that his tongue is stuck to his palate and that he has been placed in the dust of death (xv), the psalmist continues: "I will tell of thy name to my brethren,/ and praise Thee where they are assembled" (xxiii)

and this may well be connected to don Manuel's later exhortation to Angela to pray for Him too (1146).

San Manuel Bueno, mártir also contains intriguing maternal references. The priest is nostalgic about a "nogal matriarcal" (1134, 1148), which reminds him of his youth. Ángela, though a young virgin, experiences maternal feelings towards him in moments of high tension. And during his re-enactment of Christ's agony in the Valverde de Lucerna church, his own mother responds "desde el suelo" (1136-37), indicating a position of lowliness of which there is no indication in the Gospels or in traditional iconography (one of the most famous evocations of the crucifixion begins "*Stabat* mater dolorosa").[10]

Finally, the priest's interest in the welfare of children (and in that most childlike of creatures, Blasillo) may be unremarkable, both on a spiritual and a practical level, but the emphasis that Ángela places on this is, perhaps, worthy of note. Furthermore, his views on the innocence of children are puzzling, and those on infant death virtually incomprehensible. On a common-sense level, how could he have convinced even the most admiring of parishioners that their articulation of devout resignation ("¡teta y gloria!" and "angelitos al cielo") in the face of such a tragedy could constitute "una de las mayores blasfemias" (1134)? The obvious implication that the joys of life have been unjustly denied to such children is incompatible with the phrase "la cruz del nacimiento", which is echoed when don Manuel quotes from *La vida es sueño*: "el delito mayor del hombre es haber nacido" (1147). And it is, at the very least, puzzling that he should link infant death and suicide, bracketing them together as "los más terribles misterios" (1134).

These three categories by no means exhaust the stock of unanswered, and possibly unanswerable, questions suggested by the text, but it is difficult to find a common denominator for the others. Eventually they may tie in with the father/mother/child triad, but at this juncture the only option appears to be to list them haphazardly. To begin with, we might ask why Ángela uses so many possessive adjectives. And why physical words and phrases are used *a lo divino* (for example, "el padre de mi espíritu", 1129; "Don Manuel [...], de quien [su madre] estaba enamorada —claro que castísimamente", 1129; and "el pueblo [...] se sentía lleno y embriagado de su aroma", 1129).[11] Why did Ángela reject the idea of being a

---

[10] The Gospel according to St John says: "Near the cross of Jesus there stood His mother, His mother's sister, Mary the wife of Cleophas, and Mary Magdalene" (19, xxv). The *Stabat Mater* has long been attributed to the Franciscan Jacopone da Todi (*c*.1230-1306), though this is now in some doubt. See Marina Warner's section on this in *Alone of All her Sex. The Myth and the Cult of the Virgin Mary* (London: Weidenfeld and Nicolson, 1976), 213.

[11] Linguistic connections between the physiological/carnal and the spiritual are common in Unamuno; we have only to think of terms such as "anemia mental", "agonismo", "lo cardíaco", "lo biótico" and "ovíparo".

teacher? What was the real reason for her losing touch with her best friend? Why was marriage an impossible option? *Why did she assume that don Manuel would understand her motives* ("Ya sabe usted, padre mío, por qué", 1143)? Why emphasize the power of don Manuel's eyes (later pointing out that they were closed when he died) and his voice (1129)? Why is she like a "sonámbula" after the final Holy Week communion service (1147)? And why does she classify the story of her charismatic mentor as a confession (1129), adding: "es curioso que [el obispo] no lo haya sospechado" (1153)?

As for don Manuel himself, both his obsessive concern with gossip and his somewhat peculiar theories on envy ("La envidia [...] la mantienen los que se empeñan en creerse envidiados" 1133), seem to merit further consideration, as does his deterministic claim that he was not born to be a hermit, which is followed by a reference to the temptations of the desert (1135). Even more disturbing is his fear that Ángela's mother might have said something about him ("¿qué es lo que te han dicho de mí? ¿Qué leyendas son ésas? ¿Acaso tu madre?" 1136). Also, it is hard to understand his declaration that there is no hell for Ángela (other than in the sense that there is no hell for anyone at all if death means extinction), or his conviction that her disquiet —unlike his— is merely literature.[12] Why does she suspect that he is in some kind of danger without her? Why, as she herself fruitlessly asks, did he not deceive her as —she alleges— he did others? Why should he, an unbeliever, "resuscitate" Lázaro? Why was he so preoccupied with hygiene?[13] Is it significant that he plays the *tamboril* (1134)? (This is yet another case of *divinización*, since he converts a physical activity —dancing— into something resembling a "rito religioso".) Why was he so given to tearful trembling? Why is he now considered a martyr? And by whom? The author, the narrator, or all the villagers?

Let us begin by considering Ángela's repetition of "mi"/"mío", together with "padre", early in the narrative ("mi verdadero padre espiritual, el padre de mi espíritu, del mío", 1129). The possessive indicates her perception of exclusivity here, and even later on in the text, when ownership is collective, the implication is the same ("*nuestro* don Manuel"; "*nuestro* lago"). What is even more interesting is that the syntax of "mi verdadero padre espiritual" makes it impossible for us to avoid temporary assimiliation of the locution "mi verdadero padre" as a semantic

---

[12] Nothing in the text suggests that Ángela is consciously mendacious. The reader must accept that recounted episodes containing dialogue between her and the priest "took place". For example, we have no reason to doubt that on one occasion, when pressed on the subject of the afterlife, Don Manuel sobbed, refused to reply, and then asked her to pray for him and to absolve him.
[13] We recall that hygiene was also one of Pío Baroja's hobby-horses.

entity before reading the second adjective. Although psychologists tell us that the eye does not really perceive words sequentially,[14] it is difficult to disagree with Seymour Chatman when he claims that "verbal structures [do present themselves] as if they were linear".[15] Thus the substitution of don Manuel for Ángela's (absent and, by implication, false) earthly father is suggested *sin querer*, and the immediate repetition of the phrase with altered syntax ("el padre de mi espíritu") may be a hasty, semi-aware, corrective clarification. She can, I suggest, be classified as a daughter in a Lacanian stage of imaginary possession.

Her earthly father had been a "forastero", a stranger in the immutable, exclusive, chosen, enclosed space that is the village. Ángela and her mother, Simona, have always clung to this: "¡Sois como las gatas, que os apegáis a la casa!" claims Lázaro (1138). Simona, whose perfunctory prayers are the only manifestation of any recollection of her dead —and alien[16]— husband, is also devoted to don Manuel, adopting the role of submissive wife *a lo divino*. Again the language is revealing, as it juxtaposes *adorar*, with its religious connotations, and *estar enamorada*, after which corrective clarification is again deemed necessary: "Don Manuel, a quien [...] adoraba, de quien estaba enamorada —claro que castísimamente"(1129). Ángela identifies with her mother via a common object of desire —a surrogate father— in discourse which demonstrates that repressed female desire (Lacan's desire to desire) will always find a voice.

Everything Ángela tells us about don Manuel reveals his fitness for the role of patriarch. He replaced her father and supplanted his own to the extent that the existence of the latter is never referred to. Only the priest's relationship with his mother, the *Dolorosa* to his agonizing Christ, the Virgin whose presence in a Catholic scenario is as essential as that of Joseph would be redundant, is mentioned. Paternal absence is constantly underlined. The *titiritero* whose wife dies in childbirth —Julia Kristeva's consecrated (religious or secular) representation of femininity[17]— is not actually present when he becomes a father once again, but his substitute, don Manuel, is. The episode of Perote, shanghaied into marrying the

---

[14] Marianna Torgovnick makes this point in *The Visual Arts, Pictorialism, and the Novel* (Princeton: Princeton University Press, 1985), 31: "[it has been] shown that the eye does not really perceive paintings holistically, nor really perceive words sequentially".
15 *Coming to Terms*, 8.
[16] There is a notional indication of parricide here; Ángela's father, like the alien Moses — who is, of course, mentioned later in the text in connection with his substitute, don Manuel— has been eliminated, but the phallocentric line retains its legitimacy.
[17] Julia Kristeva, in her "Stabat Mater", *Histoires d'Amour* (Paris: Denoël, 1983), 225-47 (originally "Hérétique de l'amour", *Tel Quel* 74, Hiver, 30-49), says: "... nous vivons dans une civilisation où la représentation *consacrée* (religieuse ou laïque) de la féminité est résorbée dans la maternité".

"desgraciada hija de la tía Rabona, que se había perdido y volvió, soltera y desahuciada, trayendo un hijito consigo" (1131), contains yet another false paternal presence. The girl's reprehensible behaviour involves abandoning what Lázaro classifies as her "feudal and mediaeval" village, which again suggests an equivalence between its monolithic isolation and chosen authenticity (a manifestation of the concept of intrahistorical *Volksgeist*) and the hope of salvation.[18] Lexically, the departure of this prodigal daughter is linked to a loss of self ("se había perdido"), and she is without hope (*desahuciada* indicates insecurity as well as homelessness), having forfeited any claim either to grace ("des-graciada") or to her birthright. However, what is vital is don Manuel's conviction that for her innocent child, as for his widowed sister's children, the acquisition of *any* father is essential.

His coercion of Perote reveals the quasi-despotic patriarchal authority of the priesthood, for which there are both traditional and experiential bases. A priest's power may be derived in part from elements as superficial as distinctive clothing, uniqueness within the community, the intriguing and differentiating condition of celibacy, hypnotic vocal qualities (this is one reason why the voice is emphasized by Ángela) and a superior education (here we discover that in his seminary days don Manuel "se había distinguido por su agudeza mental y su talento, y había rechazado ofertas de brillante carrera eclesiástica", 1130); but mostly it stems from a presumed level of immaculate virtue that inspires sentiments of submission, even fear, in his parishioners. In Valverde de Lucerna, the community's experience of don Manuel's energy, lack of pretentiousness, non-ascetic love of nature[19] and humanitarian common sense has contributed to the creation of an image that is especially admirable. Experience has confirmed traditional beliefs, and in this way a mandate is granted to a substitute for the Name-of-the-Father/the Law/ *Logos*/ God to give a prodigal daughter in marriage to another false father, Perote, thereby replicating don Manuel's symbolic status in a real (within the fiction) context.

If Ángela semi-knowingly sees herself as don Manuel's virgin daughter—and therefore, according to the theories of Georges Dumézil, the guardian of paternal power[20]— her unconscious also classifies her as his wife. Her adolescent

---

[18] The only other character with the temerity to leave Valverde de Lucerna is the radical Lázaro, and he too is redeemed by returning.

[19] Robert H. Thouless, *An Introduction to the Psychology of Religion* (Cambridge: Cambridge University Press, 1928), points out that ascetics deliberately repress any emotional attitude towards nature, and he mentions both Thomas à Kempis and St Augustine, the latter having made the relevant claim that when "[m]en draw thither to admire the heights of the mountains and the powerful waves of the sea—[they wish] to turn away from themselves" (35, 36). Moreover, of course, any emotional relationship with natural objects may be judged dangerously similar to that with another human being.

[20] Georges Dumézil, *La Religion romaine archaïque* (Paris: Payot, 1974), referred to by Julia Kristeva in her "Stabat Mater".

preoccupations had been far from exceptional as they fluctuated between female pair-bonding founded on religious sentimentality ("una compañera que se me aficionó desmedidamente, y que unas veces me proponía que entrásemos juntas a la vez en un mismo convento, jurándonos, y hasta firmando el juramento con nuestra sangre, hermandad perpetua", 1130) and dreams of love and romance ("novios y [...] aventuras matrimoniales", 1130). But a sudden textual break highlights her recognition of what is truly important to her: "Por cierto que no he vuelto a saber de ella ni de su suerte," she says (1130), firmly closing the door on frivolous and, after all, irrelevant memories. That an intimate friendship, once so central to Ángela's life that she recalls details of it forty years later, could be dismissed without comment points to the moment when desire became paramount and the signifier of its object unmistakable: a priest/father, in a Lacanian sense its ideal incarnation because "the very structure at the basis of desire always lends a note of impossibility to [its] object".[21] Ángela's report of her friend's discourse makes its psychological subject quite clear, and it ends, climactically: "¡Qué suerte, chica, la de poder vivir cerca de un santo vivo, de carne y hueso, y poderle besar la mano! Cuando vuelvas a tu pueblo escríbeme mucho, mucho, y cuéntame de él" (1130). This Ángela never did, for he was her don Manuel in her Valverde de Lucerna, where there was no place for *forasteros*.[22]

The once-popular theory of erotogenesis maintained that all religious faith is a misinterpretation of sexual desire, and those that contributed to this school of thought in the early decades of the century concluded that therefore all religious feelings were discredited. While this view is unquestionably debatable,[23] there are indeed countless links between religious sentiment and sexuality.[24] For example,

---

[21] Jacques Lacan, "Desire and the Interpretation of Desire in *Hamlet*", in Shoshana Felman, editor, *Literature and Psychoanalysis. The Question of Reading: Otherwise* (1977) (Baltimore and London: The Johns Hopkins University Press, 1989), 36.

[22] Malinowski's claim that "the charter of the clan is given in the mythology of a common ancestor" (Bronislaw Malinowski, *A Scientific Theory of Culture and Other Essays* [1944] [New York: Oxford University Press; A Galaxy Book, 1960], 163) is metaphorically applicable here, with the integrity of the "clan"/ village guaranteed by adherence to a heritage of devout Catholicism mixed with a certain smug *menosprecio de corte*. The incarnation of this perceived "common ancestor" is the priest, for Ángela the leader of a superior subgroup constituted by herself and Lázaro. This is explicitly revealed in Ángela's comment when she and Lázaro discuss their secret: "Si intentase, por locura, explicárselo [a los vecinos], no lo entenderían" (1151).

[23] Thouless points out that for the mystics "love of God has seemed to be the end of those desires which they thought could find only imperfect satisfaction in human love": *An Introduction to the Psychology of Religion*, 135.

[24] See Thouless, *An Introduction*, Chapter Ten.

"certain types of religious excitement and certain phases of religious development show a correspondence with the times of the crises of the sex-life".[25] This connection is relevant to *San Manuel Bueno, mártir* because at the age of fifteen Ángela rejects the possibility of a conventional future based on marriage and a family; her only wish is for don Manuel to dictate the course of her life (1130).[26] Although this may not qualify as a conversion, it is interesting to consider the phenomenon of adolescent conversion: the peak age, we are told, is sixteen, but "the event comes earlier in general among females than among males".[27] Ángela's focus has been definitively set and she channels her natural drives into what is, conventionally speaking, an unnatural direction. Marriage is out of the question and past friendships can be dispensed with as irrelevant to her newly-acquired sense of purpose. The prospect of a teaching career also loses its appeal: apart from her disinclination to abandon her birthplace again (which may also have to do with don Manuel), there is the fact that the acquisition of authority, however limited, will be incompatible with the humble passivity required of a wife.

Paradoxically, religious sentiment is frequently expressed by means of the language of human love; in this text, I am suggesting, the ostensibly spiritual language serves to disguise human sexuality. The carnal expressions all involve a kind of *double entendre*.[28]

Other human drives have to be be suppressed if a religious call is to be answered: meekness and solitude are also keys to the spiritual life. There is no doubt that meekness would have come easily to a woman in Ángela's position, but it is worth remarking that by rejecting family life she opts for an extraordinary level of solitude.

We can only guess at the extent of the narrator's awareness of the stages in her development —suggestibility > desire-love > torpor ("Me levanté sin fuerza y como sonámbula", 1147) when don Manuel is dying[29]— but repeated instances of

---

[25] *Ibid*, 130.
[26] She shows no desire to become a nun since this would take her away from don Manuel.
[27] Thouless, *An Introduction*, quotes Starbuck's *Psychology of Religion* on this (131).
[28] For example, "el pueblo [...] se sentía lleno y embriagado de su aroma" ostensibly refers to the priest's sanctity, but could be understood differently. The supposedly spiritual power of his eyes recalls the mediaeval *flechazo* theory of the source of irresistible sexual attraction, and in many folk-tales conception takes place when a man looks at a woman (of course, the fact that Don Manuel's eyes are closed in death indicates the end of his *physical* power). The male voice, too, has always had symbolic sexual connotations and these are emphasized in the story of the Annunciation. In Lacanian psychology, the voice and the gaze (*regard*) are incorporated into Freud's biological theories of desire.
[29] "El pueblo todo observó que a don Manuel le menguaban las fuerzas, que se fatigaba" (1146). Two more indications of his waning powers (see the previous note) are that he was

clarification of words or phrases that might otherwise be misinterpreted are not the only indications that her discourse is semi-knowing. Thus devotion to the priest constitutes one explanation of her classification of her story as a confession (1129), even if, as in the case of some other bisemic locutions, this label could also be seen as denunciatory: it may be her obsession with don Manuel that might have aroused the bishop's suspicions (1153).

There is some suggestion that the priest himself was not entirely unaware of the process of positive transference on the part of Ángela, as dependence on the father turns into a substitute relationship complicated by adult desire and emotion. Don Manuel's horror of gossip could therefore be defensive and his concern that Ángela's mother might have warned her about him ("tú tiemblas de mí ¿no es eso?" 1136) is easily explicable. However, Ángela herself disingenuously hints that he knows that *she* is motiveless: there can be no hell *for her*, she has him say. Clearly, she insinuates, this is because he realizes that her (supposed) psychogenic blindness stems from the inability, not a refusal, to see. The compulsion to talk about the object of her desire does not affect her need to be judged the most innocent of sinners. Again, her discourse is semi-knowing and rhetorical. There may even have been a sexual basis for her otherwise unaccountable tears when, at her first confession after returning home from school, she is almost incapable of reciting the "yo pecador" (1136). It is also feasible that she sees don Manuel's antipathy toward the life of a hermit as arising from a fear of the presumed nature of the "tentaciones del desierto" (1136): her wishful unconscious equates his determinism ("no nací para ermitaño", 1136) with suppressed carnality. Her emphasis on his abhorrence of idleness may also suggest sublimation. That he considers Ángela's disquiet to be "literature" —that is, mimetic fantasizing— while his is authentic, indicates to her his superior awareness of all aspects of life, not just of theological and ontological concerns. The modern reader could be forgiven for noting an element of counter-transference when Ángela claims that he knows why she has no intention of marrying.

In addition to indications that don Manuel is both a surrogate father and the object of Ángela's desire, there are signs that she sees him as her child, preoccupied as she is with his falling into danger without her. Her admitted, but uncomprehended, maternal feelings towards him ("Empezaba yo a sentir una especie de afecto maternal hacia mi padre espiritual; quería aliviarle del peso de su cruz del nacimiento", 1138) reflect the demands of the libido as she subconsciously completes "the threefold metamorphosis of a woman in the tightest parenthood

---

unable to keep his eyes open and that "Su voz misma, aquella voz que era un milagro, adquirió un cierto temblor íntimo" (1146).

structure".[30] The Virgin was Christ's daughter and wife as well as His mother, as Kristeva has underlined.[31] Of these aspects of Ángela-the-woman, the maternal element, with Mary as paradigm, is not the least important, for by means of auto-assimilation into virginal maternity, sin and death are dramatically eliminated[32] and this provides yet another explanation for her assumption that there can be no hell for her. Moreover, suppression of her memories of an earthly father emphasizes a symbolic Immaculate Conception. And if her humble passivity reflects the traditional attitude of a devoted wife, it could also be seen as the maternal humility which is manifest in the lowly posture of don Manuel's mother during the communion service. According to Kristeva, for the real and the symbolic mother, humility "is accompanied by the immeasurable pride of the one who knows she is also [her son's] wife and daughter".[33] A kind of sempiternal unity is achieved within the symbolic register.

All these observations oblige us to consider the question of the location of the subject in *San Manuel Bueno, mártir*, to pose that most rudimentary of questions: who is at the heart of this text? At first, both its title and Ángela's emphasis on don Manuel's alleged spiritual complexity encourage us to concentrate on him. However, the perceptions of another are indicated by the title, as well as by the first-person format. But because of the ambiguity of the subjectively-orientated human/symbolic relationship we then have to classify this Other as an unreliable narrator. Indeed, one of the reasons for the continuing fascination of this *novella* in a postmodern age is precisely the *general* air of ambiguity which envelops, if not eclipses, that which specifically surrounds don Manuel. A high level of participa-

---

[30] The English version of Kristeva's "Stabat Mater" is by Léon S. Roudiez, in *The Kristeva Reader*, edited by Toril Moi (Oxford: Basil Blackwell, 1986), 160-86. The original French is: "En effet, *mère* de son fils et *fille* de celui-ci, Marie est aussi, et en outre, son *épouse*: elle réalise par conséquent la triple métamorphose d'une femme dans le système le plus étroit de la parenté".

[31] Jung also talks of a "hierogamous" relationship between Mary and Christ. C.G. Jung, *Answer to Job* (Princeton: Princeton University Press, 1969).

[32] Duns Scotus' well-known concept of *praeredemptio* (the idea of the Immaculate Conception was made dogma in 1854, but had been current since the end of the first century and is discussed in several apocryphal texts, particularly *The Secret Book of James*).

[33] "Stabat mater": "... la tête baissée de la mère devant son fils ne l'est pas sans orgueil incommensurable de celle que se sait aussi son épouse et sa fille". Kristeva also points out that Catherine of Alexandria (said to have been martyred in 307) imagined receiving a wedding-ring from Christ, that Bernard of Clairvaux classified Mary as "beloved and wife" from 1135 onwards, and that Catherine of Siena (1347-80) went through a mystical wedding with Him. And with regard to the interchangeability of the mother/son relationship, she quotes Dante's lines from the *Divina Commedia*: "Vergine Madre, figlia del tuo figlio".

tion on the part of the reader is demanded because this text emanates from an unusually complex, interested and insecure psyche, and it is, perhaps, worth repeating that it is unlikely to provide easy answers to our questions. As Shoshana Felman has observed, literature is not simply "a body of language to interpret, nor is psychoanalysis a body of knowledge with which to interpret, since psychoanalysis is equally a body of language, and literature also a body of knowledge".[34]

If we start from the premise that the text is actually "about" Ángela Carballino, three ingenuous questions arise. The first is whether her portrayal of don Manuel is accurate. Then (if we decide that it may not be), what is the purpose of the complex web of fantasy that she may have woven around him? Finally, we must ask ourselves why she commits the story to paper in a *memoria* which might, and indeed does, fall into someone else's hands. The word "secreto" (1153) is rendered meaningless not only by the act of writing but also by the dissemination of the text by an author who refuses to divulge details of how he acquired it ("He aquí algo, lector, *que debo guardar en secreto*", 1153, my italics). Does the word "confession" indicate Ángela's need for absolution from the weight of past sins, imagined or otherwise? Is this text a talking/writing cure?

As for the accuracy of her account of don Manuel's actions, discourse and world-view, the fact that we are obliged to choose what to believe cannot be overemphasized. Suspicions arise precisely because of the shifting impact of a narration in which there is no corroboration for what is being alleged —though it may be reasonable to assume that the *non-contentious* facets of the priest's biography are, so to speak, true. The reason for their inclusion may not always be immediately discernible, but their significance often is. One example is what seems to be a gratuitous reference to don Manuel's concern with hygiene, which can be located within the framework of other current social preoccupations. Man's basic need for health has provoked many different cultural responses, from witchcraft and sorcery (disease, a manifestation of bad magic, was originally contested by means of good magic, as Malinowski has observed) to the emphasis on communal and personal hygiene so much in evidence among intellectuals in the first two or three decades of this century.

In fact, there is insufficient textual evidence to prove that don Manuel's "secret" was invented by Ángela and there is a certain affinity between psychoanalytic readings of *San Manuel Bueno, mártir* and of Henry James's *The Turn of the Screw* (1888), another short novel which has divided its critics. Both Unamuno and James have recourse to an unmarried female narrator who is exercised by the supernatural (conventional religion in the first case, *das Unheimliche* in the

---

[34] Shoshana Felman, "To Open the Question", in *Literature and Psychoanalysis*, 6.

second), and preoccupied by good and evil. In the first text, Ángela is ostensibly concerned with salvation; in the second the governess is convinced that she must "*save* the children from the ghosts, [and] engage in a ferocious moral struggle against `evil'".[35] Ten years after its publication, James himself pointed out —not, it seems, without a certain astonishment— that his story "[had drawn] behind it a train of associations".[36] This statement came long before Edmund Wilson's notorious 1934 reading, which classified the text as a study of neurosis and gave rise to debates between "Freudians" and "metaphysicians" (or "anti-Freudians"). Indeed, in the words of a contemporary critic, the James work is *still* "groaning under the weight of post-Freudian analysis of its unnamed governess's sexual traumas".[37] This phrase scarcely indicates wholehearted approval of this critical approach, and many commentators have been even more energetic in their condemnation,[38] but it is surely counterproductive to disregard psychoanalytic considerations in any investigation of ambiguity.

Even so, ambiguity is but one of the features that *The Turn of the Screw* and *San Manuel Bueno, mártir* have in common. Both female narrators may be judged neurotic, though the causes of their neurosis may vary: James's governess is a hysteric, according to Lacan's definition of hysteria as the manifestation of unsatisfied desire. Ángela, on the other hand, the fulfillment of whose desire is impossible (desire for the representative of what condemns desire), could be classified as obsessive.[39] Nevertheless, Ángela's abnormal insistence on self-examination may lead us to see her as a hysteric, too, if we remember that Breuer claimed that hysterics suffer mainly from reminiscences and that Freud was

---

[35] I am indebted to Shoshana Felman's article on *The Turn of the Screw*, "Turning the Screw of Interpretation", in *Literature and Psychoanalysis*, 94-207 (this quotation: 95). Her observations on the Henry James *novella* suggest many points of interest to readers of *San Manuel Bueno, mártir*.

[36] Henry James's so-called New York Preface (1908).

[37] Jonathan Keates, "James, Henry 1843-1916", in *Makers of Nineteenth Century Culture*, edited by Justin Wintle (London: Routledge & Kegan Paul, 1982).

[38] In fact, Robert Heilman, in his "The Freudian Reading of *The Turn of the Screw*", *Modern Language Notes* LXII, 7 (November 1947), 433, claims that "it is probably safe to say that the Freudian interpretation of the story [...] no longer enjoys wide critical acceptance" and adds: "[it] does violence not only to the story but also to the [1908] Preface".

[39] "... hysteria is characterized by the function of an unsatisfied desire and obsession by the function of an impossible desire. [...] the obsessive neurotic always repeats the initial germ of his trauma, i.e. a certain precipitancy, a fundamental lack of maturation. This is at the base of neurotic behavior, in its most general form: the subject tries to find his sense of time [*lire son heure*] in his object, and it is even in the object that he will learn to tell time [*lire l'heure*]." Jacques Lacan, "Desire and the Interpretation of Desire in *Hamlet*".

convinced that hysteria produces stories. Her obsession with don Manuel also borders on the paranoid. Then, both texts contain elements that may well be symptomatic projections (the ghosts in *The Turn of the Screw*; don Manuel's ontological dilemma in *San Manuel Bueno, mártir*) and female protagonists who, not without feelings of superiority, see and understand more than anyone else.[40] Furthermore, both texts reproduce stories that have been kept secret: that of the governess is revealed forty years after the event by Douglas, who hands over her manuscript to the narrator even later than this, when he himself is dying. His faith in her, based on her attraction for him, leads him to endow her with narrative authority.[41] The same is true of the Unamuno persona —though for a different reason, as we shall see. There are other significant common threads: in *The Turn of the Screw*, it is the governess who brings up the topic of her possible insanity (which would "explain" everything), while Unamuno makes Ángela herself refer to the key question of her possible lack of faith: "Y yo ¿creo?"/"Y yo no sé lo que es verdad y lo que es mentira, ni lo que vi y lo que sólo soñé —o mejor lo que soñé y lo que sólo vi—, ni lo que supe ni lo que creí. [...] ¿Es que supe algo? ¿es que creo algo?" (1152). And both women serve a "master"; in *The Turn of the Screw* he is the governess's employer, but Ángela's situation is more subtle: her master is the desired Ideal in the form of father, son (conceived without sin), and husband.

I suggest that in both texts answers are impossible to locate. Felman rightly points out that the basic weakness in Wilson's reading of *The Turn of the Screw* is precisely that he and later Freudian critics are persuaded that they have been "called upon to *answer*", to provide "an analytical response", when the meaning of the text, "far from being clear, is itself a *question*". In effect, the key question (which applies equally to *San Manuel Bueno, mártir*) is: does James's text authorize any particular reading of itself?[42] What misleads us is that in both cases a clearcut and explicit solution does *seem* to be a possibility. In *The Turn of the Screw*, it is only too tempting to espouse one of three explanations:

    (a) that the children have been possessed by evil in a house haunted by the perpetrators of horrendous corruption;

    (b) that the governess is completely insane. (This harks back to nineteenth century rational explanations for *contes fantastiques*.)

---

[40] For example, in the the James story, the governess classifies the housekeeper as "a magnificent monument to the blessing of a want of imagination", while Angela Carballino is scornful on the subject of the intelligence and capacity for understanding of the inhabitants of Valverde de Lucerna.

[41] Shoshana Felman, "Turning the Screw of Interpretation", 131.

[42] Shoshana Felman, *ibid*, 104, 105.

(c) that the governess is a frustrated neurotic, and the ghosts and other hallucinations are projections of her repressed sexual desire for the master.

Equally, *San Manuel Bueno, mártir*'s critics tend to fall into two groups. The first asserts that Angela is presenting, as reliably as is humanly possible, the story of the puzzling incompatibility between morality and faith as embodied in her spiritual mentor. This can then be considered by an audience that will, of necessity, be as perplexed as she is. The second, that she is a spinster tormented by unfulfilled and unfulfillable desire. The difficulty is that the texts themselves refuse to furnish enough evidence to support either of these hypotheses. The traditional (spiritual) interpretation of *San Manuel Bueno, mártir* reduces Unamuno's admirable ambiguity to a simple narrative with a philosophical nucleus that is unnecessarily adorned with extraneous features and disturbing psychosexual indicators. But the exclusively post-Freudian interpretation suggested by the text's undeniable emphasis on sexuality risks undervaluing its spiritual dimension. It is as impossible to answer for this text as it is for *The Turn of the Screw*, but at least we can afford it a close reading, noting "lo que se diga sin querer", much of which (for reasons of *bienséance*) is sexually based, but always suspecting the disconcerting possibility that, as James himself said, "the story *won't* tell" —at least, "not in any literal, vulgar way".

Let us, then, assume that Ángela's vision of don Manuel is based on desire (though not necessarily that the vision is false) and consider her point of view; this will necessarily illuminate her injudicious recording of his story. There are two important factors in this text that should not be ignored. One is Ángela's perpetual quest for meaning and her constant self-examination. The other, her lifelong obsession with don Manuel. It would be tedious to enumerate all the allusions to the first preoccupation, but it is worth pointing out that the text itself is also a search for meaning. For the reasons we have already referred to, don Manuel might well have been considered a fount of knowledge and consolation, but, like Christ Himself, he invariably avoided answering direct questions.[43] (The story of Perote, at least as recounted by Ángela, demonstrates his habit of keeping his deepest thoughts to himself.) We cannot know if he was religious even if it can be

---

[43] Miles's answers to the governess's questions in *The Turn of the Screw* are equally evasive. After the child has mentioned "this queer business of ours," we find:
"Of what queer business, Miles?"
"Why, the way you bring me up. And all the rest!" [...]
"What do you mean by all the rest?"
"Oh, you know, you know!"

confidently asserted that he was a good man, perhaps even a saint. We are as perplexed as Angela was because we cannot be sure.

Angela is a *reader* of the text which is don Manuel, and, as such, she too feels constrained to seek a convincing explanation for the man as mystery: to "make it out", in the words of James's governess. If this godlike, ideal figure, aspects of whose humanity and insecure individuality are so unsettling, does not know, then —surely?— it must be because he does not believe. She projects her own doubts on to him, at the same time as she unconsciously reinforces her fragile self-sufficiency regarding faith (we recall that at one point she is prepared to absolve *him*). What she perceives as her intimate relationship with him, with her sense of possession and exclusivity perpetually frustrated, leads her to put her conclusions in writing. Her motives are almost certainly not charitable. There may be the desire for a kind of misguided revenge, and her sense of power is also in evidence: possession of don Manuel's supposed vital secret is tantamount to possession of him, since she is now in a position to control his posthumous fate. The Church may grant him sainthood, but Angela's text can turn him into an unwitting martyr. "Wherever the hysteric goes, she brings war with her", it is said,[44] and it is hard to avoid a comparison with the ultimately fatal nature of the Jamesian governess's *idée fixe*.

What I am suggesting is that in *San Manuel Bueno, mártir* we have a secretive, insecure —even neurotically unstable— female narrator who is bent on "saving" the signifier of her desire by means of the vicarious articulation of a (possibly unnecessary) confession. ("He'll confess. If he confesses he's saved," says the governess in *The Turn of the Screw*.) Ángela is not the object of the male gaze or a male reader; rather, don Manuel has been —and after death still is— the object of hers. It is she who creates and bestows identity, and in her elaboration of the priest's presumed lack of faith, desire is no longer mute. From a position of envy of his self-sufficiency, she relates encounters in a way that suggests that he envied hers. He himself had no time for envy, we discover, claiming that "la mantienen los que se empeñan en creerse envidiados" (1133), an affirmation that refers to *Ángela's* emotional situation. It may be no coincidence that the Latin *invidere* also means to look with malice, even to cast the evil eye, on someone. Ángela, in classic paranoid fashion, is mentally rigid and biased, is (perhaps) accurate in her perception of don Manuel's unclassifiable melancholy and tearful emotional crises, but (possibly) wrong in her diagnosis of their cause. She has confused subject and object, she is prey to a long-repressed need for control, and, ultimately,

---

[44] Moustapha Safouan, "In Praise of Hysteria", in *Returning to Freud: Clinical Psychoanalysis in the School of Lacan*, edited by Stuart Schneiderman (New Haven: Yale University Press, 1980), 57-58.

after so much time has passed and the possibility of don Manuel's canonization arises, there is no longer any chance of her story being challenged by the other person involved in the events. She now injects her own confusion into her portrait of the priest in a kind of Freudian reconstructive retrospection, with a mental aggressivity that is almost a form of the evil eye. And, once again in a semi-knowing way, she directs us to her motives with the *double entendre* behind the word "confession," for if her text constitutes posthumous calumny, it is she who has sinned. "If he *were* innocent what then on earth was *I*?" as James's governess asks.

Any search for Chatman's "locus of the work's intent" is made even more difficult when we remember that Ángela is the *second* narrator. The first, who appears only in the final chapter, is the Unamuno persona —the secretive author who invests Ángela's words with so much narrative authority that he refers to her portrait of don Manuel in the same breath as that of Augusto Pérez in *Niebla*, asking on the subject of the latter: "¿Sé yo si [él] no tenía razón al pretender ser más real, más objetivo que yo mismo, que pretendía haberlo inventado?" He then asserts his complete faith in "la realidad de este San Manuel Bueno, mártir" (1153), but the character whose authenticity he cannot question is not don Manuel, but Ángela. As we have seen, in *The Turn of the Screw*, Douglas, who was sexually interested in the governess, attributes narrative authority to her. With regard to *San Manuel Bueno, mártir*, the apparently unchallengeable authority that has so confused readers comes from the Unamuno persona's involvement with a character to whom he too is attracted, but in this case because she encapsulates his own ontological doubts. He projects them on to his creation and she in her turn attributes them to don Manuel, a virtuous, but real and flawed, human being with defects and problems, one of which is an inherited tendency to suicide. There are explicit references to this, but we could also interpret his nostalgia for the "nogal matriarcal" not merely as yearning for the simplicity of his childhood faith (as was Unamuno's own case) but as a desire to return to the mother, or death. His extraordinary humanitarianism may even represent his determined struggle to vanquish this desire, as he gives to others what Lázaro designates "fe en el consuelo de la vida" (1150), "resuscitates" Lázaro, dedicates himself wholeheartedly to children and condemns the resignation of the villagers in the face of infant death.

We have come full circle: there is no doubt that the text of *San Manuel Bueno, mártir* refers to a spiritual dilemma, but this can be experienced only by human beings, who, by definition, are also subject to psychosexual pressures and demands. The story does not tell us what we passionately want to know, but if we do not take into account its sexual substratum we cannot even formulate an appropriate question.

Dalí's Oedipal Version: "The Great Masturbator"

JAVIER HERRERO

I could as well have called this paper "Dalí: The Freudian Mystic", or "The Hero of the Unconscious", or any other title that conveyed the very serious, indeed the deeply religious and revolutionary quality that *masturbation*, as an exaltation of desire and the Imaginary, carried for Salvador Dalí. In one of his earlier contributions to *La Révolution surréaliste*, Dalí has this to say about a young man who exposed his erection to a young woman in the Paris subway:

> En el pasado mes de mayo, en el trayecto Cambronne-Glacière, un hombre de unos treinta años, sentado frente a una muy bella joven, separó hábilmente una revista que parecía leer, de modo que no fuese visto más que por la joven, y descubrió su sexo en erección completa y magnífica. Cuando un cretino advirtió este acto exhibicionista, acto que había infundido a la joven una enorme y deliciosa confusión, sin que expresase la menor protesta, eso bastó para que el exhibicionista fuera golpeado y expulsado por el público. Nosotros no podemos menos de expresar toda nuestra indignación, y todo nuestro desprecio por una conducta tan abominable contra uno de los actos más puros y más desinteresados que un hombre sea capaz de realizar en nuestra época de envilecimiento y de degradación morales.[1]

Was Dalí being funny? Far from it. In his famous (or infamous) lecture to the Ateneo de Barcelona, in which the young prophet expanded, before a traditional and patriotic (Catalanist) audience, the new gospel according to Freud, Dalí, after singing the praises of *paranoia* as a "forma de enfermedad mental, que consiste en organizar la realidad de manera que la haga servir para el control de una construcción imaginativa", compares it favorably, as a means of achieving truth,

---

[1] Salvador Dalí, "Intellectuels castillans et catalans-Expositions-Arrestations d'un exhibitionisme dans le métro", in *Le Surréalisme au service de la révolution* II (October 1930), 9. All the translations are my own.

with the "alucinación voluntaria, el presueño ... y la alienación mental", states far superior, in their revelatory power, to "el estado denominado normal del putrefacto enormemente normal que toma café".

Such states are superior for two reasons: they open the way to the true principle of life and knowledge, the "pleasure principle"; but, in so doing, they also powerfully contribute to the destruction of the reality principle, in fact, of the practical mechanical, material society that the young surrealist abominated:

> El placer es la aspiración más legítima del hombre. En la vida humana el principio realidad se eleva contra el principio del placer. Una defensa rabiosa le impone a la inteligencia, defensa de todo el que a través del abominable mecanismo de la vida práctica, de todo el que a través de innobles sentimientos humanitarios, a través de la bellas frases: amor al trabajo, etc., etc., que nosotros llamamos de mierda puedan conducir a la masturbación, al exhibicionismo, al crimen, al amor.
> ... los que persistan en la amoralidad de mis decentes ideas y razonables tengan la cara cubierta de mi escupitajo.
> Una figura como la del Marqués de Sade aparece hoy con una pureza de diamante, y en cambio por ejemplo y por citar un personaje nuestro, puede parecernos más bajo, más innoble, más digno de oprobio que los "buenos sentimientos" del gran cerdo, el gran pederasta, el inmenso putrefacto peludo, Ángel Guimerá.[2]

Like that of most prophets, the 24 year old Dalí's message was not enthusiastically received by the audience; in fact, Salvador had to exit the Ateneo under the protection of the police, and years later would reveal in an interview that the officer that conveyed him to a waiting taxi told him: "I don't know if you are crazy or not, but you certainly have *cojones!*"

Dalí has given multiple explanations of his paranoiac-critical method, and, of course, of its philosophical and, indeed, theological implications. The examination of his analysis, which is really self-analysis, is of great importance, not only for the light it sheds on his art, but above all for the coherence it gives to the dispersed texts of multiple Dalís (the lover, the son, the artist, the scandalous snob, etc.) which form an inevitable context to his painting. Among these self-explanations I have chosen the one given in *The Unspeakable Confessions of Salvador Dalí* because it provides the more complete description of the deepest implications of his method: through *delirium*, the artist communicates with an unconscious that is not only his "other", or the Lacanian "O-ther" (the [Father-M-other] Other through

---

[2] "Salvador Dalí: posició moral del surrealisme". Lecture in the Ateneo de Barcelona (22 March 1929) in *Manifiestos, proclamas, panfletos y textos doctrinales. Las vanguardias artísticas en España. 1910-1931*, edited by Jaime Brihuega (Madrid: Cátedra; Cuadernos Arte Cátedra), 179-183.

which Desire and the Name of the Father, the Law, intermingle), but a Cosmic, Divine-Other that seems to have some formal analogies with Jung's universal unconscious, although remaining, from the point of view of its content, radically faithful to Freud:

X
HOW TO BECOME PARANOIA-CRITICAL

I am living, controlled delirium. I am because I am in delirium, and am in delirium because I am. Paranoia is my very person, though both dominated and exalted by my consciousness of being. My genius resides in that double reality of my personality; the marriage at the highest level of critical intelligence and its irrational and dynamic opposite. I overthrow all boundaries and continually establish new structures for thinking.

Long before 1933 when I read Jacques Lacan's admirable thesis, *De la psychose paranoïque dans ses rapports avec la personnalité* (Of Paranoiac Psychosis in Its Relationships to Personality), I was perfectly aware of what force was mine. Gala had exorcised me, but the deeper intuition of the quality of my genius had always been present in my mind and principally in my work. Lacan threw a scientific light on a phenomenon that is obscure to most of our contemporaries—the expression: paranoia— and gave it its true significance.

Psychiatry, before Lacan, committed a vulgar error on this account by claiming that the systematization of paranoiac delirium developed "after the fact" and that this phenomenon was to be considered as a case of "reasoning madness". Lacan showed the contrary to be true: the delirium itself is a systematization. It is born systematic, an active element determined to orient reality around its line of force. It is the contrary of a dream or an automatism which remains passive in relation to the movingness of life. Paranoiac delirium asserts itself and conquers. Surrealist actions bring dream and automatism into the concrete; but paranoiac delirium is the very essence of Surrealism and needs only its own force.[3]

That is to say, before Lacan, he was already conscious of the revelatory character of his visions, which brought him into contact with a truth (expressed through deliriant images) which illuminated and exalted his *desire.*

Such visions, though, had a chaotic character which blurred their signs; a systematic construction was needed to force them into precision, to give to them their coherent reality. But was not this rational imposition, in Freudian terms this

---

[3] *The Unspeakable Confessions of Salvador Dalí as told to André Parinaud.* Translated from the French by Harold J. Salemson (New York: William Morrow and Company, 1976), 141.

"secondary elaboration", a logical addition that perverted their purity? Lacan, however, showed him that *the construction belonged to the revelation*, that it also was the language of the unconscious and, consequently, part of the vision. The structure, in fact, constituted the separate visions into a cosmos, a super-reality, an *erotic reality*, deadly enemy what the *putrefactos* call "real":

> All my art consists in concretizing with the most implacable precision the irrational images I tear out of my paranoia. My method consists of spontaneously explaining the irrational knowledge born of delirious associations by giving a critical interpretation of the phenomenon. Critical lucidity plays the part of a photographic developer, and in no way influences the course of the paranoiac force ...
> The true real is within us and we project it when we systematically exploit our paranoia, which is a response and action due to the pressure —or depression— of cosmic void. I believe my paranoia is an expression of the absolute structure, the proof of its immanence. My genius consists of being in direct contact with the cosmic soul ... I believe that the universe around us is but a projection of our paranoia, an enlarged image of the world we carry within us, I think that the object our eyes isolate from the real or that we invent is a pure expression of our delirium crystallized. A simple secretion. Objectivity is but in temporary suspension.[4]

I have quoted Dalí's *Unspeakable Confessions* at length because they provide us with a *master text*, a contextual discourse which, like all discourse and all text, is in itself a tissue of the wider textual horizons which occupied the attention of his contemporaries. As such, other texts, to which I shall refer presently, will receive meaning from it and, finally, will illuminate the pictorial texts whose analysis is the subject of my paper. Visions, then, bring with them messages from an Other that, we have seen, is a divine Eros; but ... which visions? I shall go directly to the heart of the matter: these signs of the Other, the messengers that Dalí receives from Eros, are the GRASSHOPPER, ANTS, the FISH, the DRY OR SWOLLEN HEAD (his own head), the LANDSCAPE OF CADAQUÉS (PORT LLIGAT), STONES (one, two, or sometimes many), the HAND, and WILLIAM TELL. Some others, of secondary character, appear only occasionally. These images are, to a great extent, textual, that is to say, even if they appeared to Dalí spontaneously, they are immediately absorbed into contemporary discourse. Finally, how do they organize themselves? Obviously through the paranoiac coherence that constitutes them into a revelation of Eros, of a Divine Other. Such coherence is provided, of course, by the Oedipal structure. A structure seen through Dalinian eyes, where the Phallic

---

[4] *Ibid.*, 141-144.

Mother (who absorbs and devours the Father) cannibalistically copulates with and destroys the HEROIC SON, who tries, unsuccessfully, to counter-attack by sodomizing the Mother. A neat structure, as you can see.

Let us briefly examine each sign:

THE GRASSHOPPER AND THE FISH

I shall let Dalí speak —very early indeed; in an article published in the avant-garde magazine *L'Amic de les Arts* in 1928, he states:

> En esta misma época, en las rocas de delante de nuestra casa de Cadaqués, cogí con la mano un pez de tamaño pequeño; su visión me impresionó tan fuertemente y de una forma tan especial que lo tuve que lanzar horrorizado, acompañando la acción de un grito. *Tiene la cara igual que la de una langosta*— constaté a continuación en voz alta.[5]

But, let us note, it is the fusion of the two images, the fish and the grasshopper, that produces anguish: why? In a further article in the same journal, a manifesto that preaches the freedom of the fingers (an obvious glorification of masturbation), Dalí narrates his surprise before the amazing discoveries that an uneducated peasant, who does his military service with him, spontaneously reveals: sometimes he sees, in an hypnagogic state, a "flying phallus" that becomes, on other occasions, a "flying finger". Dalí himself confesses that he has also experienced sometimes the same excitement: "Mi pulgar me había sorprendido a menudo de repente, a pesar de la costumbre de verlo aislado saliendo por el agujero de la paleta como a alguien turbador e insólito". It is, then, the connection phallus-finger-fish-grasshopper that constitutes the anguishing structure which plays such a major part in the early Dalinian paintings.

ANTS

Given the fact that *hormigas* play such a part in the artistic imagination of Lorca, Buñuel and Dalí, it would be safe to assume that their signified of *death* and *corruption* goes back to the years of the *Residencia de Estudiantes*. That this is indeed the case is shown by the many references that we find in contemporary texts (among the group of friends of the *Residencia de Estudiantes*) to the *asno podrido*, the mythic origin of the famous "putrefactos", a term used by avant-garde friends to scornfully designate the bourgeois artist, intellectual, politician, etc. The "asno podrido" or "putrefacto" expression seems to have been introduced in the group,

---

[5] Salvador Dalí, "... L'alliberament dels dits ...", *L'Amic de les Arts* IV, 31 (Sitges, 31 March 1929), 6-7.

like so many other original ideas and witticisms, by Pepín Bello; it appears, as is well known, in *Un Chien andalou*, in several of Dalí's earlier paintings, and very early, in the mentioned article "L'alliberament dels dits", of *L'Amic de les Arts*, where Dalí describes the rotting donkey as full of flies and ants ("mosques" and "formigues").

THE LANDSCAPE OF CADAQUÉS: SEA AND ROCKS

This landscape forms one of the most persistent components of Dalí's art; it remained in his imagination (and his life) until his death. Although, as we shall see, it signifies, logically, the cruel, devouring Earth-Mother (the Phallic Earth-Mother, Mother and Father simultaneously), Dalí, in a delirium of masochism, returned there again and again, and there he died. Childhood readings, and the stories his father narrated to him, since his infant days, helped him to identify that landscape with the one he found in his school books describing the tertiarian age, with its fantastic jungles, and its newly born, monstrous rocks. His father, when he took the small boy for a walk along the rocks of Port Lligat, used to tell him that they were going (as in the books of Kipling that he was given at the time) to explore "tierras vírgenes", and pointed out to him the fossils that could be found embedded in the rocks, explaining how such rocky hills had been, in pre-historic times, at the bottom of the sea. Dalí had seen, in his father's law-office, a fossil that had the shape of the female sex organ and this gave him the idea that this ferocious example of Nature, compounded of rock and water, was a terrifying female. The time of such a landscape, because of being placed at the origin of humankind, was, for him, *dawn* ("crepúsculo matutino"), but also *twilight* ("crepúsculo vespertino"), because it was the end of a formative period in Nature. In a surprising move, and through the reading of the zoologist Fabre, who had written a fascinating book on insects, Dalí associates this crepuscular moment with the *Mantis Religiosa*, which he identifies with the grasshopper:

> A menudo me había sentido intrigado, mucho antes de entrar en el orden de las constataciones actuales y desde la primera lectura de las obras de Fabre (hará unos seis o siete años), por la complaciente repetición en su obra del tema crepuscular, el tono panteísta que arrastraba a sueños cósmicos, la nostalgia y el sentimiento de la pesadumbre elegíaca. Está claro que la descripción de un insecto evoca siempre en el analogías atávicas: "¡Qué mundo tan singular el de los locustinos, uno de los más antiguos animales de la tierra firme y, como la escolopendra y el cefalópodo, un representante "retrasado" de las antiguas costumbres![6]

---

[6] Salvador Dalí, *El mito trágico del "ANGELUS" de Millet* (Barcelona: Tusquets Editores; Colección "Los cinco sentidos"), 67.

DALÍ'S OEDIPAL VERSION: "THE GREAT MASTURBATOR"   79

The *antiguas costumbres*, the early, the atavistic ways. It is the atavistic character of the Mantis that attracts the attention of Dalí. An astonishing custom indeed! The Mantis represents an extreme case of the Oedipal complex, the one that Dalí interprets as the authentic, original one, the myth of the castrating, cannibalistic Phallic Mother. Dalí chooses to let Fabre himself describe the ferocity of the Mantis:

> Y no es éste el aspecto más trágico. En las relaciones entre los suyos, la mantis nos reserva unas costumbres tan atroces que no las encontraríamos ni entre los arácnidos, que tan mala fama tienen en ese aspecto... Un decapitado, un amputado hasta medio pecho, un cadáver persiste en querer ofrecer la vida. No cesará hasta que sea roído por el vientre, donde tiene los órganos procreadores. Comerse al macho después de consumada la boda, devorar al enano sin fuerzas, desde este momento inútil, pueden entenderse, hasta cierto punto, en el caso del insecto poco escrupuloso en materia de sentimiento; pero zampárselo durante el acto, eso sobrepasa todo lo que sería capaz de soñar una imaginación atroz. Yo lo he visto, con mis propios ojos, y todavía no he salido de mi asombro...[7]

The landescape of Cadaqués becomes, in Dalí's interpretation, the scenario of the primaeval human myth, of the terrifying and tragic act which, through Oedipal transformation, constitutes *man*: the eternal conflict of the Phallic Mother (one of whose metamorphoses is God the Father) devouring (and erotically possessing) the Son: Kronos devouring his children, William Tell shooting his bow at his son (at the apple on his head), Abraham sacrificing his son and God the Father crucifying Christ, Lenin devouring the Children of the Revolution; all are, in Dalí's words, versions of the ferocious, cannibalistic eroticism of the Mantis.

THE ERODED STONE FIGURE

Dalí finds confirmation of his interpretation of the Port Lligat landscape in a vision where two rocks appear to him as representing the peasant couple of the "Angelus" of Millet. He sees the peasant wife as the Woman-Mantis ready to jump towards the Male, who, with his hat over his groin, although appearing as respectfully praying, is really hiding an erection. Of these two rocks, one is completely pierced by holes produced by erosion; such holes, and the reduced size of the figure, represent the annihilation of the Male by the devouring Female-Mother:

> El aspecto incomprensible de la piedra agujereada y carcomida por la erosión, mucho más pequeña que la que representa a la mujer, se identifica por completo

---

[7] *Ibid.*, 120-121.

con la actual representación de la figura del hombre, *la más deformada por la acción mecánica del tiempo*. El aspecto sorprendente de la primera piedra, evocadora de la figura del hombre, formaba parte, evidentemente, del mismo sistema de representaciones que la actual escultura de la roca, pero a las simples nociones de "agujereada" y disminuida (que ya implican una idea muy clara de ruina) se añaden ahora las, mucho más completas, de extinción, de desaparición, desfiguración, circunstancias éstas que parecen aclararse por el contenido psíquico y por la riqueza que se desprende a la última consideración: *sólo quedaba de él el bloque vago e informe de la silueta que se convertía por ello en terrible y particularmente angustiosa*. Esa angustia nos parece confirmar los vestigios del sentimiento de muerte que, se adivina fácilmente, empezamos a sospechar en las particularidades ruinosas bajo las que acaba de aparecérsenos el personaje masculino.[8]

It is precisely because of this intuition of the identity of the act of love with death through female cannibalism that Dalí experienced in his youth a paralyzing horror towards sexual intercourse:

Es una época en que viví bajo el terror del acto del amor, al que confería caracteres de animalidad, de violencia y ferocidad extremas, hasta el punto de sentirme completamente incapaz de realizarlo, no sólo a causa de mi supuesta insuficiencia fisiológica, sino también por miedo a su fuerza aniquiladora, que me hacía creer en consecuencias casi mortales. Este terror se había apoderado de mí con violencia durante el principio de mis relaciones con Gala, principio que marcaba una crisis decisiva en mi vida erótica ya que el amor de Gala debía operar una cura psíquica; los recursos de ese amor sobrepasaban en intuición vital los más sutiles conocimientos del tratamiento psicoanalítico.[9]

But, how has this myth become so powerfully implanted in Dalí's imagination as to constitute the central icon of his surrealist art? He gives us two powerful images that have left this ineradicable *trace* in his psyche:

1. A story in one of his childhood books, "La por de la selva" [El miedo de la selva] in which a monster terrorizes the jungle and its inhabitants:

Una de las ilustraciones representaba al monstruo saliendo por una ventana. Se veía una parte de la cabeza y una de sus garras. Destrozaba a los niños en sus cunas antes de que la madre, apareciendo en camisón, pudiera salvarlos. Esa mujer, con los senos muy destapados, figura entre las representaciones eróticas preferidas de mi primera infancia, y la identificaba, sin duda alguna, con mi madre. Estimo que

---

[8] *Ibid.*, 79-80.
[9] *Ibid.*, 81-82.

en este caso estamos en plena posesión del sentimiento generador: los atavismos del crepúsculo.

El cuento en cuestión nos suministra directamente (sin necesidad de analizarlo) el elemento del terror, desencadenado por el monstruo a la vez que el elemento erótico determinado precisamente por la imagen de la madre.[10]

2. Dalí adds to this souvenir another, which he calls (as so often in his *Vida secreta*) a "falso souvenir", of his mother, when he was a baby, kissing him and acting as if devouring his penis. Such a souvenir he interprets as a revelation of the nature of the Mantis-Mother who, after having had intercourse with the Male-Son, cannibalistically devours him.

Finally, this iconic system, this ur-myth, allows him to interpret great works of art, and by so doing, to reach the true nature of human activity, its inevitable, radical conflict between oppression and freedom. Let us look for a moment at Millet's "Angelus". From the outside we have a couple of peasants, husband and wife, respectfully praying: a religious icon, male and female submitting to socio-religious law. But what hides behind this appearance?

> Primera fase: destacándose a contraluz del ambiente crepuscular que determina los sentimientos atávicos, los dos turbadores simulacros obsesivos encarnados en la pareja del *Angelus* permanecen uno ante otro. Es un momento de espera y de inmovilidad que anuncia la inminente agresión sexual. La figura femenina —la madre— adopta la postura expectante que identificamos con la postura espectral de la mantis religiosa, actitud clásica que sirve de preliminares al cruel acoplamiento. El macho —el hijo— está subyugado y como privado de vida por la irresistible influencia erótica; permanece "clavado" en el suelo, hipnotizado por el "exibicionismo espectral" de su madre, que lo aniquila. La posición del sombrero, cuyo simbolismo es de los más conocidos y de los más indiscutibles en el lenguaje de los sueños, denuncia el estado de excitación sexual del hijo e ilustra el propio acto del coito; sirve también para definir una actitud vergonzosa ante la virilidad.[11]

But, we finally find out, the Male-Son attitude in the myth is not exclusively passive; he avenges the Female attack by sodomizing her:

> Segunda fase: el hijo efectúa con su madre el coito por detrás, reteniendo con sus manos, a la altura de sus riñones, las piernas de la mujer. Se trata de la postura que revela en su más alto grado la animalidad y el atavismo. Esa representación

---

[10] *Ibid.*, 98-99.
[11] *Ibid.*, 129-130.

nos la suministra el cuadro por medio de uno de los objetos accesorios, la carretilla, cuya personalidad erótica es de las más indispensables. Además de las metáforas antropomórficas de una extrema complejidad y de una extrema riqueza que implica, la carretilla está cargada de una intencionalidad muy concreta y particular. Así, en la serie de fantasmas típicos de erección: vuelo, patinaje, locomoción rápida, etc. ... sabemos que la tracción penosa (caballo tirando de una pesada carreta con esfuerzos paroxísticos en lo alto de una cuesta) simboliza, por el esfuerzo desmesurado que se presta a la realización del acto sexual, los complejos de impotencia o de debilidad sexual. La carretilla se sitúa entre esas últimas representaciones; es más directa que aquellas, que comportan elementos constitutivos suministrados por el elemento de *tracción animal*. Esa circunstancia, decíamos, confiere al acto del coito un carácter de extremo e insuperable esfuerzo físico, absolutamente feroz y desproporcionado, que ilustra también el elemento de la "horca clavada en la tierra arada".[12]

In a final, and truly brilliant, twist, Dalí imposes his vision on the whole surrealist movement. As is well known, Breton assumed Lautréamont's definition of beauty as a pithy description of surrealist aesthetics: "Beauty is the accidental encounter, on an operating table, of an umbrella and a sewing-machine" ("rencontre fortuite, sur une table de dissection, d'une machine à coudre et d'un parapluie"). But what can this represent? Dalí tells us: obviously, the "machine-à-coudre" is the image of the Phallic-Mother devouring the son; the "parapluie" indicates the Son's erection, being devoured and castrated by the cannibalistic mother, and finally the "table de dissection" reveals the cruel, cutting, stabbing essence of the relation between the sexes. If Dalí is to be believed, he, like Rousseau, seems to think that desire can only avoid the terrifying pitfalls of the reality principle by remaining enclosed in the theatre of the imagination. It is true that Gala opened to him the door to the real, to status, wealth, fame and, even, to heterosexual intercourse. But he seems to have remained forever contemplating the oneiric visions of unlimited male power that he enacted in the crepuscular landscape of his dream: there, in a world when his beloved Cadaqués took on the colors of the tertiarian age, among atavistic jungles and monsters, the Great Masturbator imposed on the kneeling female the adoration of his phallus.

---

[12] *Ibid.*, 134-135.

Contextos y sextextos de Octavio Paz

PETER G. EARLE

Un ensayo (en la limitada acepción de *intento*) sobre los textos sexuales de Paz necesitaría el espacio de todo un libro. Habría que considerar para cualquier investigación de sus sextextos ciertas estrofas de "Piedra de sol", ciertos pasajes de *El laberinto de la soledad*,[1] la mayor parte del libro *Conjunciones y disyunciones*,[2] el curioso introito a *Nueva picardía mexicana* de A. Jiménez,[3] el ingenioso repaso a las teorías del Marquis de Sade y de Charles Fourier en "La mesa y el lecho",[4] y no sé cuántos escritos más.

Por ahora me limitaré a unos pasajes de su poemas y *El mono gramático*.[5] Daré especial atención a la analogía que Paz gusta de hacer entre el acto sexual y el acto de escribir poemas. Él parece decirnos que en los dos casos el sujeto, sea amante o poeta, acaba su quehacer en una interrogación. Al terminar el orgasmo que podría ser un poema, o el poema que podría ser un orgasmo, ese sujeto no sabrá definir lo que ha experimentado. En cambio habrá sentido o percibido ciertas paradojas o dicotomías: al poeta como al amante le impresiona una alternancia del cuerpo o visión presente con el cuerpo o visión ausente. También sentirá que lo físico tiene su desenlace en lo metafísico y, como Octavio Paz repite *ad infinitum* en verso y en prosa, todo ser se siente, al mismo tiempo, otro ser.

Permítaseme, antes de empezar, una observación más. *El arco y la lira*, el mejor libro de Paz en prosa,[6] es una teoría de la poesía en el contexto de la modernidad. Pero

---

[1] Octavio Paz, *El laberinto de la soledad*, 2ª edición (México: Fondo de Cultura Económica, 1959).
[2] *Conjunciones y disyunciones* (México: Joaquín Mortiz, 1969).
[3] "Introito a guisa de carcocapsa saltitans", en A. Jiménez, *Nueva picardía mexicana*, 14ª edición (México: Editores Mexicanos Unidos, 1979), 9-11, 157-159, 39-40, 260-265.
[4] "La mesa y el lecho", en *El ogro filantrópico* (Barcelona: Seix Barral, 1979), 212-234.
[5] *El mono gramático* (Barcelona: Seix Barral, 1974).
[6] *El arco y la lira*, 2ª edición (México: Fondo de Cultura Económica, 1967).

es, al mismo tiempo, una experiencia de la poesía en ese mismo contexto. Mis lecturas a Paz me han llevado a concluir que su teoría (elemento persistente que surge de repente en los raptos mas líricos) está fundada en su experiencia y no al revés. Y un elemento básico de esa experiencia es cierto *voyeurisme*, la fulminante curiosidad que lo ha llevado a delinear en sus ensayos y gran parte de su poesía una erótica de la vida que es, además, una erótica del arte y de las palabras.

Amor, sexualidad, poesía

Pienso en dos muros muy distantes entre sí: uno está cubierto de lianas, humedades y manchas. Pertenece a una casa arruinada en un pueblo abandonado de la India. Pero es también una muralla imaginada por Octavio Paz en *El mono gramático*, sextexto culminante de sus obras. Las manchas o lianas o humedades son sombras; es decir, frases de una obra en el proceso de escribirse que se leen sobre el muro imaginario. Paz dice: "Son las sombras proyectadas por el fuego de una chimenea encendida por dos amantes que son el catálogo de un jardín botánico tropical que son una alegoría de un capítulo de un poema épico que son la masa agitada de la arboleda..." (*El mono* 55) y sigue la oración inacabable con varios etcéteras. Junto con las sombras sobre el muro, la escena de los amantes con su fuego encendido (Esplendor con su amigo) es una doble metáfora (equivalencia del sexo y equivalencia del texto), unión sexual y la escritura de un poema. Se nos dice, en efecto, que la sucesión de imágenes con que la mente y los nervios estimulan el acto sexual tiene su paralelo en otra sucesión de imágenes, echada a luz por los mismos órganos (la mente, los nervios) y que acaba en la creación de un poema.

El otro muro, largo y pintado de blanco, está en la ciudad de México, frente a la casa de Gabriel García Márquez. Éste nos cuenta en un breve ensayo, "Love and Romance Make a Comeback" (publicado primero en Lima y traducido al inglés para *World Press Review*) que alguien —amante anónimo y tal vez poeta— ha escrito en la pared con letras muy grandes: "MARGARITA, DAME UN BESO". Para García Márquez el mensaje a Margarita es una sobrevivencia feliz o un feliz augurio, respuesta implícita a ciertas advertencias —impersonales, sombrías— que se hallan en tranvías y otros sitios públicos y que señalan los peligros del amor sin precauciones. El novelista celebra, si bien en forma sólo tentativa, un retorno al amor romántico en la sociedad hispánica. Termina diciendo:

> A few days ago, my 18-year-old son asked his mother to teach him the bolero, which has made a comeback. In the cities of Latin America and Spain dimly lit discos are opening to experience it anew. I have always believed that love would save the human race, and these signs, which might seem regressive, are not; they are rays of

hope. That is why I'm hoping that Peggy will read the message that someone has written across the street from my house. Please, Peggy, give him a kiss.[7]

El contraste de dos muros que también son textos me sugiere que es mucho más fácil para un narrador moderno que para un poeta moderno escribir sobre el amor (palabra —he notado— que no aparece en el título de este simposio, y tal vez esa omisión —voluntaria o involuntaria— resulte simbólica), posiblemente porque la novela y el cuento asimilan mejor que la poesía, de por sí más autorreflexiva que la narración, ciertas actitudes y perspectivas particularmente vulnerables en nuestra época: la esperanza, la inocencia, la cristalización romántica así como la concibió Stendhal, la desilusión lírica, la vaga espiritualidad —en fin, todo lo susceptible que son la sensibilidad y sentimientos del sujeto. El poema como interrogante, como visión oblicua, como juego autónomo, y hasta como instrumento crítico y epistemológico, son las funciones que cada vez más le han interesado a Paz. Ellas son, por decirlo así, formas de una aventura. Desde los primeros manifiestos de Huidobro hasta nuestros días esas formas son el núcleo de una modernidad hispanoamericana que persiste todavía, a pesar de las teorías hoy no menos persistentes de la posmodernidad. Aparte de su frecuente afinidad erótica, el aventurismo implica, para todo poeta o artista de vanguardia (de cualquier época), la impunidad.

La aventura de la modernidad

En una curiosa nota al pie a "Poema circulatorio" (*Vuelta* 88) Octavio Paz rescata a Arthur Cravan, efímero poeta y olvidado boxeador, quien en 1916 busca en España refugio de la primera guerra mundial. Dos de las hazañas abortadas de este aventurero son dignas de mención: la de ser noqueado por el prestigioso Jack Johnson en el primer round de una pelea en Madrid y, un año después en Nueva York, la de ser arrestado en el acto de desnudarse mientras dictaba una conferencia pública sobre el arte moderno. "*Quelle belle conférence!*" —se dice que comentó Marcel Duchamp (otro evidente entusiasta de la desnudez) en aquella ocasión. Figura complementaria de varios vanguardistas de la época —el violento Filippo Marinetti, el ambicioso Vicente Huidobro, el chiflado Jacques Vaché— el indisciplinado Cravan quiso expresar mediante actos simbólicos su impunidad estética. Así, sus gestos creativos merecieron la atención de Paz, heredero directo y portavoz él mismo del modernismo: no hispanoamericano —se entiende— sino internacional, al que Cravan había aportado su llamativa demostración. Me refiero al experimentalismo amplio y

---

[7] Gabriel García Márquez, "Love and Romance Make a Comeback", *World Press Review*, 38 (May 1991), 5, 34.

flexible, fruto de la práctica y la reflexión, que se define en términos históricos en *El arco y la lira* y *Los hijos del limo*.⁸

A mí como estudioso de la modernidad (en la línea iluminada intuitiva y también teóricamente por Paz) me interesan todas esas rupturas y extravagancias: el atrevimiento, el desnudamiento como acto estético, el *voyeurisme* técnico hoy en día de muchos lectores académicos, la publicación de la primera edición de *Blanco*⁹ en una sola página de cinco y pico de metros que se desplegaba en forma de acordeón, el malabarismo semiótico de muchos universitarios posmodernistas (que en el fondo no son más que unos modernistas exasperados); la vuelta triunfal al Occidente de Venus y Eros en la primavera de 1968.

En ese contexto he querido dividir la obra lírica de Paz en dos etapas mayores de veinte años cada una. (La simetría, mas no la sustancia de ellas, es casual.) La primera va de 1950 a 1970; la segunda, de 1970 a 1990. Digo "etapas mayores" en reconocimiento de dos menores: la inicial (1930-1950), en que el autor escribe mucha poesía y muchos artículos y reseñas, pero sin desarrollar plenamente el arte del sexteto que comentaré más adelante; y la segunda, que es la actual, post-nobeliana, de imprevisible duración, ya que el escritor a fines de 1990 tenía 77 años y el deber extra-literario de disponer gentilmente del más lucrativo de los premios para escritor.

Después del acto, o la Desmaterialización

La primera etapa (1950-1970) se distingue por un proceso de materialización; la segunda (1970-1990), por otro de desmaterialización: "Soy la sombra que arrojan mis palabras" es el verso con que termina su poema *Pasado en claro* (1975; edición revisada, 1978).¹⁰ En su segunda etapa Paz nos declara en forma múltiple y con gran riqueza metafórica que el poeta moderno no es pequeño dios, ni inventor, ni artífice, sino un receptor y luego articulador de rumores y paisajes; aspira a que en las cuerdas de su lira vibre el lenguaje del universo. Persisten los interrogantes: ¿De dónde vienen las palabras? ¿Quién ha sido su primer enunciador? Pero poco le interesan en sentido activo esos misterios; lo principal son los espectros que quedan, el residuo abstracto pero cada vez más potente que son los verbos y los nombres. En eso consiste la desmaterialización, proceso en que la sexualidad y la historia se diluyen en una especie de catarsis platónica involuntaria. Es cierto que el desenlace de otro importante poema de la segunda etapa, "Nocturno de San Ildefonso" (1976),¹¹ es un paisaje fluido en que se funden la luna, el lecho, la mujer, y su amante; pero en los versos testimoniales de

---

[8] *Los hijos del limo* (Barcelona: Seix Barral, 1974).
[9] *Blanco*, en *Ladera este* (México: Joaquín Mortiz, 1969), 143-169.
[10] *Pasado en claro* (México: Fondo de Cultura Económica, 1975).
[11] "Nocturno de San Ildefonso", en *Vuelta* (Barcelona: Seix Barral, 1976), 71-83.

esta misma composición se define en términos nuevamente abstractos la relación entre poesía e historia:

> Entre el hacer y el ver,
>   acción o contemplación,
> escogí el acto de palabras:
>   hacerlas, habitarlas,
> dar ojos al lenguaje.
>
>   La poesía no es la verdad:
> es la resurrección de las presencias,
>   la historia
> transfigurada en la verdad del tiempo no fechado.
>
>   (*Vuelta* 79)

Entonces la desmaterialización es una metamorfosis que acaba en imágenes de lo fugaz; la desmaterialización es optar por un "acto de palabras" que no se atreve a intervenir directamente en los actos físicos del mundo y se limita a jugar con otras palabras. Ese mecanismo de espejos es, en efecto, lo que Paz asimila de los poetas de vanguardia. Sin embargo, algo del pasado muy concreto del poeta nos queda, también, en esa "resurrección de presencias". Su memoria sigue siendo nuestro vínculo y punto de referencia a la realidad. Por otra parte, como se ha visto en *Pasado en claro*, Paz acaba por desmaterializarse hasta a sí mismo: "Soy la sombra que arrojan mis palabras". La gramática del verso no admite dudas: las palabras son el sujeto activo; él, simple sombra, es el complemento directo de ellas.

En poemas más recientes —los de *Árbol adentro* (1987)[12]— la sexualidad se recuerda, pero —como en el soneto, "La Dulcinea de Marcel Duchamp"— al mismo tiempo se disipa:

> Mujer en rotación que se disgrega
> y es surtidor de sesgos y reflejos:
> mientras más se desviste, más se niega. (*Árbol* 111)

En "La casa de la mirada" del mismo volumen dos versos con mayúscula, EL CORAZÓN ES UN OJO y CREAR PARA VER (*Árbol* 128 y 129), confirman el punto de vista; eso es: la creación y el corazón que la estimula se reducen al ejercicio de la visión; y toda esa casa, que es un poema transparente, es producida por y para los ojos. Tradicionalmente, los poetas ven para crear; Paz, en su inacabable tarea de desmaterializar el mundo desde 1970, crea para ver, porque todo se mueve, se

---

[12] *Árbol adentro* (Barcelona: Seix Barral, 1987).

transforma y huye al instante; la única posibilidad para el poeta es ver lo que aparece y desaparece y registrar el espectáculo de las imágenes. Ésa llegó a ser la labor primordial (y la experiencia vital) del creador en esa casa de la mirada, Laberinto de la Modernidad.

Carnal Knowledge, *o la Materialización*

En la obra lírica de Paz la metáfora dominante de las funciones —tanto las sintácticas como las orgánicas— en forma velada o abierta, perspectivista o pornográfica, es nada menos que el hallazgo y experimento de la Primera Pareja (ya practicado antes desde milenios innumerables por protozoos y moscas, y confirmado muchos milenios después por grandes gramáticos): la cópula. Paz no ha perdido de vista los variados matices de la maravillosa palabra: el biológico; el lógico y el gramatical ("término que une el sujeto con el atributo" es la discreta acepción apuntada en el diccionario de María Moliner); y, por supuesto, el sexual.

Volviendo a Galta, es decir, a las ruinas y al muro de *El mono gramático*, lugar de "realidades sentidas, imaginadas, pensadas, percibidas y disipadas" (*Mono* 53), el legendario mono Hanumán (sabio, mago, volador, gramático) enseña al autor en el capítulo 13 un extraño cuadro sexualizante o —¿cómo diríamos?— el sexorama pintado en un álbum hacia 1780: un retablo copulativo de doble nivel, borrosamente reproducido frente a la página 73 de *El mono*. Al fin del capítulo dedicado a esa extraña obra el poeta resume así su meditación:

> Asimetría de las dos partes: arriba, copulación entre machos y hembras de la misma especie; abajo, copulación de una hembra humana con machos de varias animales y con otra hembra humana —nunca con el hombre. ¿Por qué? Repetición, analogía, excepción. Sobre el espacio inmóvil —muro, cielo, página, estanque, jardín— todas esas figuras se enlazan, trazan el mismo signo y parecen decir lo mismo, pero ¿qué dicen? (*Mono* 73-74)

Pero hay más; integrada al delirante mosaico que es el *El mono gramático* tenemos la imagen móvil de Esplendor, "que no es cuerpo sino el río de signos de su cuerpo" (*Mono* 64). Luego sucede (tenía que suceder) una fluida, rítmica, luminosa, múltiple-dimensional y fantasmagórica copulación entre ella (Esplendor) y el hombre ya aludido en mi primer párrafo. En pocas palabras, ellos son y no son, están y no están, aparecen y desaparecen como las palabras que se escriben en un poema. La pregunta retórica citada arriba en el contexto del panorama copulativo, i.e., el contexto de "repetición, analogía, excepción", se hace ahora de nuevo:

> ¿Qué dicen todas esas figuras?

Porque al final de este capítulo 11 (como al final del último capítulo), Esplendor se desintegra y se desvanece como cualquier otra visión del poeta. En conclusión: Paz nos ha dicho aquí, como en muchos otros pasajes, que el ejercicio de la poesía, como el ejercicio sin restricciones de la erótica, del arte amatorio, se hace sobre una página, un muro, una cama, un mar, un espacio cualquiera; porque la poesía, como la sexualidad, es "repetición, analogía, excepción". Ambas alternan en su materialización y desmaterialización. Ambas recorren su interminable camino de Galta: iluminación y goce, descubrimiento y misterio fundidos, *via crucis* del conocimiento.

Buñuel and *Tristana*; Who Is Doing What to Whom

PETER W. EVANS

One of his most coherently organized, "classical" narratives, inspired, like *Robinson Crusoe*, *Cumbres borrascosas*, and *Nazarín*, by a major Realist novel, *Tristana* departs from the the more anarchic modes of *Un Chien andalou*, *La Voie lactée* and *Le Fantôme de la liberté* without ever seriously distancing itself from Buñuel's pervasive surrealist allegiances. For all the dismissive remarks about Freud (e.g. in *Mon Dernier Soupir*, and the Ambassador of Miranda's derogatory off-the-cuff platitudes in *Le Charme discret de la bourgeoisie*), Buñuel turned repeatedly, whether consciously or not, to Freudian theory and obsessions, above all, of course, to eternal questions about the legitimation or disavowal of sexual desire. His approach to these questions differs significantly from the French lyricists of *amour fou* since, as many others (notably Robert Havard) have pointed out, Buñuel could never deny the legacy of *desengaño*, cynicism and irony bequeathed him by the dominant trends of native peninsular cultural traditions.[1] Even when released from its various social and psychological constraints, desire proves to be, as *Tristana* makes unambiguously clear, no truly liberating force, often, instead, causing even greater havoc and grief in the daily routines of ordinary human lives.

The narrative of an orphaned girl's seduction by her uncle and guardian, whom she eventually marries and murders —interrupted by a brief and unsatisfactory idyll of romantic love with a young Catalan painter— hinges on Freud's work on Oedipal rites of passage towards the socialization of the self. The quasi-incestuous involvements of Tristana and Lope trace the vicissitudes and traumas of oppressive, imprisoning forms of father/daughter relationships, but alongside this re-enactment of the more negative patterns of the Oedipal drama, the film also raises wider questions

---

[1] See Robert G. Havard, "The Seventh Art of Luis Buñuel: *Tristana* and the Rites of Freedom", *Quinquereme* V (1982), 56-74. See also Gwynne Edwards' equally comprehensive study of the film in *The Discreet Art of Luis Buñuel* (London and Boston: Marion Boyars, 1982), and Joan Mellen's "Buñuel's *Tristana*", in *Women and their Sexuality in the New Film* (New York: Horizon Press, 1973), 191-202.

about the relations between the sexes, focusing especially on the enduring mixture of awe and dread, feelings often prompted by hostility arising out of mutual ignorance, leading to complicated manoeuvres to defuse or at the very least contain the perceived threat to self or social structures. In this film, as becomes clear when Lope's maid Saturna remarks to Tristana, "las leyes están hechas por los hombres, hija", the focus switches more persistently to male perspectives, to male strategies of coping with the perceived threat of the female, although the female discourse, especially in its more tormented and revenge-seeking moments, also finds room for sharply-focused and often lurid expression.

Whereas the film's last moments shift the centre of interest very firmly towards the monstrous shapes of female transgression against the nightmare of the male social order, the rest of the film largely concentrates on the male's attempts to deal with the enigma of femininity, something recognized by the narrative as a phenomenon owing as much to social construction as to genetics. As always in Buñuel, contradictions abound, and the film's rhetoric, clearly designed to expose the tyrannies of the male order, slips in unguarded moments into its own prejudices and distortions. First of all, for all his glaring faults, intolerable attitudes and behaviour towards Tristana, Fernando Rey's Lope is redeemed by humour, a certain degree of profound even if belated self-knowledge, and a genuine although of course misguided affection for the seemingly credulous and virginal waif in his charge. If, as Rey has himself remarked in interviews, he became a sort of *alter ego* for Buñuel, it would seem that the *auteur* has fallen on the mercy of the viewer by shrouding guilt with charm, patriarchal victimization with appeals to recognition of all too common human frailties leading to acts of cruelty and abuse.[2] Among the more negative confessional implications of don Lope's tormented attitudes, the obsession with traditional definitions of masculinity and its exposure to the devious assaults of *afeminamiento* connects specifically with Buñuel's own curious disavowals of Lorca's homosexuality, and, more generally, with his edgy treatment of homosexuality as a whole.[3]

Secondly, among the profusion of energetic, defiant females scattered across the range of Buñuel's films, there is a liberal provision of characters who seem to frighten the life out of their creator as much as out of the males with whom they clash in the narratives. In *Los olvidados*, the mother who cruelly persists in rejecting the advances of a sympathetic, delinquent, but ultimately repentant, son; in *Belle de Jour*, the superficially perfect bourgeoise housewife who finds sexual fulfilment away from the sanitized rituals practised with her bland, unexciting, but again likeable husband, and

---

[2] See BBC TV's *Arena* interview, 11 February 1984 (BBC 2).
[3] Luis Buñuel, *Mon Dernier Soupir* (Paris: Robert Laffont: 1982), 194. See also the excellent account of Buñuel's relations with Lorca and Dalí in Agustín Sánchez Vidal, *Buñuel, Lorca, Dalí: el enigma sin fin* (Barcelona: Editorial Planeta, 1988).

in the imaginative Sadean arabesques of desire at Mme. Anaïs' house of shame; in *Cet obscur objet du désir*, the voluptuous, sultry mistress who torments an ageing and besotted Sugar-Daddy by stripping off and making love before his very eyes with her young gypsy Adonis; these are only three examples of characters who are made to behave in ways that inevitably cross unconscious as well as consciously motivated gender-based issues with the specific demands of the narrative, thus creating multiple levels of ambiguity that highlight the *auteur*'s repetitive obsessions with the motif as well as those by which the leading male characters are afflicted. Seen from one point of view, these characters are the recognizable products of a destructive ideology; from another, they embody the eternal threat posed by the enigmatic scourge of male desire, perhaps by now a force too colonized by the historical legacy of the socializing process ever to be capable of redemption, and therefore, under the circumstances, more than ever in need of effective confinement.

For all the lip-service paid to transgression of the patriarchal order, Tristana's don Lope Garrido, ignorant of the finer nuances and complexities of female psychology —especially perhaps the co-existence of male and female tendencies in the same individual— seems, in addition to much else, to seek in Tristana release from the routine women of his rakish past, going to the extreme of denying his own private code prohibiting seduction of friends' wives and innocent, vulnerable girls. Tristana's sexual allure, like that of the "collégienne précoce" of M. Husson's pleasure in *Belle de Jour*, indicates an old man's weariness and fear of age, seeking rejuvenation through the freshness and firmness of youth, and, simultaneously, control and trivialization of a captive young woman, her schoolgirl aura gratifying a fetish that at once distances and empowers the seducer. Virginity offers the additional attraction, of course, of what Freud calls "no memory of sexual relations with another", reinforcing a right to exclusive possession, something that will create a "state of bondage in the woman which guarantees that possession of her shall continue undisturbed and make her able to resist new impressions and enticements from outside".[4]

Lope's attraction to Tristana, then, is motivated by a fantasy of innocence and virginal purity, uncontaminated by worldly wickedness, the desire for someone still sufficiently vulnerable, naïve and self-effacing to be trained into serviceability, what Joan Mellen has described as a *tabula rasa* open to inscription with all the suffocating values of petit-bourgeois subservient domesticity hitherto apparently despised in a hypocritical and by now inwardly disillusioned life as a somewhat fading, rather ludicrous provincial don Juan. Even though the point is never made explicitly, we are led to feel that in addition to the diminishing availability of suitable female prey, the

---

[4] Sigmund Freud, *On Sexuality. Three Essays on the Theory of Sexuality and Other Works*, translated by James Strachey and edited by Angela Richards (Harmondsworth: Pelican Books, 1977), 265.

reality of transgressive, independent, sexually self-conscious women in the world at large has probably made Lope, now that the opportunity has seemingly offered itself, seek the consolations of a life shared with a powerless ingénue, in which he can finally exercise control over a sex, in Freud's words, "different from man, for ever incomprehensible and mysterious, strange and therefore aparently hostile", a sex, moreover, whose active hostility can in a wide variety of ways "take the extreme form of castration".[5]

Fears and threats of castration provide the motivation for repression. Everywhere characters submit themselves to an unquestioning acceptance of constraints and inhibitions of various kinds: the bell-ringer —like the blind man in *Los olvidados*— ignores or dismisses the widespread repressions all around, speaks nostalgically of the past and its strict adherence to traditions of discipline; the policeman, firing at a rabid dog, displaces onto a dumb animal the fury of a community's outrage against challenges to its embrace of reassuring, conservative traditions; passers-by in the streets of Toledo, symbol in the film's departure from the novel's original Madrid setting of everything that is at once beautiful, glorious and, in all negative senses, provincially-minded, fulminate against the failure to abide by accepted standards of decency when they see a couple kissing openly and unashamedly in a street. Here women as much as men are the slaves of ideology, high rank (as in the case of Josefina, Lope's sister), seduced no less than low (as in the case of Saturna, Lope's maid), by its equivocal, powerful allure.

Of all the film's ideological Golems, none matches in grotesqueness the eventually acquired monstrousness of Tristana in maturity, married to her loathed but apparently necessary former guardian, accepting her victimization by the socializing process, yet simultaneously striking out through her treatment of Lope against the system's callousness of which he is so vivid a projection. Before her radical transformation from obedient daughter-surrogate and complaisant mistress into the crippled scourge of a patriarch, Tristana represents a male fantasy of innocence and naïvety imposed upon the as yet developing instincts and urges of a woman denied independence and self-fulfilment. In the essay on "Femininity", Freud exposes the dangers of identifying masculinity with agressiveness, femininity with passivity.[6] Women, he argues, expressing a banal truth only astonishing for its necessary anti-patriarchal formulation, may often give preference to passive aims and modes of behaviour, but that is largely the result of powerful social processes causing, additionally, the development of strong masochistic tendencies. Undeniably, though, in the pre-Oedipal phase of female development, a phase that subjects the female to

---

[5] Sigmund Freud, *New Introductory Lectures on Sexuality*, translated by James Strachey and edited by Angela Richards (Harmondsworth: Pelican Books, 1973), 145.
[6] See "Femininity", *New Introductory Lectures*, 148-150; 165 *et seq.*

the "socializing processes of the Superego and the taking up of her place in society", phallic, masculine impulses co-exist with feminine ones, traces of which survive even in the post-Oedipal phase.[7] Their surfacing makes even clearer why women remain an enigma to some men.

While the phallic urges, paradoxically further nurtured and developed by the repressions to which Tristana initially submits in don Lope's household, reach their most monstrous form after the amputation of her leg, they are in evidence right from the start. In another of the film's many ambiguities, during the scene of the football match in which Saturna's son Saturno has been reprimanded for tripping one of the opposing players, Tristana is shown offering Saturno an apple. Absent from the scene, Lope has not witnessed this most mythic of female gestures. The innocent Tristana of Lope's fantasies, the longed-for, impressionable and subservient virgin serves notice even at this early stage of a desire to release an active, aggressive libido. The sexually pure and innocent orphan is also Eve, oldest of *femmes fatales*, embodiment of the very nightmare from which Lope is in flight. Yet, the scene remains ambiguous: either, in refusing to make more overt connections between an act of generosity (a middle-class girl offering fruit to a handicapped proletarian boy), judgment is deliberately reserved for the eye of the beholder, implicated more directly in the scene now, and left to form an opinion on the basis of innocence or prejudice; or, given the history of Buñuel's equivocal portrayal of women, and on the basis of his various shifts of emphasis from the novel's original patterns (especially the transformation of the novel's more optimistic though still satirical ending, where Tristana settles down to a respectable marriage with Lope, into the far bleaker moment of her fatal decision not to summon the doctor when following a heart attack Lope is on the point of death), the scene really does warn of treachery lying at the heart of innocence.

The film's ending, in which Tristana proves to be a *femme fatale*, Eve and Judith rolled into one, creates resonances beyond the purely formal demands of the narrative. The dream sequences in which Tristana sees Lope's decapitated head replacing the bell clapper at the top of the church tower are, after all, perhaps not exclusive to Tristana. They may, arguably, also belong to Lope, and by extension, to all men troubled by the terrible enigma of femininity. The image of the head is twice linked directly to Tristana, who is of course a nightmare construction of patriarchal repression. Intriguingly, though, on one occasion don Lope also awakes in terror from a nightmare, though we are denied a glimpse of the nightmare itself. Has he, too, seen his own decapitated head, severed by the woman on whom he has lavished his care, affection, generosity (and lust?). Like the apple incident, and like the moment of defloration, when the dog, mischievously defined *alter ego* of the viewer, is thrown out of the room,

---

[7] *Ibid.*, 165.

as doors shut all around Tristana, creating an effect not only of entrapment but also of refusal of access to the viewer (compare the obliteration of sound in other films, e.g. *Le Charme discret de la bourgeoisie*), the scene remains deliberately opaque, mysterious, sphinx-like in its challenges to interpretation, in its appeal to the viewer's complicity, a complicity potentially arousing the mixed responses of awe and dread in the presence of attractive women by which the Saturnos—retreating into the bushes at the sight of a woman's exposed breasts—the don Lopes or even the don Luises are eternally gripped. Buñuel engages the viewer in a battle for control over the image of a woman, but the transformation of Tristana from healthy young woman to cripple, like the transformation of Catherine Deneuve from impassive, devastatingly frigid "White Devil" of desire into a pastiche of the middle class Iberian temptress, remains fascinatingly ambiguous throughout. The choice of Deneuve, pallid synthesis of French chic, elegance and beauty, seems at first to clash with the film's ambiance of intensely Castillian provincialism. Buñuel himself admits that Deneuve and Galdós' Tristana are worlds apart.[8] And yet even if realist conventions are flouted by Deneuve's presence and mystique, the universalizing, iconographic force of her place in the film's narrative, taking the film out of strictly-defined cultural contexts, clearly offered Buñuel irresistible opportunities. Catherine Deneuve as Tristana not only reactivates obsessions with the quasi-Hitchcockian surface cool blonde/ inwardly dark and libidinal Fury of other films; she also represents, more generally, a dream image of beauty, an aloofness, an Olympian pallor and distance all the more suitable, from a male point of view, as Molly Haskell argues, for demystifying a powerful fantasy.[9] The first step in the process leads to a metaphorical as well as a literal defloration.

As the man who deflowers Tristana, Lope unleashes what Freud, in the lecture on virginity, defines as archaic feelings of hostility, unwittingly transforming her into the Judith whose dream of Holofernes' decapitation takes on the symbolic significance of castration.[10] Defloration here becomes not the hoped-for binding of the woman lastingly to the man, but the hideous expression of an archaically-rooted, even primitive form of hostility against the male aggressor. In the process of her apparent transformation from obedient, virginal daughter into both devouring mother (she is maternal towards Saturno, and reduces Lope to a kind of infantile dependency), and castrator, where the wish-fulfilment dream of castration becomes the reality of murder, Buñuel offers a darkly hyperbolized dramatic conceit of Freud's description and

---

[8] See Agustín Sánchez Vidal's excellent, informative and analytical *Luis Buñuel. Obra cinematográfica* (Madrid: Ediciones J.C., 1984), 325.
[9] See Molly Haskell, *From Reverence to Rape* (Chicago: University of Chicago Press, 1987), 304-5.
[10] See Freud, "The Taboo of Virginity", *On Sexuality*, 281.

analysis of the weaning of the daughter from the mother to the father. Significantly, the film begins with Tristana's mother's death, an action resonant with ideological as well as narrative meaning.

Although contentiousness surrounds Freud's analysis of the processes leading to the daughter's transferred attachments from mother to father —with all the implications of pain resulting from loss of the mother's breast, nursery discipline, denial or punishment of multifarious sexual urges, and, above all, the castration complex and the vexed question of penis envy— reference to such matters and their handling by Freud seem useful in the context of a surrealist text not itself completely liberated, for all its brilliant artifice, from contentiousness or even prejudice.[11] At the very least, though, the Freudian model allows Buñuel room for formulating his sombre misgivings about the social as well as the personal consequences of such processes.

For Freud, of course, the castration complex is the most important of these considerations. Developing his argument by pointing to the drive to acquire the longed-for penis, Freud refers to the daughter's belief in the mother's castration, as a result of which she abandons masturbation of the clitoris and becomes increasingly passive as she turns to the father, in the process replacing a wish for the penis with the desire for a baby. Ultimately, these twin wishes, traced back by Freud to primitive sources, become conflated as the daughter submits to the socializing processes of the Oedipal drama. The film seems to accept the logic of Freud's argument, but presents it dramatically in a way that stresses its negative and, as in the particular instance of Tristana's relationship with Lope, its often horrific consequences. The way the argument is developed in its implicit formulation within the narrative once again hovers between rhetoric on the verge either of misogyny or of feminist awareness, with scenes like the one in which a birdcage appears in frame as Tristana talks to the conservative bell-ringer, or where she discusses her desire to be a concert pianist with the ultimately conservative Horacio, her painter lover, suggesting that the text too is conscious of itself as the product of some of the very processes it seeks consistently, and in the face of all its own in-built prejudices, to interrogate.

But this ambivalent treatment of the castration complex finds its most grisly formulation not only in the decapitation of don Lope but also in the amputation of Tristana's leg. While the amputated leg is another of the fetishes, or ghoulish Calanda-inspired substitutes for the mother's penis the little boy once believed in and still refuses to give up, through which Lope disavows the threat of his own castration, the severed head represents the female's castration of the male by the woman who has become another of the film's cannibalizing mothers. Lope progresses from a position of benign parental concern over Tristana's necessary mutilation to one of collusion with male

---

[11] See "Femininity", *New Introductory Lectures*, 158-63.

medical control of the female body, to increasingly fetishistic obsession, a development matched by Buñuel's own many self-mocking, self-conscious allusions to foot fetishism (cf. *The Diary of a Chambermaid*, *Viridiana* and so on), here further emphasized by the almost gratuitous showing of the false leg in scenes of no direct concern to Lope. On the other hand, what Buñuel and Lope do to Tristana is matched by the action of the castrating mothers: not including Tristana, the film's most destructive mother is Saturna, Lola Gaos' wizened, weasel-like, gravel-throated custodian of tradition, female version of the progeny-devouring god so unnervingly depicted by Goya: like Galdós, Freud, and the Old Testament Holofernes and Judith text, one of Buñuel's great sources of inspiration in this film. The man-eating mother and castrator here has struggled to wrest control from the male, has, perhaps in restricted ways, often unconsciously, transgressed the legitimizing norms of the social order, yet is herself ultimately too traumatized by entry into patriarchy ever to be able seriously to damage the system, let alone achieve its overthrow. In the clash of male and female discourses —epitomized by the power relations governing the fatally entangled lives of Tristana and don Lope— the female only ever appears to triumph. For, as in *Viridiana*, say, where Don Jaime's continued influence over Viridiana's life is signified by the prominence of his portrait in the living room, so here the triumph of conformist ideology is marked by the visual transformation of Tristana into the highly ironic "Otra" (Horacio's word), not of a truly alternative, liberated world, but of bourgeois ideology itself, the heavily made-up, traditionally dressed, imperious, and ultimately murderous monster of male desire, her colonized appearance most vividly and gaudily pronouncing the triumph of the old order.

In Buñuel's world of Sadean torment and worldly hypocrisy, rebels are scarce. But wherever they exist, and whatever their ultimate failings, their denials or refusals of a debilitating social system —whether through humour, through sexual or political or other forms of transgression against reason's dream of monsters— bear witness to the survival of truly human desires for survival and knowledge. These in the end are what save Tristana and Lope from merely reflecting the projections of individual or collective phobias, anxieties or dread. Though they are both ultimately annihilated by the system, they each enjoy moments of isolation from the brutish, sanctimonious, reason-cursed multitude, through their acts of marvellous, even exhilarating and fulfilling defiance unmasking the arbitrary follies of a life-denying order.

---

* *I am indebted to generous grants from the British Academy and the Small Grants Committee of the University of Newcastle upon Tyne, enabling me to carry out this research and to deliver this paper at Pittsburgh.*

La periferia del deseo: Julián del Casal y el pederasta urbano

ÓSCAR MONTERO

Casi todos los críticos de la obra de Casal han aludido tanto al "problema" de su sexualidad como a la riqueza de su erotismo textual. La división del territorio ya es de por sí reveladora: por una parte, la sexualidad del individuo, diversamente nombrada y finalmente anónima, el célebre amor que no osa decir su nombre; por la otra, el erotismo de las representaciones en la obra. Semejante escisión es ambigua, incluso arbitraria; pero por eso mismo, las zonas opacas que sugiere son atractivas, es decir, convidan a una lectura.

El mismo Casal contribuyó al misterio sobre su sexualidad y sus contemporáneos se encargaron de complicarlo. Sería difícil y tal vez infructuoso proponer un modelo epistemológico o un conjunto de definiciones como gesto fundador de un comentario sobre las repercusiones de la sexualidad y el erotismo en la obra de Casal y en la ciudad donde vivió. Por el momento, prefiero la latitud, las ambigüedades y la deriva a la imposición prematura de definiciones y esquemas dignos del lecho de Procrustes. Se trata de enmarcar a Casal y su obra con el retrato de la Habana gay en 1889, basándose en una crónica del poeta cubano y en dos tratados pseudo-científicos coetáneos.

La crónica de Casal se titula "A través de la ciudad. El Centro de Dependientes", y se publicó por primera vez en el periódico habanero *La Discusión*, 28 de diciembre de 1889. Los dos tratados son los siguientes: *La prostitución en La Habana* del Dr. Benjamín Céspedes (1888); y *El amor y la prostitución. Réplica a un libro del Dr. Céspedes* de Pedro Giralt y Alemán (1889).[1] En las páginas que siguen los tres textos citados se superponen no sólo para aclarar un aspecto poco conocido de la sexualidad

---

[1] La crónica de Casal también se encuentra en *Prosas*, Tomo 2, Edición del Centenario (La Habana: Consejo Nacional de Cultura, 1963), 17-20. El libro de Céspedes, *La prostitución en La Habana*, se publicó con un prólogo de Enrique José Varona en La Habana: Tipografía O'Reilly, 1888; el de Pedro Giralt y Alemán, *El amor y la prostitución. Réplica a un libro del Dr. Céspedes* en La Habana: La Universal, 1889. Las citas que siguen remiten respectivamente a estas ediciones y se darán parentéticamente.

habanera en el fin de siglo sino para sugerir una nueva ruta hacia la sexualidad y el erotismo de Julián del Casal.[2]

Siguiendo *grosso modo* las sugerencias de Bataille, podría decirse que bajo el nombre de erotismo se agrupan las transgresiones del cuerpo en determinado contexto; el erotismo contradice y contamina el orden de la realidad hegemónica; es también un aspecto de la vida interior del individuo y de la pérdida de sí.[3] En la segunda mitad del siglo XIX, las oposiciones binarias, normal/anormal, fértil/estéril, natural/artificial, rigen múltiples zonas de un saber que todavía determina los recursos epistemológicos contemporáneos más diversos; en el contexto de dicho saber, el erotismo de Casal es un "secreto abierto", velado y a la vez revelado en un contrapunteo dialéctico.[4] El saber científico del XIX transformó una práctica sexual heterodoxa, la sodomía, en una especie social, la homosexualidad, que llegó a amalgamar toda práctica sexual considerada aberrante y que por supuesto se opuso radicalmente a su contrario, también recién acuñado, la heterosexualidad. Las clasificaciones del saber decimonónico revelan el deseo no de suprimir sino de codificar y parcelar: de definir "un orden natural del desorden", en la frase de Foucault.[5] En las ciencias que dominan el saber en la segunda mitad del siglo XIX se cumple el proceso de transformar las prácticas sexuales en diversos discursos, es decir en "sistemas de utilidad". La "perversidad" y la "decadencia" de la literatura del fin de siglo responden dialécticamente a esa sistematización utilitaria de los deseos del cuerpo. Frente a las versiones insulares de ese saber, ¿qué forma toma la respuesta estética de Casal? ¿Cómo se inscribe su erotismo en relación a los "sistemas de utilidad" que cumplían una compleja etapa de desarrollo histórico precisamente en el momento en que escribe?

Es sorprendente la abundancia de las referencias a la sexualidad de Casal, desde los comentarios de sus contemporáneos hasta la crítica más reciente. Sin embargo, se trata de diversas versiones que aluden a los mismos incidentes, que se basan ya en el anecdotario biográfico ya en la obra, ambos de los cuales se nutren de un dato desconocido o indecible, a saber la identidad sexual del individuo, o más bien su orientación sexual, ya sea hacia la homosexualidad o hacia un ascetismo casi masoquista. La "degeneración" de las diversas agrupaciones artísticas del fin de siglo,

---

[2] Utilizaré la palabra "pederasta" en el sentido que evidentemente tiene en la época de Casal, es decir casi sinómino de "homosexual", que, dicho sea de paso, no aparece en los documentos cubanos que consulté. Ver Nota 9.
[3] *El erotismo*, traducción de Toni Vicens (Barcelona: Tusquets, 1980).
[4] Eve Kosofsky Sedgwick, *Epistemology of the Closet* (Berkeley-Los Angeles: University of California Press, 1990), 67-90.
[5] *The History of Sexuality*, vol. 1: *An Introduction*, traducción de Robert Hurley (Nueva York: Vintage, 1980), 15-49. Publicado originalmente con el título de *La Volonté de savoir* (París: Gallimard, 1976).

por ejemplo, decadentes y simbolistas, tuvo su definición más explícita y probablemente más influyente en el célebre libro de Max Nordau, *Entartung* (Berlín, 1892). Para Nordau el erotismo, o lo que llama la "erotomanía", es el denominador común de la obra de los decadentes y es sinómino de la "egomanía". El artista decadente y "degenerado" es incapaz de traer "una representación borrosa y liminal" hacia "el brillante círculo focal de la conciencia".[6]

Los primeros críticos de Casal se basan en las mismas fuentes positivistas que utilizó Nordau y aluden constantemente a la relación entre la degeneración física y moral y la producción literaria. Para Nordau, las anomalías, las aberraciones y las enfermedades características de todos los "ismos" decadentes contaminan el cuerpo social sano. En su biografía de Casal, Emilio de Armas sintetiza la cuestión sobre la sexualidad en "la leyenda" sobre Casal, "que gustosamente acogerían sus contemporáneos como pieza romántica de primera calidad". Como toda leyenda, se nutría de un secreto: "Sus amigos solían hablar de él en el tono de quienes comparten un secreto de iniciados".[7] Casal contribuyó a ese "misterio" el "secreto de mis males" de "Rondeles", que comienza: "De mi vida misteriosa,/ tétrica y desencantada,/ oirás contar una cosa/ que te deje el alma helada".[8]

Emilio de Armas comenta el anecdotario y la crítica sobre el tema, donde se alternan el detalle de carácter biográfico y la alusión a la obra. Las lecturas que cita de Armas tienden al psicologismo característico de cierta crítica a partir de fines del siglo XIX. Por ejemplo, José Antonio Portuondo señala en Casal "un intenso sentimiento de culpabilidad"; Gustavo Duplessis se refiere a la "sexualidad impura" del poeta adolescente que "entraba en pugna feroz con su erótica exaltada e idealista". Para Carmen Poncet, Casal era "un tipo sicológicamente intersexual", uno de esos individuos poseedores de "un mecanismo sexual perfecto; pero que frecuentemente se inhiben por la falsa conciencia que experimentan de su capacidad" (35-40). Cómo se enteró la profesora Poncet del estado de perfección del "mecanismo sexual" de Casal, casi medio siglo después de su muerte, debe constituir otro misterio. En fin de cuentas, el tema de la sexualidad vital y del erotismo estético de Casal en manos de amigos y críticos "nos lo complica con anécdotas y episodios menudos que interpretan

---

[6] Cito de la traducción al inglés, Max Nordau, *Degeneration* (1892) (New York: Appleton, 1895). La traducción al español es de Nicolás Salmerón y García, *Degeneración* (Madrid, 1902). Las citas de la edición de Nueva York, traducidas por mí al español, se darán parentéticamente.

[7] Emilio de Armas, *Casal* (La Habana: Letras Cubanas, 1981), 33. Las citas que siguen se darán parentéticamente.

[8] *Rimas, The Poetry of Julian del Casal*, 3 vols. editado por Robert Jay Glickman (Gainesville: University of Florida Press, 1976), vol. 1, 209. Las citas de la poesía de Casal remiten a esta edición y este volumen y se darán parentéticamente.

demasiado a su arbitrio", en la conclusión sensata de Monner Sans (41). Si el estudio de los deseos desconocidos del poeta es problemático, es inexorable la vuelta dialéctica al texto, a su representación de la sexualidad, iluminada o enmascarada, según sea el caso, por el secreto en cuestión.

En el sinuoso circunloquio sobre la sexualidad de Casal, se destaca sobre todo su singularidad; cabría decir su unicidad. El gesto fundacional del pánico homosexual, evidente en la crítica sobre Casal, no es la intolerancia —después de todo a Casal se le admira por sus dones poéticos— sino la marginación: Casal es diferente, único, tanto como poeta como individuo.[9] La sexualidad de su cuerpo no sólo carece de nombre, sino que se reduce a la categoría de lo anómalo, lo marginado y lo aislado. El vocabulario psicológico utilizado por la crítica muy tempranamente ha definido esa marginación. La soledad de la figura de Casal, tan poderosamente evocada por Cintio Vitier, un Casal algo torpe en el andar, más corpulento de lo que uno podría imaginar, bamboleándose por la calle tropical, reclamaba mi atención, quizá porque correspondía, porque yo quería que correspondiera, a la soledad peculiar que siente uno cuando reconoce que es gay y cuando sospecha que nadie más puede serlo. También me atraía esta pregunta: ¿cómo era el ambiente gay en la Habana de 1890? Me atraía porque sabía con toda certeza que "ambiente" había, sin tener, sin embargo, la menor idea de sus diversas manifestaciones ni de cómo investigarlas. Mi primer paso fue separarme provisoriamente de Casal y su obra, y sobre todo distanciarme por el momento de la tradición crítica y su compleja urdimbre metafórica donde la enfermedad, la orientación erótica y la producción literaria se traspapelan para producir diversas lecturas, torpes o acertadas según fuera el caso, pero animadas todas por un secreto indecible.

---

[9] Aunque la versión alemana de la palabra "homosexual" se utiliza por primera vez en 1869, no aparece en los otros idiomas europeos hasta 1892 y no circula ampliamente hasta casi mediados del siglo XX. Ver David Halperin, *One Hundred Years of Homosexuality and Other Essays on Greek Love* (New York: Routledge, 1990). Moliner, *Diccionario del uso de español* (Madrid: Gredos, 1967), todavía conserva como sinónimos "invertido" y "sodomita", y se refiere a "afeminado". Martín Alonso, *Diccionario del español moderno* (Madrid: Aguilar, 1966), la define como "inclinación sexual hacia personas del mismo sexo"; la vigésima edición del diccionario de la Real Academia (1984) como "inclinación manifiesta u oculta hacia la relación erótica con invididuos del mismo sexo". Al menos en una ocasión, la crítica del siglo XX se refiere a Casal como un "intersexual", uno de los términos que se utilizaron para reemplazar "homosexual"; otros términos fueron "homoerotismo" y "uranismo", mencionados en Lily Litvak, *Erotismo fin de siglo* (Barcelona: Bosch, 1979), 155. Ver George Chauncey, "From Sexual Inversion to Homosexuality", *Salmagundi*, núm. 58-59 (1982-1983), 114-146. Sobre el pánico homosexual, la incertidumbre etimológica y el impacto ideológico de los términos, especialmente "homosexual" y "gay", ver Sedgwick, *Epistemology*, 16, 36-39.

Por eso quiero reconstruir parcialmente un aspecto del ambiente de la Habana contemporánea de Casal, para que esos personajes sociales constituyan una presencia coral en la lectura ulterior de la obra. Sé que Casal pasó por esas mismas aceras; no podré jamás afirmar, o negar, si rechazó ese ambiente o si lo conoció, o si simplemente cruzó a la acera de enfrente. En todo caso, para acercarse a lo que Lezama llamó "el quitasol de un inmenso Eros" en su "Oda a Julián del Casal", para compartir los versos que dicen "Nuestro escandaloso cariño te persigue", hay que mencionar el silencio de esos otros, los paseantes de las afueras del Parque, diagnosticados por un saber que todavía hace estragos. De esta manera tal vez se transforme el secreto y el castigo urdidos en torno a lo sexual en simpatía erótica a la distancia.

Desde un comienzo, la crítica puso sobre el tapete, por así decir, la cuestión de la sexualidad de Casal, fundando una leyenda basada en ciertos datos biográficos y sobre todo en una lectura causalista de la obra; el tema se menciona y en seguida se pasa a otros temas aledaños, como el de la enfermedad corporal y el desgaño espiritual, o el consabido contraste vida/arte; de esta manera se alude al tema y a la vez se borra la incertidumbre epistemológica que evidentemente provoca. Semejante espejismo opaca el asunto, y suponiendo que ese haya sido el deseo del mismo Casal, no tiene por qué serlo el de la crítica, cuya labor inevitablemente parcela y reordena los textos disponibles para tratar de entenderlos mejor, no para participar consciente o inconscientemente de su simulación original. Es decir, la investigación se desplaza del plano psicológico, donde se reproducen ciertos prejuicios originales a la definición misma de la homosexualidad, hacia el plano social.[10] Si en la Habana finisecular las prácticas sexuales aberrantes o "anormales" se desconocían, lo cual es altamente dudoso, o si simplemente no se nombraron en lo absoluto, lo cual es más probable, no habría manera de documentar dicho plano social en el cual contextualizar la persona poética de Casal, su respuesta estética, y los comentarios sobre su rareza y su degeneración vital y literaria que sirvieron de base a la crítica posterior para seguir rondando el citado misterio. No hay evidencia para situar a Casal en un ambiente homosexual; sin embargo, se habla de la importancia de lo sexual en Casal porque se trata de una sexualidad marginal que por su carácter heterodoxo se manifiesta insistente y diversamente en su obra. El comentario que sigue sobre la presencia real de prácticas sexuales heterodoxas en la Habana finisecular es un intento de desmistificar el aspecto social de esa sexualidad marginal para agrietar un tanto el secreto de Casal,

---

[10] Al desplazar el territorio en cuestión de factores psicológicos a factores sociales, Eve Sedgwick, *Between Men: English Literature and Male Homosocial Desire* (New York: Columbia University Press, 1985) ha liberado a los críticos de la tendencia a enmarcar sus comentarios en términos de un discurso que ignora sus propios prejuicios. Parafraseo el comentario sobre Sedgwick de Richard Dellamora, *Masculine Desire. The Sexual Politics of Victorian Aestheticism* (Chapel Hill: University of North Carolina Press, 1990), 9.

para que no resurja de nuevo como un misterio indecible cuando se comente la obra, para ir más allá de las alusiones y los circunloquios sobre una represión de carácter exclusivamente psicológico y para leer más eficazmente los temas y los desvíos retóricos que constituyen las imágenes textuales que representan dicho secreto.

Es muy probable que la crónica de Casal sobre el "Centro de Dependientes" respondió a un debate contemporáneo sobre la homosexualidad en la capital, y específicamente sobre el comportamiento sexual de los dependientes, un debate ventilado en dos libros publicados unos meses antes de la crónica. El léxico explícito de los dos tratados donde se comenta, o se niega, la homosexualidad de los dependientes, donde del cuerpo se pasa a la ciudad y a la cuestión nacional, contrasta con la descripción en la crónica de Casal, donde se alude a uno de los tratados, pero donde la relación entre los jóvenes se representa en términos de amistad y cariño fraternales pero no sexuales y donde la descripción prolija del salón principal del centro ocupa casi la mitad de la breve crónica. Los tres textos, que se publicaron en La Habana dentro de un período de dos años, demuestran que "el problema" de la homosexualidad se comentaba abiertamente, incluso como correlato de la cuestión nacional, es decir la cuestión del destino político y cultural de la isla. Por otra parte, los dos tratados confirman el hecho de un ambiente gay habanero en plena movida.

El doctor Benjamín Céspedes publicó *La prostitución en La Habana* en 1888. En su prólogo al estudio, Enrique José Varona lo alaba porque "nos invita a acercarnos a una mesa de disección, a contemplar al desnudo úlceras cancerosas, a descubrir los tejidos atacados por el virus" (xi). Según Varona, el cuerpo enfermo es el de la ciudad y la "disección" del doctor es útil puesto que señalar el mal es de algún modo comenzar a sanarlo. La metáfora médica de Varona, sin embargo, no permanece en el plano de la retórica; encuentra su referente en uno de los moradores de la ciudad enferma, entrevistado y examinado por un colega del doctor, "un distinguido facultativo". Un capítulo del libro de Céspedes se titula "La prostitución masculina", donde se presenta detalladamente el ambiente "pederasta" de la ciudad. Vale la pena citar parte del párrafo inicial de este capítulo no sólo por la definición que presenta de la homosexualidad sino porque se trata de una "aberración" evidentemente tan socializada como la prostitución:

> Y aquí en la Habana, desgraciadamente, subsisten con más extensión de lo creíble y con mayor impunidad que en lugar alguno, tamañas degradaciones de la naturaleza humana; tipos de hombres que han invertido su sexo para traficar con estos gustos bestiales, abortos de la infamia que pululan libremente, asqueando a una sociedad que se pregunta indignada, ante la invasión creciente de la plaga asquerosa; si abundando tanto pederasta, habrán también aumentado los clientes de tan horrendos vicios (190).

El doctor comenta la tendencia de algunos de los tales pederastas a fraternizar con las prostitutas, pero más perturbadora es la presencia de los clientes, que sugiere un comercio que ha transformado la capital en una "de esas ciudades sodomíticas", una versión criolla de "la Roma decadente". Inmediatamente sigue la clasificación irrisoria de los pederastas en "tres clases": "el negro, el mulato y el blanco". La clasificación es una de las maneras de marcar la objetividad científica y de distanciar al observador de una comunidad aparentemente dispersa por toda la ciudad, "repartidos en todos los barrios de La Habana". Como la prostituta y como el vampiro, "por la noche se estacionan en los puntos más retirados del Parque y sus alrededores más solitarios". Sigue una descripción del pederasta "afeminado" que cito por su carácter arquetípico; valdría tanto en la Roma decadente como en el Nueva York de mañana. De más está decir que la descripción del ambiente que escandalizó al buen doctor produjo en mí un sentimiento peculiar de simpatía y nostalgia:

> Durante las noches de retreta circulan libremente confundidos con el público, llamando la atención, no de la policía, sino de los concurrentes indignados, las actitudes grotescamente afeminadas de estos tipos que van señalando cínicamente las posaderas erguidas, arqueados y ceñidos los talles, y que al andar con menudos pasos de arrastre, se balancean con contoneos de mujer coqueta. Llevan flequillos en la frente, carmín en el rostro y polvos de arroz en el semblante, ignoble y fatigado de los más y agraciado en algunos. El pederasta responde a un nombre de mujer en la jerga del oficio (191).

Llama la atención en la descripción la actitud de la policía, los representantes inmediatos del poder que deben vigilar el comportamiento de los ciudadanos y que sin embargo parecen no hacer caso a la presencia de los pederastas, o de las prostitutas; es decir, la parcelación del espacio urbano se da por sentada dentro del "orden natural del desorden" mencionado por Foucault. El estereotipo del afeminado, casi un travestí, tan verídicamente representado, se complica con la mención del rostro "agraciado" de algunos y más adelante de sus "amantes preferidos" y de las fiestas que celebran "entre ellos", donde "fingen" partos y bautizos. Siguiendo la pauta del cientifismo decimonónico, el doctor trata de relacionar el comportamiento homosexual con la criminalidad y la enfermedad, pero su objetividad científica no le permite caer en el panfletismo; por ejemplo, anota que "no siempre son pasivos en sus relaciones sexuales" y que "se prestan a ser activos". Su descripción ratifica la existencia de un ambiente gay en la Habana finisecular prototípico del de cualquier gran ciudad al menos hasta 1969, el año de Stonewall.[11]

---

[11] En junio de 1969, frente al bar Stonewall en el Sheridan Square de Greenwich Village, Nueva York, un grupo de hombres y mujeres gays se enfrentó violentamente a la policía que los

El vicio *contra naturam* descrito por Céspedes tiene otro lugar preferido, los talleres y establecimientos donde hacían vida común los jóvenes aprendices y los empleados públicos, que llegaban a la capital del interior o del extranjero y que a falta de familia o del consabido tío, pernoctaban en los lugares de trabajo o en algunos recintos organizados con el fin de albergarlos. El capítulo sobre "La prostitución masculina" concluye con una entrevista a uno de esos jóvenes "como de quince años de edad", que viene a consultar al doctor porque creía "estar dañado por dentro". El médico le diagnostica un "chancro infectante sifilítico" y luego fija su atención en él: "noté lo afeminado de su rostro, tan agraciado como el de cualquier mujer, y lo redondo y mórbido de sus formas de adolescente", "mórbido", por supuesto, en el doble sentido de "suave, blando, delicado" y "que padece enfermedad o la ocasiona", uno de los adjetivos claves de los diversos decadentismos finiseculares y de sus detractores porque rubrica tanto la enfermedad como la "erotomanía" y la "egomanía", para citar la bestia negra bicéfala de Max Nordau.[12]

La entrevista del doctor con el muchacho, que es dependiente en una tienda de ropas, revela otro aspecto de la vida gay de la época. En el lugar donde pernocta, los compañeros "acarician" al muchacho y "hacían conmigo ciertos manejos"— "Con casi todos," responde a las preguntas insistentes del médico, porque "me pegaban," dice en un comienzo, y luego añade: "Me besaban y me cogían la mano y yo tenía que hacerles." Entre esos "todos", "Habían [sic] dos que dormían juntos, pero a esos se les miraba con más respeto." En la entrevista del médico, citada verbatim por el doctor Céspedes, en medio de tanta referencia a lo grotesco y lo enfermizo, el "respeto" de los compañeros hacia los dos que "dormían juntos" es sorprendente y conmovedor. En cuanto a la autoridad, en este caso el "*principal*" del comercio, es tan indiferente como la policía, y "con tal de no aflojar dinero, en lo demás no se mete en esas cosas feas", dice el muchacho (194), sugiriendo la relativa tolerancia hacia las prácticas en cuestión. El estudio del doctor Céspedes reproduce los dos aspectos básicos de la definición de la homosexualidad en el siglo XIX: por una parte, es una enfermedad con síntomas identificables, especialmente cuando el cuerpo, como el del chico

---

acosaba. Jonathan Katz, *Gay American History: Lesbians and Gay Men in the U.S.A.* (Nueva York: Avon Books, 1976), 508. La Rebelión de Stonewall, como llegó a llamarse el incidente, marca el comienzo del movimiento de liberación gay y la transformación del ambiente homosocial urbano, donde proliferan nuevos y diferentes tipos de comportamiento y donde la marginación tradicional se integra de diversas maneras a la cultura dominante. Antes de Stonewall, la marginación del homosexual en el espacio urbano y su "comercio" con los "clientes" descritos en *La prostitución en La Habana* son característicos. Por otra parte, la epidemia del SIDA ha provocado nuevas formas de marginación.

[12] Nordau utiliza las dos categorías casi sinónimas a través de su *Entartung* (*Degeneración*). Ver nota 6.

entrevistado, está marcado por "chancros"; por otra parte, ampliando la metáfora, es una enfermedad social que "infecta" el resto del cuerpo político sano. Las metáforas somáticas del mal tienen una fuente evidente, "científica", en el cuerpo del muchacho; pero incluso antes de que se le entreviste, las metáforas antropomórficas, que ya eran moneda corriente, se aplican a la ciudad, de la misma forma que se aplican a los aspectos "decadentes" de la obra de Casal. En la descripción del ambiente gay de la Habana finisecular se dibuja la red metafórica que constituye un aspecto fundamental del saber de la época, un saber que se aplicó tanto al crimen, la enfermedad y la homosexualidad como a las prácticas simbólicas, específicamente toda escritura donde predomine "el adorno del exterior" y la incapacidad de "dibujar", es decir de significar nítidamente, "en el luminoso círculo focal de la conciencia" —otra vez Nordau (61).

Significativamente, en el análisis del doctor Céspedes la homosexualidad se sitúa ambiguamente entre la enfermedad y la práctica simbólica; los "pederastas" son seres "viciosos", marcados por los síntomas de las enfermedades venéreas, que además "fingen" los comportamientos sociales que en ese momento definen "la mujer", particularmente la prostituta, es decir se maquillan con polvo de arroz, se contonean al caminar.[13] Si no se puede ni se quiere situar al individuo Casal en el ambiente, ni siquiera en su periferia, descrito por el doctor Céspedes, se debe en cambio reconocer el impacto, y la violencia, de sus metáforas en los comentarios críticos sobre la obra de Casal, en las descripciones del cuerpo enfermo y corrupto en algunas de sus propias crónicas y poemas, y en la identificación tópica, pero finalmente enfática y subjetiva, en Casal, de la ciudad tanto con el mal y la decadencia como con la creación poética, resumida en los célebres tercetos, de los cuales recuerdo los dos primeros:

> Tengo el impuro amor de las ciudades,
> y a este sol que ilumina las edades
> prefiero yo del gas las claridades.

---

[13] En la *Crónica Médico-Quirúrgica de la Habana*, vol. 16 (1890), 79-81, en una sección titulada "La pederastia en la Habana" un tal Dr. Montané nota, entre otros detalles, "el relajamiento del esfínter" en siete de 21 pederastas, que además divide entre "insulares" (17) y "europeos" (4), de La Habana, del interior, etc.; también menciona, como lo hace Céspedes, su forma de pintarse y adornarse y "su extraño gusto por los perfumes y objetos brillantes, su monomanía por las fotografías, en las que se hacen representar en trajes de teatro o de mujer". El doctor hizo circular "entre los miembros del Congreso" a quien se dirige "algunos ejemplares que pudo procurarse", se supone que de fotografías, tal vez todavía conservadas en los archivos habaneros. Le agradezco a George Chauncey el regalo de una fotocopia de las páginas citadas.

A mis sentidos lánguidos arroba,
más que el olor de un bosque de caoba,
el ambiente enfermizo de una alcoba (251).

El ambiente descrito por el doctor Céspedes es absolutamente marginal; los pederastas viven en "guaridas" y aunque circulan por el centro de la ciudad, se limitan a la periferia del centro y a las horas nocturnas: "se estacionan en los puntos más retirados del Parque y sus alrededores más solitarios" (190). La entrevista con el muchacho se desarrolla en consulta, ni siquiera la del autor sino en la de un "distinguido compañero", donde "el médico tiene el deber como el confesor de ser reservado en todos los asuntos de sus clientes" (193). Para distanciarse y marcar su autoridad, y sobre todo su diferencia, representada como la ausencia de lo sexual, el doctor utiliza los recursos del narrador privilegiado del naturalismo;[14] es un "especialista" que nombra la enfermedad y hace entrar el cuerpo en "el círculo focal" de su propia representación, que correlativamente niega toda representación ajena: los pederastas "fingen" como fingen los "impostores" decadentes de Nordau.

Los pederastas del doctor Céspedes son marginados no sólo por sus preferencias sexuales sino también implícitamente por su clase; muchos son criminales de oficio, son "desaseados y alcoholistas", "lavanderos, peluqueros y criados de las prostitutas". Los dependientes y empleados de las tiendas pertenecen a la clase obrera, y el doctor afirma que las condiciones de vida de este grupo facilitan el desarrollo de la homosexualidad. Salvo en la mención fugaz de "los clientes", la clase de los letrados y profesionales, y del mismo doctor, queda fuera del comercio con el grupo en cuestión, reificado en aras de la ciencia y presentado como objeto de estudio, como la monstruosidad de un museo de historia natural. Finalmente, la solución ofrecida por el doctor no es de carácter moral ni psicológico sino social: los "mancebos célibes" no deben recluirse en falansterios donde la ausencia de la mujer los conduce a la "incontinencia bestial entre hombres" (195).

El libro del doctor Céspedes tuvo una respuesta casi inmediata, que amplía significativamente el panorama, aunque sin duda ése no fue su propósito. En 1889, un año después de aparecido el libro del doctor, Pedro Giralt publica un folleto ambiguamente titulado *El amor y la prostitución. Réplica al Dr. Céspedes*. Su propósito es defender la virilidad de los dependientes y señalar "los vicios" de la burguesía y las clases profesionales, específicamente las clases criollas, puesto que el médico, "hombre vulgarísimo y completamente inepto para especular seriamente en los altos y sublimes principios de la Ciencia", ha imputado "a todo un grupo social los

---

[14] Josefina Ludmer, *Onetti. Los procesos de construcción del relato* (Buenos Aires: Sudamericana, 1977), 122-123.

defectos aislados de uno de sus individuos" (83). En el tono iracundo del panfletista, el autor ataca el "fanatismo del criollismo" en la "obra pornográfica" del doctor, porque cree que éste ha sugerido que la prostitución y la homosexualidad son males de origen europeo que han contaminado la isla.

Un gran número de los habitantes de los albergues de empleados y dependientes descritos por el doctor Céspedes era de origen extranjero, en su mayoría españoles recién emigrados, y Giralt pretende llevar las "necedades científico-sociales" del doctor al plano del debate contemporáneo sobre el nacionalismo. Giralt excusa el comportamiento de los que hacen "papel de hembras" porque lo hacen no por placer sino para "ganarse el sustento" y muchos de ellos pagan su deuda con la sociedad pues han sido enviados a la Isla de Pinos por el Gobernador Civil. Con una cita sorprendente del célebre soneto de "Sor Juana Jesús de la Cruz" [*sic*] sobre cuál es más pecador "la que peca por la paga/ o el que paga por pecar", Giralt desata su ira no sobre los pederastas sino sobre sus clientes, que no son dependientes sino miembros de la élite urbana:

> ¿Cómo calificaremos, pues, a estos pederastas activos y paganos que van o iban a solicitar a los maricones para ocuparlos pagándoles con dinero? No obstante estos, más culpables que los pasivos, no han sido deportados, y se están paseando por las calles de la Habana. ¿Serán dependientes? ¡Ah, si se pudiera decir ciertas cosas que la vergüenza pública prohibe revelar; si fuera lícito contar con nombres y apellidos ciertas historias íntimas y secretas cuyos detalles se cuentan *sotto voce* por los corrillos; las confidencias de algunas mujeres a sus comadres y de éstas a sus íntimos, aparecerían a la luz del sol con toda su repugnante fealdad más de cuatro entes, al parecer bien educados, que llevan levita y ocupan señalados puestos (83-85, énfasis de Giralt).

La terminología anti-científica de Giralt tiene todo el valor de lo explícito: esos "más de cuatro entes", sinécdoque de una muchedumbre, son tan maricones como el chico más afeminado que se pasea por el Parque. Sus comentarios además sugieren que la marginación de los pederastas en la descripción médico-social del doctor Céspedes es una ficción no sólo homofóbica sino clasista.

Los menos afortunados, es decir los de la clase obrera, fueron a parar a la cárcel de la Isla de Pinos, pero sus clientes se pasean impunemente por plena Habana porque su buen nombre, su educación, en fin su clase social, la clase de los "que llevan levita y ocupan señalados puestos", los protege. Al defender "la honradísima y sufrida clase de Dependientes del comercio", Giralt señala la amplitud y la difusión de las prácticas homosexuales en la Habana de 1889. Además, al rechazar el cientifismo del doctor, los argumentos disparatados de Giralt transforman el diagnóstico del cuerpo enfermo del muchacho y de cierto sector de la ciudad en una oposición socio-política entre la clase obrera, en este caso compuesta en su mayoría de peninsulares recién llegados, y la burguesía profesional criolla, que desde la prensa dirigía, como lo hizo el propio Casal, diversos ataques más o menos velados a las autoridades coloniales.

Como se mencionó antes, el libro de Céspedes, prologado por Varona, se publicó en 1888; el de Giralt, el próximo año. Casal regresó de Madrid en enero de 1889 y es poco probable que haya desconocido los libros de Céspedes y de Giralt. Lo más probable es que se le asignó la crónica para *La Discusión* con la intención de suavizar los términos del debate entre criollos y peninsulares, exacerbado por los ataques de Giralt, y de borrar la escabrosa cuestión de la homosexualidad en los centros de dependientes.

La crónica de Casal, "A través de la ciudad. El Centro de Dependientes", apareció, firmada con el pseudónimo de "Hernani", en *La Discusión*, el 28 de diciembre de 1889 (2:17-20). La crónica fue el resultado de una visita al Centro, situado "en los altos del teatro Albisu", uno de los tantos "centros", "liceos" y "colonias", instituciones gremiales, docentes y sociales que se propagaron por toda la isla. Casal describe las condiciones que han llevado a los jóvenes a abandonar su provincia española, el esfuerzo de su trabajo y la integración de muchos de ellos a la sociedad cubana. El Secretario del Centro guía al cronista por todo el recinto, que resulta ser un verdadero falansterio con salones de lecturas y de clases, donde tienen acceso gratuito al curriculum de una escuela de comercio, y un salón de fiestas, que recibe todo un párrafo descriptivo. La crónica de Casal parece haber sido provocada por el deseo de investigar una situación curiosa o interesante, o al menos ése es el pretexto que sugiere Casal: recoger "los datos que reclamaba nuestra insaciable curiosidad" (2:18). Sin embargo, a diferencia de otras crónicas, donde se representa la reacción subjetiva del escritor, la crónica sobre los dependientes parece más bien la visita de un reportero al lugar de los hechos.

En la obra de Casal, la consulta del médico, el circo, el museo y las aceras urbanas están poblados de cuerpos, los cuerpos escultóricos del *museo*, la descripción detallada de un herpe en la consulta, la multitud sofocante del circo; por lo tanto, en la crónica sobre los dependientes es sorprendente el vacío total de las habitaciones por donde circula el cronista. En cambio, como si quisiera llenarlo, detalla los muebles de las aulas y el decorado del salón de fiestas; como si quisiera cubrir lo sexual indecible, desata una serie de significantes que enmarcan y reducen vertiginosamente el salón descrito. Las paredes, "pintadas de óleo de un color azul pálido", están:

> ornadas de simétricos *panneaux*, formados con varillas de madera dorada, que resaltan al brillo de la luz que despiden las arañas de cristal. Dentro de un *panneau* hay una luna veneciana, sujeta por ancho marco de bronce, y en otro una copia de un cuadro célebre, pendiente de fino cordón de seda azul turquí (2:19).

Sigue la descripción del techo, de una tribuna, y de "un teatrito precioso, alegre como una pajarera y reluciente como una caja de juguetes". La reducción estetizante, casi violenta, del salón clausura la posibilidad de que un cuerpo lo atraviese: un salón ornado de *panneaux*, que contiene una luna veneciana, sujeta por ancho marco de bronce, donde también hay un "teatrito precioso", que se reduce aun más en "una caja de juguetes", como si la metonimia jadeante se agotara y se clausurara a sí misma. Ese "teatrito precioso" se reduce a tal punto que no toleraría representación alguna; ningún cuerpo contamina la "escena" de un gabinete, valga decir un "closet", vacío. Sin embargo, del Centro de Dependientes viene el cuerpo, visiblemente marcado por la sexualidad, del joven pederasta entrevistado en el tratado del doctor Céspedes.

En la crónica de Casal el Centro está totalmente vacío, salvo por la presencia borrosa del Secretario. Para mostrar que en los centros no existía el ambiente descrito por el muchacho entrevistado por Céspedes, Giralt se había referido a su "régimen disciplinario" y al hecho de que "está prohibido hablar de política". Casal parece citarlo cuando dice que allí "está permitido hablar de todo menos de política" y continúa con una descripción casi pastoril de los jóvenes:

> ¿No es más agradable comunicarse sus ensueños de riqueza y sus proyectos para lo porvenir? ¿No es más bello recordar la patria lejana, donde se ha pasado la infancia y donde hay seres queridos que nos aguardan? De este modo ¿no se obtiene más pronto el fin apetecido, que es el de estrechar cada día más los lazos de cariño, simpatía y amistad entre los dependientes? (2:19)

En los tratados de Céspedes y Giralt, se comenta la homosexualidad con franqueza sorprendente, a la vez que se trata de limitarla al cuerpo y sus síntomas; en cambio, en la crónica de Casal, los dependientes se pierden en un plural incorpóreo y abstracto como si el cariño, la simpatía y la amistad que se tienen entre sí dependiera de esa ausencia. Lo innombrable en la crónica no es sólo la homosexualidad sino el cuerpo erótico, que debe transformarse estéticamente, o que debe pasar a otro registro del erotismo, que debe figurar de otra manera y en otros recintos, en el circo, en el museo, en la pesadilla, los lugares predilectos de su representación.

More Notes on the Presentation of Sexuality
in the Modern Spanish American Novel

DONALD L. SHAW

In an earlier article on this theme,[1] I attempted to sketch the broad outlines of the evolving attitude towards sexuality on the part of some major modern Spanish American fiction writers. It was not possible to do more than scratch the surface of this subject in a few printed pages, and I therefore cheerfully embrace the opportunity to amplify the discussion. A question to which I did not devote much attention in 1982 was that of origins. If Luis Alberto Sánchez was right in suggesting in 1942 that the bulk of mainstream Spanish American fiction up to then had been virtually asexual,[2] where can we look to find an alternative to the suppression of all but sporadic references to this fundamental area of human behaviour? The obvious answer is: to *modernismo*. Here we encounter a surprise. A glance at the extensive bibliography on the movement compiled recently by Luis Iñigo Madrigal[3] reveals that although *modernismo* seems to have been studied from almost every conceivable angle, hardly a single item exists that deals with it specifically from that of its treatment of sexuality and eroticism. An exception with regard to Peninsular *modernismo* is Lily Litvak, who begins her *Erotismo fin de siglo* (Barcelona: Bosch, 1979) by remarking: "La crítica literaria moderna ha visto de cerca el papel desempeñado por el erotismo en movimientos como el Surrealismo o el Expresionismo. Sin embargo, ha dejado prácticamente sin tocar el análisis de este aspecto del modernismo, aun cuando es uno de los leitmotifs de su plástica y su literatura" (1-2). She then correctly associates the *modernistas'* exploration of eroticism with their deeper awareness of the *fin de siglo* crisis of

---
[1] See Donald L. Shaw, "Notes on the Presentation of Sexuality in the Modern Spanish American Novel", *Bulletin of Hispanic Studies* LIX (1982), 275-82.
[2] Luis Alberto Sánchez, *América, novela sin novelistas* (Santiago de Chile: Ercilla, 1940), 29-30.
[3] Luis Iñigo Madrigal, "Bibliografía del modernismo literario hispanoamericano", in Luis Iñigo Madrigal, editor, *Historia de la literatura hispanoamericana* II: *Del neoclasicismo al modernismo* (Madrid: Cátedra, 1987), 549-61.

ideals and beliefs; "aquella época," she writes, "descubre que Eros no sólo produce placer, sino también soledad, desesperación, melancolía, *spleen*. Precisamente son la misantropía y el pesimismo del erotismo fin de siglo lo que nos muestran su fundamento espiritual" (3-4). She goes on to affirm, *à propos* Valle-Inclán, "El modernismo, a la búsqueda no tanto de una religión, sino de una religiosidad, encontró en el erotismo místico un éxtasis que sustituyó al religioso" (107).

Joseph Feustle amplifies this statement in an article which emphasizes, for instance, how often Darío uses references to the Eucharist in order to confer a kind of sacramental quality on the sexual act.[4] But a serious ambiguity persists, especially in *modernista* fiction. In that *vademecum* of the movement's ideas and attitudes, Silva's *De sobremesa*, the hero, Fernández, gives free rein to his sexuality, but in the last resort, like Juan Jerez in Martí's *Amistad funesta*, sees in woman "más el símbolo de las hermosuras ideadas que un ser real".[5] Germán Gullón, writing of *modernista* fiction in general in Spanish America, comments: "Ya estamos en otro mundo. El narrador está convocando una mujer bella, de tal género de belleza que tiene algo de sobrenatural, no es un ser de carne y hueso".[6] However this generalization overlooks a figure like Niní Florens in the Venezuelan Pedro César Dominici's *La tristeza voluptuosa* (Madrid: Bernardo Rodríguez, 1899), whom the hero, Eduardo, "amaba rabiosamente, sin el menor asomo de idealismo, por sus encantos corporales" (100). As Juan Ramón Jímenez pointed out a few years later, the aspiration of the *modernistas* was to "entrar en el mundo ideal de la mujer, por medio de la pasión",[7] that is to say, as we can see quite clearly in Darío, to use the senses, and especially eroticism, as a means of opening the doors of perception on to a hidden world of harmony. This is what Litvak means by "el erotismo místico". We see it in the poems of the Darío of "Eros vita lumen", specifically, for example in "Garçonnière" (*Prosas profanas*) where the "amantes de la eterna Dea" (Venus) "oyen el mensaje de la vasta Idea" —we notice the capitalization. Exploration of the senses, rather than mortification of them according to the Christian ascetic tradition, is what leads to life-enhancing insight.

Here, then, is what seems to be the modern origin of that whole trend in twentieth-century Spanish American fiction which, as suggested in 1982, associ-

---

[4] Joseph Feustle, "El secreto de la satiresa en la poesía de Rubén Darío", *Actas del Sexto Congreso de la Asociación Internacional de Hispanistas*, edited by A. M. Gordon & E. Riggs (Toronto: Toronto University Press, 1980), 239.

[5] José Martí, *Amistad funesta (Lucía Jerez)* (Madrid: Gredos, 1969), 72.

[6] Germán Gullón, "Técnicas narrativas en la novela realista y en la modernista", *Cuadernos Hispanoamericanos* 286 (1974), 83.

[7] Juan Ramón Jíménez, "Ideas líricas (1907-8)", *Libros de prosa* I: *Primeras prosas* (Madrid: Aguilar, 1969), 271.

ates eroticism with a means not only of overcoming the *otredad* of the sexual partner and the solitude of the individual, but also existential insecurity. This trend was noticeably absent from the phase of fiction which overlapped with that of *modernismo*: the regionalist novel, or *novela criolla*, represented by writers like Rivera, Güiraldes, Gallegos or Mariano Latorre. It seems to be because, as C. J. Alonso has recently affirmed,[8] the basic preoccupation of the regionalist writers was with national or ethnic identity and values. To these eroticism was irrelevant. In Azuela's novels, we notice, sexual behaviour was used in an ultraconventional way as part of the moral commentary incorporated into the text. In *Los de abajo*, for instance, the downward spiral of Demetrio's character is illustrated by his behaviour with Camila. Similarly, the moral degradation of Anastasio and La Codorniz is underlined by references to venereal disease. Characteristically, in *Don Segundo Sombra* there is almost no room for sexual relationships; and while Fabio, the hero, eventually becomes aware of the possibility that man may be carrying on a lonely struggle against an adverse human condition, love and sexuality never form any part of the answer. Again, in *La vorágine*, although the first paragraph contains the *modernista* topos, "ambicionaba el don divino del amor ideal que me encendiera espiritualmente", all that Cova finds is Madona Zoraida, "la hembra bestial y calculadora". Both in *La vorágine* and *Doña Bárbara*, love and sexuality are highly conventionalized, with marriage and conjugal affection (a dream for Cova, a future reality for Santos Luzardo) set against the possibility of a degrading relationship with an older, sexually rapacious woman. But this last remains no more than a possibility for Gallegos. In fact, in *Doña Bárbara*, Santos never feels anything but pity and contempt for Bárbara. For her part, if it is indirectly suggested in the first edition that she amused herself by sleeping with the *peones* on her ranch, this notation was carefully removed from the second and subsequent editions. The deletion is symbolic. Emphasis on sexuality, especially female sexuality, in the regionalist novel was incompatible with the representative roles conferred on the major characters.

Thus the key-figure in this period was inevitably Roberto Arlt. Not for nothing does one of his most percipient critics, J. M. Flint, devote the longest chapter of his *The Prose Works of Roberto Arlt* (Durham: Durham University Press, 1985) to "Sexuality and the Sex War" in Arlt's writings. Arlt is beyond question the greatest precursor of the Boom in Spanish American fiction, bringing it back from rural to urban themes and from *criollismo* to serious interest in the universal human condition. For our purpose the specific importance of Arlt is connected with his

---

[8] Carlos J. Alonso, *The Spanish American Regional Novel* (Cambridge: Cambridge University Press, 1990), 66: "the *novela de la tierra* purports to write a literary text that incorporates the autochthonous essence."

reintroduction of explicit sexuality into the novel and more especially his reintroduction of it in an existential context. Arlt was deeply conscious of the all-pervading influence of *modernismo* when he began writing, commenting, "Cuando las nuevas generaciones vengan y puedan ver algo de todo lo que se ha escrito en estos años, se dirá ¿Cómo hicieron esos tipos por no dejarse contagiar por esa ola de modernismo que dominaba en todas partes?"[9] One of his ways of resisting its contagion was by parodying its *erotismo místico* repeatedly in his work. Arlt, that is, was just as aware of the modern spiritual crisis as the *modernistas* (and, of course, far more so than the *criollista* novelists in general, which is what makes him historically so important). The anguish of modern man erupts into his first novel *El juguete rabioso* (1926) and remains a fundamental motif in the rest of his writing. Not surprisingly, in view of the *modernista* precedents, it is accompanied by an almost obsessive preoccupation with sex on the part of his characters, male and female alike. But Flint underlines the paradox that while "there exist strong links between the concepts of anguish and humiliation and the relations between the sexes, hardly anyone has sexual relations in Arlt's writings" (50). Equally, Óscar Masotta in his *Sexo y traición en Roberto Arlt* (Buenos Aires: Jorge Álvarez, 1965) refers to "Esa severidad religiosa con la que el sexo es visto en las novelas de Arlt" (99). In fact, Arlt consistently denigrates and degrades sexual activity in his novels, a process which reaches its logical climax in *Los lanzallamas* (1931), when Hipólita, after a chequered sexual career, at last finds a soul-mate in *El astrólogo* because he is castrated! Many of Arlt's major characters share the yearning of the *modernistas* for the ideal as a counterbalance to anguish, but they utterly reject Darío's notion that the way to find it was to "unir carne y alma".

The treatment of sexuality by Arlt forms the best way into the subject of its varied treatment in later fiction. It raises a slight smile, for instance, when we read that an original feature of Onetti's fiction is his attitude to sexuality in which "las mujeres oscilan siempre entre adolescentes y prostitutas sin que exista un lugar para la mujer sana, adulta, compañera".[10] Similarly when Skármeta suggests that sexuality really came into its own as a theme with his generation,[11] one wonders how, as a former professor of Spanish American literature, he came to forget about Arlt as the great predecessor.

---

[9] Cit. Jack M. Flint, "Disintegration Techniques in the Prose Writings of Roberto Arlt", *IberoAmerikanisches Archiv* 10 (1984), 104.

[10] Jorge Ruffinelli, "Juan Carlos Onetti, un escritor", in Reina Roffé, editor, *Espejo de escritores* (Hanover N.H: Ediciones del Norte, 1985), 30.

[11] Antonio Skármeta, "Al fin y al cabo ...", in Raúl Silva Cáceres, editor, *Del cuerpo a las palabras: la narrativa de Antonio Skármeta* (Madrid: LAR, 1983), 132.

The Brothel Theme

Although the brothel theme in modern Spanish American fiction dates at least from Federico Gamboa's *Santa* (1903), it does not become significant in the present context until much later. Again, Arlt is the key-figure. Gamboa had been interested in prostitution as a social phenomenon. When for instance the match-seller in his story "Uno de tantos" (*Del natural*, 1903) kills himself when his girl friend is forced into a brothel, Gamboa is protesting against poverty and the sexual oppression of women in an unjust society. But when Erdosain at the beginning of *Los siete locos* seeks out the most squalid brothel he can find, his problem is not in the first instance socially determined. Its root, as critics from González Lanuza to Gnutzmann have perceived, is metaphysical. Like another character in the novel, Ergueta, Erdosain is seen going "de burdel en burdel y de angustia en angustia".[12] Instead of postulating triumphant sexuality as a way to find an ideal which will confer meaning on life, Arlt reverses the direction of the search and paradoxically posits the need to seek an ideal of purity and a deeper vision of our own personalities in the vilest manifestations of sexuality and self-degradation.

Gnutzmann cogently compares Arlt's attitude to sexuality to that of Onetti, arguing that both writers seem to be unconsciously affected by religious considerations, that is, by the tendency in Christianity to connect sexuality with the fall of man. At the same time, less convincingly, she contrasts his outlook with that of Sábato.[13] The link with Onetti is highly significant. On the one hand, Onetti takes over in *La vida breve* Arlt's notion of sexual self-degradation and rebellion against orthodox standards of morality as a means of exploring one's hidden identity. On the other hand, in *Juntacadáveres*, Onetti both carries the brothel theme to its parodic extreme and gives a new twist to the idea if self-discovery through sexual activity.

We may note in passing that this theme figures in Borges' late story "La noche de los dones", the only one in which the brothel theme figures prominently. The youthful narrator initially believes that his first sexual experience and the spectacle of the killing of Moreira which follows leave him with indelible memories. These guarantee in some sense the continuity of his personality and relieve any possible ontological insecurity. But at the end of the tale Borges characteristically pulls the rug from under our feet. Even the recollection of sexual initiation is perceived to be no more than the routine recollection of the words formerly used to describe it. Any sense of the ongoing reality of the self drains away.

---

[12] Roberto Arlt, *Los siete locos* (Buenos Aires: Fabril, 1968), 91.
[13] Rita Gnutzmann, *Roberto Arlt o El arte del calidoscopio* (Bilbao: Universidad del País Vasco, 1984), 44-5.

Of the various well-known modern novels in which the brothel theme appears, Donoso's *El lugar sin límites*, Vargas Llosa's *La Casa Verde* and Sarduy's *Colibrí*, for instance, *Juntacadáveres* is probably the most significant because in it the brothel functions in three different ways. One of Onetti's primary concerns is to rub his readers' noses in the dirt of their own personalities. Thus, at the most obvious level, the brothel in *Juntacadáveres* functions as a mirror held up to the hypocrisy and pseudo-morality of the inhabitants of Santa María, where it is situated. Set up by means of a squalid political manoeuvre mediated by the unpleasant and —ironically— homosexual Barthé, with the connivance of the local doctor, the building in which it functions is owned by the local newspaper proprietor, who, however, forbids his son to frequent it. Its closure is brought about not by decent citizens who are standing up for minimal civic standards, but by moral blackmail on the part of a pack of fanaticized schoolgirls.

However, there is more to it than a sarcastic and contemptuous commentary on the behaviour of the inhabitants of Santa María seen as typical of human behaviour everywhere. Onetti looks back to Arlt in his presentation of the founding and collapse of the brothel in terms of the (parodic) fulfilment of a vocation by the pimp Larsen. With cold irony Onetti uses the brothel image to degrade the search for a life-directing ideal. His comment on Larsen, the "filatélico de putas pobres", the dream of whose life is to create the ideal knocking-shop ("Yo lo veo como un artista en su afán del prostíbulo perfecto"),[14] reveals again the anti-*modernista* thrust of the existential metaphor in this case. Onetti is not just ironizing about the existential quest. He is subverting the almost universal human longing to transcend the purely contingent. Larsen, like his adversary Padre Bergner, is a man of vocation; he hears its call at an early age, suffers for it, dreams of its fulfilment, pursues it year after year, and finally clutches at it in Santa María: "fundar el prostíbulo era ahora, esencialmente, como casarse in articulo mortis, como creer en fantasmas, como actuar para Dios".[15] The language in Chapter 14 of *Juntacadáveres* —*fe, predestinación, destino, convicciones* and the like— creates a pattern which presents a parodic anti-religious "calling", in which sex is the mediating factor. N. Perera San Martín takes the issue even further, arguing that the brothel itself, as an extension and manifestation of Larsen's "vocation" comes eventually to function as a source of transcendence which rivals Padre Bergner's church so far as the male citizens of Santa María are concerned: "No cabe ninguna

---

[14] Juan Carlos Onetti, in the interview with Ruffinelli (note 10 above), 35.
[15] Juan Carlos Onetti, *Juntacadáveres* (Madrid: Alianza, 1981), 166.

duda: el escándalo del prostíbulo está en esa competencia con la iglesia, en ese ofrecer a los hombres otro 'más allá'".[16]

The other major novel which comes to mind in connection with the brothel image in a parodic quasi-religious setting is Donoso's *El lugar sin límites*. As Moreno Turner and Philip Swanson have convincingly argued, the brothel in El Olivo is the central symbol of a novel whose basic theme is the inversion of all conventional Christian values.[17] As Swanson writes, "The brothel-symbol implies a degraded reality, the opposite extreme from the patriarchal family home of the nineteenth century, the repository of stable values, the social nucleus, the example of hierarchy and cohesion" (50). The central sexual episode, the orgasm of the homosexual Manuela in bed with La Japonesa, is crucial in this respect: a woman behaving like a man becomes pregnant by a man who feels himself to be intrinsically a woman, without love, in a brothel, for money, at the behest of a God-figure, don Alejandro, who looks on approvingly. The parodic juxtaposition of inverted Christian myth and human sexual ambiguity leaves the message in no doubt. Don Alejo is an evil, not a benevolent, God, one who creates only in order to destroy, who grants his favour capriciously (and in fact with cruel irony), and who in any case is losing his powers. The sexual ambiguity of Manuela, Pancho, La Japonesa and La Japonesita symbolizes their lack of identity while the surroundings and circumstances in which they live imply total absence of hope. In a world without positive God-given order, bereft of values, man has nothing on which to base his identity. At the same time Manuela's "femininity" (expressed *inter alia* by her adoration of don Alejo and her belief in his all-powerful protectiveness), when he/she was born biologically male, could suggest that man's readiness to adore and depend on a God who might be wicked is a betrayal of his true nature. Sexual ambiguity, in other words, takes on spiritual overtones in a now familiar fashion. In the case of Pancho, Moreno Turner and Swanson both misinterpret the mythic element in his character, seeing it as related to Lucifer's rebellion against God. But the very presence of a sexual prohibition declares the Genesis story to be the referent here. Pancho is Adam, La Japonesita is Eve and

---

[16] Nicasio Perera San Martín, "La adjetivación insidiosa de J. C. Onetti en *Juntacadáveres*", *Travaux* XXIV (Université de St. Étienne, 1976), 103.

[17] Fernando Moreno Turner, "La inversión como norma. A propósito de *El lugar sin límites*", in Antonio Cornejo-Polar, editor, *José Donoso: la destrucción de un mundo* (Buenos Aires: García Cambeiro, 1975), 73-100; Philip Swanson, *José Donoso. The Boom and Beyond* (Liverpool: Francis Cairns, 1988), 48-66. See also Donald L. Shaw, "Inverted Christian Imagery and Symbolism in Modern Spanish American Fiction", *Romance Studies* 10 (1987), 71-82.

Octavio is the tempter. Once more, sexuality is linked to man's ambiguous relationship with God, just as is the case with the homosexual rape at the end, when Manuela hopes that don Alejo (God) will redeem his promise to "save" her, but in vain.

Not all users burden the brothel image with quite such a weight of metaphysical implication as Arlt, Onetti and Donoso. In Vargas Llosa's *La Casa Verde*, and indeed even more so in his *Pantaleón y las visitadoras*, the presentation of sexual behaviour and the use of a brothel, whether fixed in the former novel or peripatetic in the latter, is designed primarily to express what the author sees as a moral rottenness in Peruvian society, (which may perhaps be akin to what one critic has called the "gangrene" in García Márquez's Macondo[18]). From *La ciudad y los perros* on, degraded sexual behaviour is seen as a metaphor. It expresses an adulteration of values. In the case of *Cien años de soledad*, the figurative incest is emblematic of the supplanting of a social relationship, a bonding institution, by a non-social, non-bonding relationship based on a pre-existent blood tie, the punishment for which is solitude. Hence García Márquez's supposedly explanatory statement that in the novel, *soledad* is the opposite of *solidaridad*. In *La Casa Verde* the sexual behaviour of the major characters is emblematic of a self-degrading society, that is to say one in which the majority of the characters are not, contrary to what José Luis Martín suggests,[19] victims of external forces, but instead collaborate with the process of their own corruption.

What does the Green House symbolize? George McMurray sees it as standing for Spanish America's "impoverished cultural heritage", Jean Franco as symbolizing "las convenciones del machismo", Dick Gerdes as connected with the all-devouring Amazonian jungle, Baldori as indicative of the rebellion of natural instincts, Oviedo as emblematic of "la reprimida sexualidad colectiva".[20] None of these explanations is satisfactory. The Green House is a bar, a dance-hall and a brothel. Martín correctly refers to it as the "encarnación de la podredumbre social" (125). But in which sense? In the sense, surely, that what it panders to is immediate

---

[18] Claude Bouché, "Mythe et structures dans *Cien años de soledad* de Gabriel García Márquez", *Marche Romane* 23 (1974), 237-49.
[19] José Luis Martín, *La narrativa de Vargas Llosa* (Madrid: Gredos, 1974), 123.
[20] George R. McMurray, "The Novels of Mario Vargas Llosa", *Modern Language Quarterly* 29 (1968), 332; Jean Franco, "El viaje frustrado en la literatura hispanoamericana", *Actas del Tercer Congreso de la Asociación Internacional de Hispanistas*, edited by Carlos Magis (Mexico City: Colegio de México, 1970), 369; Dick Gerdes, *Mario Vargas Llosa* (Boston: Twayne, 1985), 55; Rosa Baldori de Baldussi, *Vargas Llosa, un escritor y sus demonios* (Buenos Aires: García Cambeiro, 1974), 105; José Miguel Oviedo, *Mario Vargas Llosa, la invención de una realidad* (Barcelona: Barral, 1970), 135.

gratification. Freud, we remember, associated lust for immediate gratification with infantilism and postponement of it with maturity. We notice that each major section of *La Casa Verde* ends with a scene involving the "Inconquistables" and the degradation of Lituma and Bonifacia. This repeated pattern seems to imply an effect. The Green House itself implies the underlying cause.

When Gerdes ends his chapter on the novel by suggesting that in it "Vargas Llosa has singled out the need for an individual and moral rebellion against the problems of society" (74), he is correct to the extent that Vargas Llosa clearly perceives the problem to be moral rather than social. But whether individual moral rebellion could ever be possible, still less successful, in the sort of society which he depicts, is rather questionable. In any case, cultural reform is unlikely to take place at the behest of literary writers. Before leaving Vargas Llosa we must notice that in *Pantaleón y las visitadoras* the novelty with respect to *La Casa Verde* lies in the parallel between the moral self-degradation implicit in the ever-widening spread of the mobile brothels and the spiritual self-degradation implicit in the no less rapid spread of the cult of el hermano Francisco. Here once more we perceive, as in Arlt, Onetti and Donoso, the attempt to postulate a link between the erotic and the religious or metaphysical. In this case it is much more explicit and therefore simplified than in the earlier novels. What is interesting, none the less, is the way both Onetti and Vargas Llosa use degraded manifestations of religion (the schoolgirls' fanaticism and that of the followers of Francisco) to comment on the degraded sexuality associated with the brothel image.

There is much more to be said about the brothel in modern Spanish American fiction, in Marechal's *Adán Buenosayres*, for instance, in García Márquez's *Crónica de una muerte anunciada*, or in Fuentes' *La muerte de Artemio Cruz*, where Artemio's chief act of political treachery is decided in a brothel. But perhaps the most obvious recent example of a novel which incorporates this image in a prominent position is Sarduy's *Colibrí* (1983), where La Casona, as González Echevarría has noted,[21] is in part a re-make of *La Casa Verde*. Like all Sarduy's novels after *Gestos*, *Colibrí* resists any attempt at straightforward interpretation, partly because of its nonrealistic content in the first place and partly because of the ludic narrative strategies that Sarduy employs. Roberto González Echevarría's suggestion that the theme is partly power and that Colibrí at the end comes almost to symbolize the dictatorial tradition in Spanish American politics (236) does not seem entirely convincing. Set like *La vorágine* and parts of *La Casa Verde* in the Amazonian jungle, *Colibrí* amusingly parodies the tone and the deep theme of the

---

[21] Roberto González Echevarría, *La ruta de Severo Sarduy* (Hanover N.H: Ediciones del Norte, 1987), 230.

novel of the jungle and indeed of the *criollista* novel in general. As we saw, one element those novels had lacked was sexuality. Sarduy privileges it as a theme but at the same time deliberately subverts it by making Colibrí an active homosexual. His fight with the Japanese wrestler at the beginning corresponds to Santos Luzardo's taming of the stallion and subsequently of Paiba and Doña Bárbara. But Colibrí the handsome, he-man brawler, overturns machistic values by subsequently enjoying a sexual experience with his adversary. The Casona certainly represents a power-structure, but —given that it is in part a (chiefly homosexual) brothel— it initially represents a sexual power-structure governed by money. When at the end Colibrí, having fled from it, is brought back, but succeeds in destroying it in order to replace it with a new Casona, he seems to be rebelling against institutionalized sexual repression, discrimination and exploitation. Although it is not clear what the new Casona will be like, from the fact that Colibrí will be in charge, we can assume that some elements of true sexual liberation will be built in.

As we leave the brothel image as a factor in modern Spanish American fiction, we may notice that one of the reasons why it figures so prominently is that in brothels sexuality is completely divorced from love. In the work of the Boom novelists love very rarely figures. The splendidly written scene between Artemio and Catalina in *La muerte de Artemio Cruz*, in which both long to break down the barriers of pride and resentment which separate them and offer to each other understanding, forgiveness and love, without being able to do so, is paradigmatic. We may compare the situation in *Crónica de una muerte anunciada*, where conjugal love between Ángela and Bayardo never has a chance, but where the prostitute María Alejandrina is utterly idealized, so much so that she alone, as A. M. Penuel points out, "offers precisely what the Church would deny: instinctive fulfilment, tenderness and consolation".[22] The parallel with the brothel in *Juntacadáveres*, also seen in competition with the Church by Perera San Martín, as we mentioned above, cannot be overlooked.

In fact, the characteristic feature of sexual activity in García Márquez is precisely its divorce from love. Both in *Cien años de soledad* and in *El otoño del patriarca*, the idea of "incapacidad para el amor" and in the second case "incapacidad de amor" are key phrases. Thus the exercise of sexuality is reduced

---

[22] Arnold M. Penuel, "The Sleep of Vital Reason in Gabriel García Márquez's *Crónica de una muerte anunciada*", *Hispania* 68 (1985), 759. See also in this general connection T. Avril Bryan, "La sexualidad femenina en las novelas de Gabriel García Márquez", *Actas del Noveno Congreso de la Asociación Internacional de Hispanistas*, edited by Sebastian Neumeister (Frankfurt am Main: Vervuert Verlag, 1989), 485-9.

to an activity which is at best a substitute for love and at worst a form of pleasure-seeking behaviour, combined in the case of the men with exploitation of women as sexual objects. As in *La Casa Verde*, it becomes the symbol of shallow immediate self-gratification. Although in García Márquez it does not contribute to the degradation of the individual as it tends to do in Vargas Llosa's novel, it reveals itself to be ultimately unfulfilling. A significant comment occurs in *El otoño del patriarca*:

> Vale más estar capado a mazo que andar tumbando madres por el suelo como si fuera cuestión de herrar novillas, nomás que esas pobres bastardas sin corazón ni siquiera sienten el hierro ni patalean ni se retuercen ni se quejan como las novillas, ni echan humo por los madriles ni huelen a carne chamuscada, que es lo menos que se les pide a las buenas mujeres, sino que ponen sus cuerpos de vacas muertas para que uno cumpla con su deber mientras ellas siguen pelando papas y gritándoles es a las otras que me hagas el favor de echármele un ojo a la cocina mientras me desocupo aquí que se me queme el arroz, sólo a usted se le ocurre que esa vaina es amor, mi general, porque es el único que conoce.[23]

A second interesting feature of García Márquez's later work is the tendency of the women to refuse sexual passivity. We recall that in *Crónica de una muerte anunciada* Ángela's mother is proud that her daughters "han sido criadas para sufrir".[24] But Ángela's only real act of self-assertion is to lose her virginity before marriage. We can regard it as an act of rebellion and self-emancipation from a paternalistic and phallocratic society. Although it destroys Ángela's life, it liberates her sexuality at least to the extent that she can write to Bayardo later about "las lacras eternas que el había dejado en su cuerpo, de la sal de su lengua, y la trilla de fuego de su verga africana" (123-24). This shift from sexual passivity towards the assumption of full sexual identity on the part of women, combined with the final achievement of love, is strongly developed in *El amor en los tiempos del cólera*, in which a form of "educación sentimental" is prominent. But as Robin Fiddian has noted,[25] we must be careful not to jump to the conclusion that the ending contains an affirmation of hope, life and love. Just as in *Cien años de soledad* when love and sexuality conjoin the curse is fulfilled, so in *El amor en los tiempos del cólera*, when Florentino and Fermina finally discover and consummate their

---

[23] Gabriel García Márquez, *El otoño del patriarca* (Barcelona: Plaza y Janés, 1975), 28.
[24] Gabriel García Márquez, *Crónica de una muerte anunciada* (Bogotá: Oveja Negra, 1981), 44.
[25] Robin Fiddian, "A Prospective Postscript: À Propos of *Love in the Time of Cholera*", in Bernard McGuirk & Richard Cardwell, editors, *Gabriel García Márquez: New Readings* (Cambridge: Cambridge University Press, 1987), 198-99.

reciprocal love, not only is it (ironically once more) after a lifetime of conjugal "condena sacramental" on her part and crapulous sexual adventures on his, but in addition is immediately attended by the symbolic suicide of América Vicuña. Florentino's sexual self-gratification has produced the death of the young girl, while at the same time physical decrepitude and imminent death threaten to turn the long-delayed idyll of Florentino and Fermina into a caricature of the love-ideal. Although, as Alfred MacAdam has pointed out, there are notable elements of "sexual comedy" in *Cien años de soledad* and indeed in much of García Márquez's subsequent work,[26] the underlying tone is nearly always disenchanted and the implicit metaphor negative and disturbing.

The Boom novelist who more explicitly than any of the others takes up in a new context the *modernista* association of sexuality and the spiritual yearnings of modern man is Sábato. It is he who spells out in *El escritor y sus fantasmas* that in the modern novel "el sexo adquiere una dimensión metafísica".[27] The most explicit illustration of his use of sexuality as a weapon against the solitude of the individual in a post-Christian, non-Providential world is the lovemaking between Martín and Alejandra in Chapter 9 of *Sobre héroes y tumbas*. The dominant metaphors here with regard to human relationships are those of the "island" and the "abyss". Each of us is on a separate island in the sea of existence, cut off from one another by an abyss of otherness. The artist can use his art as a bridge; but for the average human being love and sexuality are the (potential) bridging elements. Thus when Martín makes love to Alejandra, this is seen as an "intento de comunicación", by means of which he "trataba de hacerse oír por el otro que estaba del otro lado del abismo". At the same time "Alejandra quizá luchaba desde su propia isla, gritando palabras cifradas".[28] We also see that, since the sexual act is seen as a response to the abyss of separateness, it is associated with the opposite of falling into an abyss, that is, climbing a mountain. The climax of the lovemaking is identified with Martín's reaching "una altura antes nunca alcanzada ... alturas incomensurables sobre los pantanos oscuros y pestilentes en que antes había oído chapotear a bestias deformes y sucias" (270). There are additional references to "elevadísimas cumbres ... majestad y pureza ... fervoroso silencio ... éxtasis solitario ... en los grandes picos" (274). Unhappily, the words "silencio" and "solitario" prefigure the failure of this attempt to find refuge in sexuality from solitude and existential despair. One of the clearest indications of the same failure

---

[26] Alfred MacAdam, *Modern Latin American Narratives. The Dreams of Reason* (Chicago: Chicago University Press, 1977), 86.
[27] Ernesto Sábato, *El escritor y sus fantasmas*, 3rd. ed. (Buenos Aires: Aguilar, 1967), 135.
[28] Ernesto Sábato, *Sobre héroes y tumbas*, in *Narrativa completa* (Barcelona: Seix Barral, 1982), 334.

is visible in the absurdist short story of Virgilio Piñera, "Fusilamiento" (from *El que vino a salvarme*, 1970), in which Teodoro, who has been sentenced to be shot, refuses sexual consolation from his wife, symbolizing by his action the inability of sexuality to ward off anguish and the sense of the imminence of death.

To conclude this survey of sexuality in the modern Spanish American novel, it is necessary to make some reference to the very marked shift of outlook which has taken place among some Post-Boom writers. I have argued elsewhere in an article on the Post-Boom[29] that it is a complex and many-sided movement about which it is hazardous to generalize. However it seems possible that future historians of Spanish American fiction may include among the characteristics of the Post-Boom a more positive evaluation of love and sexuality than was the case with the Boom novelists. Signs of this occur quite early. With hindsight it seems clear that one of the writers who marks the transition from Boom to Post-Boom is Puig. There are valid reasons for suggesting that the end of *Boquitas pintadas* (1969) marks a significant turning point. In the novel Nélida, one of the girls associated with the provincial Lothario, Juan Carlos, leaves her commonplace husband and makes a passionate pilgrimage to Cosquín, where Juan Carlos died. However, for unexplained reasons, she then returns to the capital and to banal domesticity and later dies fulfilled by her marriage and her children. Nothing could be more different than this from the mainstream of the Boom, unless it were Antonio Skármeta's first significant short story, "La Cenicienta en San Francisco" (1962), in which a moment of epiphany accompanies the casual but affectionate love-making between Antonio and Abby after a party in a hippy apartment.[30] The situation has much in common with the one alluded to above in Sábato's *Sobre héroes y tumbas*, which had just appeared. Like the typical Boom hero, Antonio is afflicted with "la madrecita soledad que tan mal venía tratándonos a nosotros pobrecitas criaturas del Todopoderoso".[31] But, as the slightly self-ironic tone of the quotation implies, although he mentions in regard to himself "tu cuerpo y tu alma que testimonian el enigma, esgrimiendo como una joya tu angustia pasajera, tu sin sentido no tan pasajero" (16), he is really not as afflicted by solitude, anguish and the sense of existential futility as Sábato's Martín or Castel. Above all, whereas the sexual act between Martín and Alejandra fails to overcome otherness and despair, here it triumphantly succeeds in producing a moment of reconciliation

---

[29] Donald L. Shaw, "Towards a Definition of the Post-Boom", *Bulletin of Hispanic Studies* LXVI (1989), 87-94.

[30] Donald L. Shaw, "'La Cenicienta en San Francisco' by Antonio Skármeta", *Revista de Estudios Hispánicos* 21, 2 (1987), 89-99.

[31] Antonio Skármeta, "La Cenicienta en San Francisco" in his *El entusiasmo* (Santiago de Chile: Zig-Zag, 1963), 14.

with the human condition in all its contingency. It is the first of a series of similar epiphanic moments in Skármeta's stories and novels, the most symbolic of which is without doubt that of his short story "Basketball" (from *Desnudo en el tejado*, 1969) in which the sexual act is a threshold experience for the young narrator, releasing even his creativity as a writer. As Ariel Dorfman aptly comments: "Para Skármeta el sexo es regeneración, nacimiento, implica siempre otro ser humano, se une a las facultades imaginativas y estéticas del hombre".[32] In Skármeta's most recent novel, *Match Ball* (1989), sexual activity is specifically identified with living life to the full and seen as a kind of absolute in itself, to be pursued regardless of the consequences if the threat posed by middle age and humdrum bourgeois conformity is to be resisted.

This re-evaluation of sexuality in the Post-Boom and its association with self-fulfilment is especially visible in some of the women writers who form such an important sector of the movement. Rosalind Coward has written: "The confession of sexual experience is one of the most characteristic features of contemporary feminist writings. Like the confessional novel in general, the novels by feminists also present the experience of sexuality as the significant experience of the novel".[33] This seems to be true whether the writers in question are overtly feminist or not. There is room for a book on the subject of the treatment of sexuality as part of modern feminine and feminist discourse in contemporary Spanish American fiction. Though examples immediately spring to mind from works by Allende, Valenzuela, Poniatowska and others, to examine them would indefinitely prolong this survey.

In brief, the significant conclusions which have presented themselves to me since my 1982 article concern:

1. The virtual abandonment of references to sexuality as a means of conveying moral commentary.

2. The general tendency to react against the *modernista* exaltation of sexuality as a road to new perceptions either about the self or the human condition. Sexual behaviour as leading to self-liberation exists as a theme in the Boom, but only as a minority phenomenon, and even then it tends to be divorced from love.

3. The significance ot the brothel image.

4. The marked shift of attitude, including the realignment of sexual activity with love, which seems to be a feature of the Post-Boom, in which women writers are playing a leading part.

---

[32] Ariel Dorfman, "Volar", *Revista Chilena de Literatura* 1 (1970), 70.
[33] Rosalind Coward, "Are Women's Novels Feminist Novels?" in Elaine Showalter, *The New Feminist Criticism* (New York: Pantheon, 1985), 133.

Perhaps the diminishing emphasis on the association of sexual behaviour with what we might call "the Devil-World Hypothesis" is the most important trend we can postulate at the present time. If it really exists, it intensifies our sense of Post-Boom fiction as being more "reader-friendly" than much of the fiction of the Boom. It is not clear, however, whether this will in the end turn out to have been an altogether desirable development.

Escritura erótica: Cristina Peri Rossi y Tununa Mercado

GABRIELA MORA

> It would be pleasantly ironic if, in pursuing an understanding of sex, it should free us from the tyranny of sex.   Rosalind Coward[1]

El epígrafe de este trabajo es en parte un homenaje a la autora que insufló mi interés en un tema que no me atraía demasiado. Las circunstancias socioeconómicas de Latinoamérica me hacía parecer frívola o secundaria una atención distraída de los problemas acuciantes de la vida y la muerte de tantas de sus colectividades. El epígrafe va también como asentimiento a la idea de que sí sufrimos de la tiranía del sexo, quizá por la misma razón de que se lo ignora, desvirtúa, mitologiza, se lo exalta o menosprecia con un temor probablemente originado en la ignorancia. Porque no se puede negar que el deseo sexual responde a una necesidad humana,[2] y es motor no sólo de la reproducción de la especie, sino de excelsos productos artísticos. A la vez, es imposible ignorarlo como espuela de acciones negativas como la violación, el estupro y otros actos violentos. Coward invita a explorar el enigma del deseo femenino, consciente de la dificultad de despojarlo de las capas descriptivas y prescriptivas asentadas por milenios en la red de discursos imperantes de acuerdo a las diferentes culturas y épocas. La estudiosa advierte también sobre lo que llama "reductismo sexual" que simplifica fenómenos más complejos y contradictorios de lo que parece, y que hoy divide a las feministas de este país.[3]

---

[1] Rosalind Coward, "Female Desire and Sexual Identity", en *Women, Feminist Identity and Society in the 1980's*, editado por Myriam Díaz-Diocaretz e Iris Zavala (Amsterdam-Philadelphia: John Benjamins Publishing Co., 1985), 36.
[2] Coward acentúa la diferencia entre el concepto lacaniano del deseo, separado de la necesidad y nunca satisfecho, y el deseo sexual, necesidad fundamental. "Female Desire and Sexual Identity", 25.
[3] La disputa divide a las feministas que defienden la pornografía bajo el derecho de la libertad de expresión y las que abogan por hacer ilegal cualquier material pornográfico. Véanse Coward, *op. cit.*, y Ronald J. Berger, Patricia Searles y Charles E. Cottle, editores, *Feminism and Pornography* (Nueva York: Praeger, 1991).

Al aproximarse al tema de la representación de la sexualidad en la literatura, de inmediato una se topa con el problema no resuelto del significado de los conceptos "erotismo" y "pornografía". La imprecisión en el uso y definición de los términos la ilustra Maurice Charney que, descontando estos vocablos por ser "más o menos sinónimos", crea el membrete "ficción sexual" para cualquier texto narrativo que tiene un interés abierto continuado por la actividad sexual.[4] No creemos que esta nueva etiqueta resuelva el problema porque, demasiado amplia, todavía deja sin diferenciar tipos de escrituras muy distintos.[5]

Los estudios sociales (psicología, sociología, historia), han influido en una demarcación entre lo erótico y lo pornográfico, que aparece en la crítica literaria, y que tiene mucho que ver con los propósitos políticos de los usuarios. En general la pornografía se considera como fenómeno negativo, de perniciosas consecuencias, que representa un acto sexual violento, en que el cuerpo es objeto de control y dominio para uno de los participantes, y degradación y humillación para el otro. El placer de uno sería el daño del otro según Eva F. Kittay.[6] La representación pornográfica se interesaría por órganos, no personas,[7] por lo que no mostraría ni afecto ni emoción.[8]

Considerada subliteratura,[9] la pornografía se estudia estrechamente ligada al efecto de comercialización masiva que ha empujado el capitalismo,[10] y su existencia sería síntoma de otros problemas sociales existentes.[11]

La literatura erótica, por otro lado, se asentaría en la noción de que el sexo es natural y saludable, celebraría el cuerpo, y representaría el placer sexual entre

---

[4] Maurice Charney, *Sexual Fiction* (Londres: Methuen, 1981), 5.
[5] La dificultad de distinguir entre lo erótico y lo pornográfico lleva a Charney a contradecirse. Por ejemplo, después de reprochar a Steven Marcus (*The Other Victorians: A Study of Sexuality and Pornography in Mid-Nineteenth Century England* [Londres: Corgi, 1969]) por considerar la pornografía como mala literatura, termina por exigir que cualquier "ficción sexual" (que incluye la pornografía) sea juzgada con el mismo criterio que cualquier obra literaria, con lo que viene a coincidir con Marcus. Maurice Charney, *op. cit.*, 3, 11.
[6] Eva Feder Kittay, "Pornography and the Erotics of Domination", en *Beyond Domination: New Perspectives on Women and Philosophy*, editado por Carol C. Gould (Nueva York: Rowman and Allanheld, 1984), 145-74 (148).
[7] Steven Marcus, *op. cit.*, 284.
[8] Susan Sontag, "The Pornographic Imagination", *Partisan Review* XXXIV, 2 (1967), 181-212 (198).
[9] *Ibid.*, 182.
[10] Véanse Darko Suvin, "Two Holy Commodities: the Practices of Fictional Discourse and Erotic Discourse", *Sociocriticism* 2 (diciembre 1985), 31-47.
[11] Véase Berger et al., *Feminism and Pornography*, 66.

individuos que lo consienten, y contendría elementos estéticos y afectivos.[12] Enraizado en manifestaciones culturales específicas, el erotismo se ha relacionado siempre con el amor, como muestra su etimología. La relación con la cultura la ha señalado bien Cristina Peri Rossi en su *Fantasías eróticas*, donde expresa: el erotismo es "a la sexualidad lo que la gastronomía al hambre: el triunfo de la cultura sobre el instinto".[13] El erotismo, asegura la uruguaya, es creación "de la imaginación y del espíritu sobre el puro instinto brutal, indeterminado y generalmente torpe".[14] Como todo producto de la cultura, el erotismo puede aprenderse, como afirma Darko Suvin al recordar que en la antigüedad griega y durante el Renacimiento, lo erótico, como "práctica cognoscitiva" educaba los sentidos y los sentimientos.[15]

La estrecha relación entre el arte y el erotismo ha sido señalada desde siempre, y es de nuevo acentuada tanto por Peri como por Suvin. Este último separa el valor de uso de la literatura como cognición estética significativa, muy distante al valor de mercancía de los textos que, indiferentes a lo estético, tienen como meta el dinero.[16] Peri Rossi, por su lado, subraya la relación entre arte y los sueños porque es el arte el que se ocuparía "de las fantasías, de los deseos, de lo innombrable", no imitando la realidad sino transmutándola, cubriéndola de emociones para hacerla más agradable y apetecible.[17]

El propósito pragmático de hacer dinero que se atribuye a la pornografía va de la mano con la meta que se le asigna: excitar sexualmente al lector. En lenguaje más burdo: provocar una erección en el hombre,[18] su usuario más frecuente.[19] Como la intención autorial no siempre es asequible al análisis, (a veces ni los mismos escritores son conscientes de ella) y el efecto en el lector es difícil de determinar (un texto erótico puede excitar, y uno pornográfico sólo aburrir), concordamos con aquellos que piensan que la calidad estética es la que importa en el análisis.[20] Habría que aplicar, entonces, al texto erótico los mismos cartabones críticos que se usan para cualquier texto literario, aún conscientes de que lo estético

---

[12] *Ibid.*, 54.
[13] Cristina Peri Rossi, *Fantasías eróticas* (Madrid: Ediciones Temas de Hoy; Colección Biblioteca Erótica, 1991), 39.
[14] *Ibid.*, 40.
[15] Darko Suvin, "Two Holy Commodities", 46.
[16] *Ibid.*
[17] *Fantasías eróticas*, 44.
[18] Alan Bold, editor, *The Sexual Dimension in Literature* (Londres-Totowa, NJ: Vision y Barnes & Noble, 1982), 205.
[19] *Feminism and Pornography* provee estadísticas que muestran mayor interés en el material pornográfico en los hombres (4).
[20] Véanse Marcus, *op. cit.*, Sontag, *op. cit.*, y el mismo Charney, *op. cit.* (11).

es fenómeno contingente, sujeto a cánones prescriptivos de las instituciones en el poder. En otras palabras, la estructura, el lenguaje, la finura y sutileza de los retratos de paisajes y personajes importarán tanto como los tópicos temáticos, asuntos que son secundarios para los textos pornográficos, de acuerdo a la opinión de la mayoría de los críticos.

Más de un estudio ha indicado ya la ausencia de escritura erótica en la literatura hispanoamericana,[21] especialmente en aquella creada por mujeres.[22] Esta ausencia o falta de interés está relacionada con muy específicas causas histórico-culturales, como son la pobreza y la represión de la Iglesia y gobiernos, entre las más importantes. Hoy día, en gran parte debido al impulso feminista, aumenta la cantidad de textos más abiertos a los tópicos de la sexualidad. No obstante, como afirma David W. Foster, lo erótico en general es sólo un aspecto entre otros que a los autores les interesa explorar.[23] Menos frecuentes son las obras en que la sexualidad es motivo central, que son las que veremos aquí.

Adhiriéndonos a la premisa enunciada antes sobre la primacía del efecto estético, apartamos obras que nos parecieron débiles en este terreno, confesando de antemano la subjetividad de la elección.[24] Basada en este juicio, y soslayando la cuestión de la incitación sexual, me referiré primero a *Solitario de amor* de Cristina Peri Rossi, y luego, con más detalle, a *Canon de alcoba* de Tununa Mercado, como ilustración de textos literarios eróticos, de acuerdo a los discutido más arriba.

Por haber analizado más extensamente en otro trabajo la concepción del amor que despliega *Solitario*,[25] aquí me centraré en tres aspectos básicos: 1) la centralidad que la novela da al placer sexual; 2) las minuciosas descripciones del goce y del cuerpo femenino; 3) la relación que se hace entre el erotismo y la palabra poética. Hay que advertir de antemano que la reducción a estos tres puntos de ninguna manera hace justicia a la complejidad y riqueza de la novela.

---

[21] Por ejemplo, D. L. Shaw, "Notes on the Presentation of Sexuality in the Modern Spanish-American Novel", *Bulletin of Hispanic Studies* LIX (1982), 275-63.
[22] William David Foster, "Espejismos eróticos: *De ausencia*, de María Luisa Mendoza", *Revista Iberoamericana* 51, 132-133 (julio-diciembre 1985), 657-63.
[23] Foster, *op. cit.*, 659.
[24] Por ejemplo, dejamos de lado la novela *La última noche que pasé contigo*, de Mayra Montero, publicada en la popular colección erótica La Sonrisa Vertical (Barcelona: Tusquets, 1991), por la pobreza de su discurso y de la historia (una sucesión de coitos).
[25] Leí trabajos sobre *Solitario de amor* (Barcelona: Grijalbo, 1988) en 1991 en la Universidad de Pittsburgh y Montclair State College. Este último prepara una edición de esa conferencia a publicarse en Ediciones del Norte.

Para el primer punto, hay que recordar que en *Solitario*, el hombre que ama es el narrador, a través de cuyos ojos y lenguaje se entrega el texto al lector. Importa subrayar, además, que en esta historia, la relación sexual no es problemática; al contrario, ambos amantes gozan intensamente la cópula. Lo que divide a la pareja es el obsesivo amor que siente el varón, amor concebido como veneno o droga que hace del enamorado un antisocial que termina por fastidiar o aburrir a la mujer.

Quizás la mano autorial femenina tenga que ver con la representación de la demorada preparación que hace el amante antes del coito. Como es imposible citar las nueve páginas que lleva describir este juego en una ocasión (87-96), basta una pequeña muestra ilustradora del lirismo del lenguaje:

> Vuelvo a alzar las manos y froto mis yemas como antes de pulsar un instrumento. Mis dedos están sensibles, alas de mariposa. Separo bien el pulgar y el índice ... y los dirijo ... hacia tus pezones. Tus pezones sobresalen de la tela negra como dos faros de piedra ... La piel se eriza y se arruga. No los veo, sólo los palpo. Pujan por salir ... Entonces, ciñéndolos bien, los ayudo a romper, como si fueran las cabezas de náufragos sobre las aguas ... Entonces, cuando ya han crecido bastante, aíslo uno ... Sobresale bajo la tela como un niño con sombrero. Tu pezón que no toco, bajo mi mirada se hincha y aumenta ... (92-93).

Es casi seguro que el empleo profuso de recursos retóricos, aun en un trozo tan breve, no interesará a un lector que persigue exclusivamente una excitación sexual.

Pero no es sólo el lirismo lo que distingue el discurso de la novela. En otras ocasiones, es la franqueza no sólo en las minuciosas descripciones del coito, sino también en la nominación de órganos, innombrables en el lenguaje amoroso tradicional. El enamorado amante dice, por ejemplo:

> No amo sus olores, amo sus secreciones: el sudor escaso y salado que asoma entre ambos senos; la saliva densa que se instala en las comisuras ... la sinuosa bilis que vomita cuando está cansada; la oxidada sangre menstrual, con la que dibujo signos cretenses sobre su espalda, la espléndida y sonora orina de caballo ... estoy amando su hígado membranoso ... la blanca esclerótica de sus ojos, el endometrio sangrante, el lóbulo agujereado, ... las amígdalas rojas como guindas, la mandíbula crujiente, las meninjes inflamadas, ... el lunar marrón del hombro, la carótida tensa como una cuerda, los pulmones envenenados por el humo, el pequeño clítoris engarzado en la vulva como un faro (15-16).

La mujer amada por el narrador, que no corresponde este amor, sabe no obstante exigir su placer sexual, consiguiendo ciclóneos orgasmos. El narrador por su parte encuentra en el amor y el cuerpo de la mujer "una lucidez repentina acerca del lenguaje" (15), que le mueve a saborear el sonido de los vocablos, y elegirlos amorosamente para su relación. El personaje mismo describe este fenómeno en la ocasión en que contempla el desnudo de su amada:

> Entonces las palabras, las viejas palabras de toda la vida, aparecen súbitamente, ellas también desnudas, frescas, resplandecientes, crudas, con toda su potencia, como si se hubieran bañado en una fuente primigenia. Como si Aída las hubiera parido entre los dientes, y una vez rota la tela de los labios ... estallaran, rojas, imberbes, iguales a sí mismas. El lenguaje convencional estalla, bosque desfoliado, nazco entre las sábanas de Aída y conmigo nacen otras palabras, otros sonidos (14-15).

El sentimiento que surge del amor en el narrador es poderosa palanca que empuja la confesión erótica, inflamando la palabra de apasionado lirismo. Pero hay que repetir: *Solitario* es una novela compleja que, fuera de la mitificación/desmitificación del sentimiento amoroso, explora la relación entre identidad, cuerpo y amor, entre otros serios aspectos de la existencia humana. Como esos aspectos han sido tocados en otro ensayo, nos ocuparemos ahora del texto de Tununa Mercado.

Canon de alcoba[26] está compuesto de siete secciones, de las cuales tres no tienen que ver con la sexualidad o el amor. Estas tres secciones elaboran material onírico ("Sueños"); político ("Realidades"), y reflexiones sobre poética de la escritura ("Punto final"). El libro tiene un total de 27 textos, algunos de los cuales califican como cuentos, y otros como breves ensayos o prosas poéticas. Entre estas últimas, la sección titulada "Eros" presenta disquisiciones sobre diferentes tipos de amor ("Amor combatiente," "Amor desaprensivo," "Amor discursivo," "Amor desaparecido"). Aquí nos detendremos especialmente en los textos narrativos.

El primer cuento, "Antieros", abre la obra, y es seguro candidato a futuras antologías, tanto por la belleza de su lenguaje como por el humor escondido bajo un estilo de apariencia distante y funcional. Narrado en tercera persona, el discurso imita la escritura del tradicional recetario de cocina con una gran profusión de infinitivos usados a la manera de imperativos. La historia, que es mínima, cuenta el quehacer mañanero de una perfecta dueña de casa. El énfasis en el orden y la limpieza de cada habitación es parodia de la rutina doméstica, blanco atacado también por otras escritoras.[27] Sin embargo, a diferencia de esas narraciones, aquí no se nos dice nada de la mujer, ni de su apariencia, nombre o edad. Sus persistentes movimientos en busca de la mancha, la arruga o el polvo, la hacen aparecer como un robot o máquina de limpiar. El cambio de robot a ser humano se da en la cocina,

---

[26] Tununa Mercado, *Canon de alcoba*, 2ª edición (Buenos Aires: Ada Korn Editora, 1989).
[27] La misma Peri Rossi hace una punzante parodia de las mujeres esclavas del orden y la limpieza en su novela *El libro de mis primos*.

transformada en recinto sagrado en que la mujer se adoba para su propio placer, en medio de una fiesta de colores, sabores y texturas:

> Volver a desabotonarse la blusa y dejar los pechos al aire y, sin muchos preámbulos, como si se frotara con alguna esencia una andivia o se sobara con algún aliño el belfo de un ternero, cubrir con un poquito de aceite los pezones erectos, rodear con la punta del índice la aureola y masajear levemente cada uno de los pechos, sin establecer diferencias entre los reinos, mezclando incluso las especies y las especias por puro afán de verificación, porque en una de esas a los pezones no les viene bien el eneldo, pero sí la salvia (16-17).

Asegurada de que "adentro todo está listo" y que nadie vendrá a interrumpir la ceremonia, la mujer se despoja de sus ropas y "con el mismo aceite con que ha freído" comienza a untarse "todo el cuerpo con mayor meticulosidad" buscando "hendiduras de diferentes profundidades y carácter, depresiones y salientes", al tiempo que huele:

> la oliva y el comino, el caraway y el curry, las mezclas que la piel ha terminado por absorber trastornando los sentidos y transformando en danza los pasos cada vez más cadenciosos y dejarse invadir por la culminación en medio de sudores y fragancias (18).

Fuera del regodeo de la palabra, evocadora de olores y sensuales texturas, la narración es insólita porque el placer se logra en soledad, sin evocación de dolores o problemas, utilizándose todo el cuerpo, convirtiendo la tarea siempre odiosa en la tradición, en una especie de rito para despertar sentidos.

Inusual es también el texto titulado "Espejismos", porque tiene como foco de atención el miembro masculino. Sea por perverso goce de "chocar al burgués" (o a la burguesa), la autora hace dos gozosos retratos de penes como si fueran objetos autónomos. El primero pertenece a un negro descrito de la siguiente manera:

> Sus pantalones, apenas sostenidos por un cordel a la cintura, tenían la bragueta abierta de par en par. Un enorme sexo gris oscuro aparecía moviéndose como un péndulo a cada paso del negro y chocando alternadamente contra los muslos. Pene y hombre iban desafiantes ... (24)[28]

---

[28] En el contexto estadounidense, la representación de un negro con un gran pene pudiera ser vista como caída en el estereotipo del poderío sexual del hombre de color. Para contrarrestar esta posibilidad, hay que pensar que en este relato el negro es visto con admiración por su caminar airoso, y que "el enorme sexo" puede ser producto de la imaginación de la narradora.

El fragmento que sigue presenta a un hombre en un tren subterráneo, llevando con tranquilidad su pene en la mano, sin que nadie altere su conducta. La sorprendente revelación final de que el miembro minuciosamente descrito sea en realidad una pera retrotrae a la mente el título de los dos fragmentos. Caemos entonces en la cuenta de que lo que leímos fueron "espejismos" del narrador o narradora, cuya vivacidad descriptiva nos hizo ver con ella (preferimos que sea ella) lo que era un deseo o sueño. Sobra decir que resulta divertido y ciertamente liberador ver por fin, para variar, una "objetivación" de una parte masculina, y que sea una mano autorial femenina la que saque a luz algo que bien puede corresponder al imaginario de muchas mujeres.

Canon de alcoba tiene entre las 27 prosas tres que contienen relaciones eróticas entre mujeres. La titulada "Oír" presenta un tipo de voyeurismo del oído al enfocarse en una muchacha que escucha a dos amigas haciendo el amor en la habitación contigua. La oyente goza al imaginar lo que se desarrolla adentro, acto que a la vez intensifica el placer de las otras dos que se saben escuchadas. Un dardo contra cierto tipo de relación heterosexual se da cuando la muchacha:

> Agradece que se le dé la posibilidad de oír un encuentro entre mujeres que no tendrá, por lo mismo, el carácter de un forcejeo, ni de una persistencia obstinada, ni de una culminación en la que no se podrá saber quién tuvo el triunfo, ni si la simultaneidad fue algo buscado que fracasó y que el ocultamiento recíproco trató de borrar en los últimos estertores (44).

La cita previa no debe llevar a pensar que el libro es de algún modo una invocación a un lesbianismo militante como con frecuencia se halla en los Estados Unidos. Al contrario, si en este relato la cuestión del lesbianismo es indiferente, los otros dos muestran mujeres que claramente no lo son. En "El recogimiento", dos amigas hacen el amor excitadas por las confidencias del pasado común en que compartieron el mismo hombre. De nuevo se acentúa el placer acicateado por sentimientos que nada tienen que ver con nociones de culpa o dolor. En cierto modo, lo que se halla aquí es el empleo del cuerpo como sustituto de la palabra:

> Advertía que los cuentos que hasta ahora se habían contado eran cada vez más una superposición de alientos entrecortados, como si la palabra, cansada, se hubiera ido secando en los labios para insinuarse en otras formas, más del pulmón que de las cuerdas vocales, más de la acechanza que crece entre dos que no se tocan que de la complicidad directa entre dos que hacen amistad (107).

El relato "Las amigas" tampoco sugiere lesbianismo, pero sí presenta el acto sexual en grupo, situación poco explorada en la literatura hispanoamericana. Aquí, tres mujeres hacen el amor como espectáculo de los hombres clientes de un establecimiento dedicado al sexo. Sin una historia central, las páginas son principalmente descripciones de actos sexuales en que las partes anatómicas se nombran con franqueza poco acostumbrada. Una intensidad semejante del placer se encuentra en "Variaciones", de la sección "Amor Udrí", que describe una relación entre pene y vagina. Apropiadamente, este trozo va seguido de una disquisición sobre la dificultad de representar el deseo sexual, titulado "El último recodo." Este fragmento, que puede considerarse una llamada metadiscursiva para aludir a los demás relatos, para algunos lectores también puede ser un elogio al pene.[29]

El relato más cercano a cierta noción de la pornografía, puede que sea el titulado "Ver", escenificación de lo que Luisa Valenzuela llama "telecoito", o amor a la distancia (*El gato eficaz* 42), aquí con el ojo y el teléfono como conductores del deseo. Una causa del efecto cómico que produce esta historia es el control de la "impersonalidad" de la narración (en inglés se diría "a dead-pan style"), y de la precisión en los detalles. El escenario es Greenwich Village de Nueva York, precisamente en la calle 10, entre la Quinta y Sexta Avenidas. Durante seis años, entre las 7 y 8 p.m., se desarrolla una especie de rito de dos solitarios. Ella se exhibe desnuda y masturbándose frente a la ventana de él, que la mira y ajusta su eyaculación para un orgasmo simultáneo. Lo que separa esta narración de otras similares es la centralidad del placer, sin que intervenga ninguno de los múltiples hechos que componen la existencia humana. Lo único que se sabe de la mujer es que es joven y bella, y que tiene el mismo horario para regresar a su casa. Del hombre, apenas se nos dice que trabaja. Sólo por inferencia podemos suponer que éstos son dos solitarios, pero como no hay indicios de los sentimientos que de costumbre se adhieren a la soledad —angustia, aburrimiento— no podemos afirmar que estos seres sean felices o desgraciados, o que tengan o no tengan una vida social fuera de esta hora que se nos narra. Hay una sola nota de aparente reproche que se desliza en la narración, comentando el carácter narcisista del goce solitario:

> La llamada se ha producido regularmente en todos estos años, desde que él observa y goza. Cuando falló, ella pareció desesperarse, pero no hizo nada para subsanar la falta. Ella no llamó y, para paliar la frustración, su acto fue más solipsista que nunca y la devoción por sí misma llegó a un paroxismo tal que a él terminó por serle insoportable, como si su puesto de mira y su acción de mirar hubieran estallado, sobrepasados por los acontecimientos (40).

---

[29] Véanse las páginas 164-65, en que el miembro masculino se describe en términos altamente elogiosos.

Como se ha visto, tanto en "Antieros" como en "Ver" los personajes son sujetos activos de su placer, sin que haya contacto físico con otro ser. La diferencia en el segundo relato es que la soledad está compartida a través de la ventana. Con estas representaciones, Mercado está desmitificando la noción tradicional de que el goce sexual necesita el amor y/o la comunicación entre participantes. Desusado resulta igualmente el hecho intimado antes de representar el placer sin traer a colación otros problemas concomitantes a las relaciones humanas, como la incompresión o la incomunicación.

El placer de la palabra, unido íntimamente a la representación que Mercado hace de lo erótico en todos los textos alusivos a él se evoca metadiscursivamente en el titulado precisamente "Amor discursivo." Aquí, una mujer y un hombre que se han conocido en el pasado, reanudan la amistad a través de un diálogo de varias horas, con secuelas emocionales y físicas sorprendentes para ellos mismos:

> Sus palabras eran como felinos que galopaban por su cuerpo ... el diálogo se encaminaba por corroboraciones que nada tenían que ver con la materia del amor pero que, extrañamente, como por una fuerza ajena a ellos, habían empezado a producir delectación física ... a él le parecía advertir que cada vez que ella cerraba un propósito a él se le estremecía algo en el plexo. Montados a las palabras y abrazados a una disquisición que siempre encontraba el asidero donde encarnarse para proseguir su desarrollo, entregados a esa práctica como quienes han descubierto una posición nueva ... no imaginaban desenlaces ni pretendían acelerar trámites. El deseo apacentaba sus criaturas, y por así decir, sus criaturas eran las palabras del diálogo (121).

Si la palabra es incentivo del deseo sexual en el fragmento citado, en "El próximo recodo" la palabra es base para reflexionar sobre la dificultad de expresar el deseo en el lenguaje. Para la hablante:

> La palabra, soplo, aliento del alma, es cuerpo en la escritura ... Crea, transforma, pero también extrae, saca de sus plantas, de su corazón, de su meollo original, la raíz donde anclaba; de adentro hacia afuera tira su raicilla y la convierte en nervadura, en tallo del que surgen ahora nuevas terminaciones, la desinencia infinita tendida hacia el deseo (159).

Se ha hecho aparente, creemos, la incidencia de lo estético en la escritura erótica de Mercado, incidencia que se hace aún más explícita en la representación de un museo como "Casa del amor", en la sección de este título. Allí se habla del efecto deseante que despierta la visión de las pinturas, explicándose que:

> No eran el desnudo, ni el acoplamiento explícito, ni la pornográfica belleza unificadora los que portaban la excitación, sino el color penumbroso, las formas insolentes de la irrealidad, la morbidez de las superficies, la rebeldía de la materia pugnando por salirse y penetrar por el ojo-órgano de la piel hasta el lugar de la cópula (93).

El no sé qué que constituye lo bello, que tiene tan intensa repercusión en el que observa, se da lo mismo que en el museo, en un claustro, casa de salud, en una hoja que cae, o un arco arquitectónico. Por esto la hablante puede afirmar que: "El deseo entonces no es cuestión del Eros acoplador, 'unificador'", sino que amenaza "a cada instante con aparecer ante las incitaciones menos clasificables" (95), que es exactamente lo que se ilustra en los textos del libro.

Es irónico que en una cultura que hace propaganda a la sexualidad a cada rato en los medios masivos, anunciando abiertamente el sexo como fundamento de la identidad y de la felicidad humana, se sepa tan poco del goce femenino. A pesar de la apertura promovida por el feminismo a todo lo que atañe a la mujer, la atmósfera de pánico que hizo fracasar la conferencia sobre la sexualidad en Barnard College en 1982 es expresiva al respecto. Carol Vance, una de las organizadoras de esa conferencia, al hacer su recuento, acusa a muchas de sus participantes de "analfabetismo y sobrerreacción" a la exposición de las materias a discutir ("visual illiteracy and literal-minded overreaction").[30] Por otro lado, no hay duda de que lo concerniente a la sexualidad femenina ha sido movilizado por discursos que sostienen el poder masculino y la subordinación femenina,[31] lo que hace razonable insistir en el exceso de abuso y violencia que han generado estos discursos en la práctica sexual específica, y social en general. Al mismo tiempo, es preciso disipar el mito de que a la mujer no le interesa el sexo, y promover el conocimiento no sólo de su fisiología sino también de su placer. Como expresara Muriel Dimen, la sexualidad no es ruta a la revolución, pero su represión fomenta la mala conciencia y la autotraición,[32] mala conciencia —agregamos nosotros— que puede tener funestas consecuencias que trascienden el mundo privado.

Las obras de Peri Rossi y Tununa Mercado dan un paso decisivo en la representación más abierta de la erotización del cuerpo y del placer femenino. Ambos textos obligan al lector a repensar su concepto del amor, y su relación con

---

[30] Carol S. Vance, "Epilogue", *Pleasure and Danger: Exploring Female Sexuality* (Londres: Routledge & Kegan Paul, 1984), 431-39 (433).
[31] Coward, *op. cit.*, 29.
[32] Muriel Dimen, "Politically Correct? Politically Incorrect?" en *Pleasure and Danger*, editado por Carol S. Vance, 138-49 (147).

la sexualidad, cuestionando ideas añejas y erradas. Las dos obras a la vez conjugan la belleza de la palabra poética con los variados cuestionamientos, poniendo de relieve la complejidad de los fenómenos representados, sin disminuir el goce que deriva de un texto literario bien escrito.

Desde afuera: asco y placer en la literatura latinoamericana

ALICIA BORINSKY

La amistad con el lector

En *En breve cárcel* de Sylvia Molloy leemos: "Qué placer recordar que alguien se cortó el pelo y dejó de comer queso, qué placer recordar que alguien se guardó la lanzadera de su madre, inútil, a pesar de que se la necesitaba. Estas líneas no componen, y nunca quisieron componer, una autobiografía: componen —querrían componer— una serie de violencias salteadas, que le tocaron a ella, que también han tocado a otros" (68).[1] Qué placer en los detalles, en la enumeración de lo cotidiano, lo fisiológico, lo doméstico, los filamentos de una memoria que no se decide a recordar sino a través de lo parcial. Rencores, presentimientos, descripción de los movimientos de la escritura, conciencia de tener sed, el aroma de un pan, caminatas, presencia de cuartos, comidas, miradas. La novela de Molloy practica una autorreflexión de lo escrito que, en vez de apartarnos del personaje para arrastrarlo (arrastrarla) en la diseminación de la capacidad alusiva del lenguaje, inventa un cuerpo y un aliento.

En breve cárcel efectúa, así, un doble ejercicio; nos recrea la imposibilidad de la memoria en tanto secuencia y nos brinda la posibilidad de ver, espiar, ser parte. Ausentes el momento histórico, el ruido y el sentido de los pasos colectivos, el universo de oficinas, burocracias, partidos políticos que de vez en cuando llamamos *realidad*.

La lectura de *En breve cárcel* se apoya en un pacto de reconocimiento, en una proximidad de lectura. Los detalles aludidos adquieren el carácter de una suerte de confidencia y ponen al lector en el papel de quien escucha y acompaña. La ficción de una voz cercana es intensificada por la restricción de lo nombrado; una estricta austeridad nutre, paradójicamente, los detalles de la novela y les da un peso decisivo. "Sólo registra lo pequeño, lo único que siente a su alcance: los cigarrillos y el encendedor, la cajita de plata que fue de Sara y que ella más tarde le había regalado a Renata para sus rituales remedios" (60). Novela eminentemente *al alcance* del

---

[1] Sylvia Molloy, *En breve cárcel* (Barcelona: Seix Barral, 1981).

lector que sugiere un contrato por el cual la esfera de lo social se desvanece para dar lugar a una estética del secreto y la complicidad. Esta prolija delimitación de un mundo y la inclusión de un lector que recibe lo leído como una carta, un vínculo, montan los efectos de intimidad en *En breve cárcel*. Si gran parte de la obra nombra la inestabilidad de las relaciones amorosas y el carácter elusivo de la memoria, también construye simultáneamente una corriente de participación con el lector. Así, la pareja solicitada a través de las menciones de las otras parejas es formada por narradora y lector.

¿Cuáles son las características de esta *otra* relación, implícita, sustrato de la posibilidad misma de las historias? Las últimas oraciones de la novela nos brindan una clave: "Desamparada, se aferra a las páginas que ha escrito para no perderlas, para poder releerse y vivir en la espera de una mujer que quería y que, un día, faltó a una cita. Está sola: tiene mucho miedo" (158). Seducir ahora al lector para que finalmente entre y tome posesión de lo que se le ha estado ofreciendo: rescatar a la protagonista, asumir la responsabilidad del círculo íntimo, entrar y encarnar no a Vera ni Renata sino al futuro virtual contenido en el presente del miedo de la protagonista.

La maniobra de la interlocución íntima en sus efectos más intensos hace del lector ese personaje maleable, esa oreja que facilita, participa, torna real, simpatiza.

La autenticidad de lo inconfesable

Los ojos azules de Alina Diaconú está narrada en primera y tercera personas, dividida en capítulos titulados alfabéticamente de A a O.

La niñez reaparece en el discurso de la narradora, esta vez a pesar suyo en la forma de un olor a cebolla que relaciona con su casa familiar. El texto cuenta un viaje que es también una prolija humillación de la protagonista. Turista por casualidad en un lugar no especificado, el viaje se convierte en una mirada interna, un develamiento de fuentes de placer y asco. Uno de los clientes del hotel donde reside la protagonista, a quien llaman "Ojos Azules", suscita la siguiente conversación: "—Le preguntaba, querida, qué es lo que a usted le da placer ... Qué es lo que a ella le daba placer. En una época, los vestidos de telas con mucho brillo y los tacos muy altos, era la así llamada 'pubertad', hace milenios de eso. -Oh, no tanto- sonríe el viejo, y sus bigotes retorcidos bajo la tintura hacen que algo torcido inunde todo su rostro, es un equívoco que la confunde, creándole un malestar" (49).[2]

Rodeada de personajes arltianos, seducida por una prostituta, partícipe en escenas sexuales donde se la manosea y orina, "Ojos Azules" nos entrega este viaje como una confesión. Hay un tono de brutalidad, de descubrimiento de algo terrible y negro en

---

[2] Alina Diaconú, *Los ojos azules* (Buenos Aires: Editorial Fraterna, 1986).

esta novela donde la proximidad con el lector reside en su ser recipiente de una cadena de cosas ocultas, inconfesables a la luz del día, una suerte de cuchicheo acerca del deseo. ¿A quién pertenece el deseo nombrado en la novela? ¿Quién experimenta el placer? Y ¿cómo responde la novela a la pregunta efectuada por el turista anciano? "Ojos Azules" recibe la comodidad del hotel como una oportunidad para recordar que en circunstancias normales no podría pagar por su estadía: "¿Qué hacer entonces en esta habitación que excede sus posibilidades de disfrutarla?" (144). La vacación en la isla reproduce a lo largo de la novela esta noción de culpabilidad que en la frase citada tiene sentido monetario. O bien ella no se merece lo que está recibiendo; es *demasiado* y sólo sirve para recordarle que es pobre y no alguien que veranea regularmente en islas, o es llevada a una intensa escena amorosa que sólo al final es reconocida como una traición. Esta traición, donde se revela que la mujer con quien ha tenido esta relación es una prostituta que espera ser pagada por sus servicios sirve también para revelar la falta de adecuación de la protagonista. Ella no sabe suficiente, no tiene una intuición que le permita construirse una narrativa comprensible y controlable. Cree entender que no debe disfrutar completamente del cuarto de hotel debido a su carencia de dinero pero se equivoca al creer que puede gozar con esa mujer porque también para eso necesitaría dinero. Vulnerable en una suerte de esencialización del ser pobre, el hotel y el orgasmo sólo cumplen la función de intensificar su falta de ubicación, la extrema debilidad que la define. A nivel estrictamente físico, su debilidad es expresada en desmayos, estados de enfermedad, percepciones desde la incapacidad física. Una suerte de ola fisiológica recubre esta novela donde el interrogante del placer es resuelto a favor de la humillación de la protagonista. Sus placeres la condenan, no éticamente sino como perceptora de sus propios avatares. El recurrente olor a cebolla la devuelve a la niñez y a lo que ella percibe como un destino.

El viaje a la isla en *Los ojos azules* es un intento de desnudar, de mostrar algo percibido como esencial. Aquí, el lector es testigo y la intimidad consiste en la recepción de imágenes eminentemente privadas, de experiencias y pensamientos. Las mezquindades y humillaciones comunicadas a través de la novela dicen al testigo como transgresor, suscitan la noción de una visión privilegiada. Al entrar en el agujero del miedo de "Ojos Azules", el lector reacciona ante cierta *desnudez*.

La presentación de las flaquezas y humillaciones de la protagonista sugiere que la estamos viendo con una proximidad que no deja nada por develar; la ilusión de autenticidad se apoya en estas referencias y pretende construir en el lector la conciencia de un cuerpo y una vida, "al desnudo". Así, la falta de control de la protagonista posibilita el control casi totalitario del lector cuya posición en el texto le permite acceso privilegiado a las verdades sólo intuidas por "Ojos Azules". Vergüenza, falta de adecuación, sentido de culpa, el lector recibe todo esto y, como resultado, cree saber quién es la protagonista. *Los ojos azules* registra la verdad como efecto de lo interior.

Y lo interior como un desequilibrio, un desacomodo, un caer a veces a propósito y otras por casualidad en situaciones donde la protagonista sólo puede hacer el ridículo. Se trata de un profundo ridículo registrado por la protagonista como autodefinición. El lector sale invicto de estos trastabilleos. La batalla no lo ha tocado porque la novela produce sus imágenes en el registro del espectáculo. Lector-consumidor, así, de una desgracia hiperbólica.

Si hay una apelación al placer de la lectura en *Los ojos azules*, éste radica en el brillo de la transgresión; en la proyección en los personajes que explotan a "Ojos Azules". La novela se cierra como una pesadilla ajena o una obra de teatro, como si hubiéramos presenciado un momento de las fantasías de un Erdosain femenino. La visión de los otros personajes y sus circunstancias a través de un distanciamiento es parte de la multiplicación de las instancias del espectáculo. Ridícula y débil, "Ojos Azules"; impenetrables pero repugnantes y amenazadores, los demás. En esta novela de Alina Diaconú la ilusión efectuada en el lector es la de un conocimiento y comprensión de la protagonista que, simultáneamente, favorece su rechazo y la coincidencia con su propio juicio de sí misma. A esa desvalorización del personaje y sus acciones debido a las revelaciones que se nos han hecho en la novela, la lectura nombra como "autenticidad". La intimidad esta aquí sostenida por el desprecio.

La vergüenza del cuerpo

En un relato muy breve recogido en su volumen *La furia*, "El mal", Silvina Ocampo intuye modos de creación de este desprecio. Un hombre en la cama de un hospital convalece de un mal que lo mantiene en un estado de incapacitación. Sin embargo hay momentos en los cuales su condición se le antoja una oportunidad de ver la realidad de otra manera: "Ahora, reconocía la diferencia que hay hasta en los gustos de una naranja y de una mandarina" (39). Esta visión optimista, traducible por el inocuo "no hay mal que por bien no venga", es inmediatamente ampliada del siguiente modo: "Cuando sentía necesidad de orinar tocaba el timbre; mágicamente aparecía una mujer, con blancura de estatua, trayendo un florero de vidrio que era una suerte de reliquia y esa misma mujer, con ojos etruscos y uñas de rubí, le ponía enemas o lo pinchaba como si cosiera un género precioso" (39).[3] Rubendariana en su carácter estatuesco y el rubí de sus uñas, esta enfermera nos cuenta un secreto. "El mal" nos invita a asomarnos y entrever aquello que convierte a la víctima en beneficiario. Terminamos el relato habiendo sido incapacitados para la compasión: el conocimiento de cómo come y cómo recibe sus enemas no se traduce en complicidad con el personaje, por el contrario el humor llena el intersticio del distanciamiento y empieza

---

[3] Silvina Ocampo, *La furia y otros cuentos* (Barcelona: Alianza, 1982).

a elaborar la destrucción de la amistad entre lector y protagonista. Los placeres corporales del personaje son recibidos como una fuente de vergüenza, nos remiten a su gozo como una confirmación de la extrema pobreza de su existencia, abren la posibilidad de una devastadora mirada retrospectiva que, con un guiño al lector, expulsa al enfermo por medio de sus propias sensaciones.

Ficción de amistad extrema en *En breve cárcel*, proyección de la visión autodestructiva del personaje en *Los ojos azules* y castigo de quien confiesa en "El mal" ... Las obras comentadas ofrecen la noción de intimidad como distintas estrategias de un compromiso de signo diferente, convirtiendo al lector en un personaje maleable a través de la hipótesis del saber acerca de un cuerpo desnudo, de cuerpos deseándose, de cuerpos en el encuentro sexual. Una noción de interioridad y de privilegio de lo privado, del detalle, de esas "violencias" a las cuales se alude en *En breve cárcel* permea la idea de verdad y autenticidad en estas obras. Las tapas de *Los ojos azules* y *En breve cárcel* nos muestran imágenes de mujeres desnudas. ¿Es ésta, entonces, la verdad acerca del cuerpo? ¿Son estos descubrimientos, denuncias, escándalos y crueldades cotidianas la historia específica, personal, la que más peso tiene para la definición de lo dicho como auténtico? Acaso el personaje de Borges que se dedica a descifrar las manchas del tigre en "La escritura del dios" se haya transmutado y ahora, absorto, contempla estos cuerpos y trata de articular lo indecible.

Desde afuera

De la contemplación del tigre no se sale hablando. Es un conocimiento que compromete lo interno, devasta la explicación, inaugura un silencio que es repliegue, abandono del yo. Desde adentro y para adentro, ficciones de intimidad del individuo o de un conocimiento ajeno, que al ser apropiado trastorna quienes somos. En última instancia los placeres de la autenticidad, las revelaciones del asco, los puentes de interlocución y sus fracasos en la danza alrededor y desde la desnudez juegan a la proximidad. Nos dan ficciones del estar cerca, conocer, saber aquello que importa.

Pero, ¿qué hacer de lo opuesto, la localización en las fisuras que separan, los avatares del no poder llegar a juntarse, no reconocer ni un yo ni un cuerpo propio y cuestionar la tangibilidad del ajeno?

Entre los textos que han delineado este mapa de contactos irresueltos y observaciones truncas, los de Felisberto Hernández sugieren el conocimiento sombrío de quien deja en suspenso la hipótesis de toda unidad en la persona. En unas páginas recogidas en el volumen *Últimas invenciones*[4] bajo el título de "El cuerpo y yo" leemos: "Cuando alguien en el mundo me llama, él es el primero que se despierta.

---

[4] Felisberto Hernández, *Obras completas*, 3 (Buenos Aires: Siglo XXI Editores, 1983).

Entonces interrumpe y espanta mis pensamientos y yo no tengo tiempo de saber si ellos huyen asustados o mueren en el acto" (292) ... "No sé si mi cara pertenece a mi cuerpo o a mis pensamientos. Pero a veces siento que mis pensamientos van acompañados de cierta actitud que toma mi cara. O tal vez ellos tienden a buscar quien los acompañe y por eso suponen una cara" (293). La literatura de Felisberto es una prolija descripción de las alternativas de esta visión. En un texto inusitadamente directo sobre la cópula, "Úrsula", Felisberto se desliza del símil a la identificación con el término comparativo. El relato empieza así:

> Úrsula era callada como una vaca. Ya había empezado el verano cuando yo la veía llevar su cuerpo grande por una calle estrecha; a cada paso sus pantorrillas se rozaban y las carnes le quedaban temblando. A mí me gustaba que se pareciera a una vaca (121).

El lenguaje del relato exacerba la fruición de lo gordo, lo mullido, lo fofo: el protagonista gusta de aferrarse a una cuerda gruesa, sentarse en sillones acolchados. La gordura de Úrsula es percibida en términos que recubren el conocimiento del mundo que nos rodea: "Su cuerpo parecía haberse desarrollado como los alrededores de un pueblo por los cuales ella no se interesaba" (122). Cuerpo, así, independiente de Úrsula pero ubicuo para quienes podamos ser habitantes de ese pueblo. Cuerpo codiciado por el protagonista no a pesar de su relación con la vaca sino debido a ella. Es como si él no sólo tuviera derecho a los pliegues del cuerpo de Úrsula sino que también le pertenecieran porque ha percibido en ella una profundidad que Úrsula misma no conoce. Cuando el protagonista decide manipular su situación para terminar contratando a Úrsula para que venga a hacer la limpieza de una vivienda que alquila, como extranjero, en las afueras de París y logra lo que buscaba, su reacción es: "no hice otra cosa que sacar la lengua en la oscuridad y guardarla inmediatamente" (124).

La relación con Úrsula se da a través de la vaca y la posibilidad de beber leche; el primer encuentro en el cuarto revela la calidad del pacto que une a ambos personajes:

> Mi amigo me mandaba decir si yo prefería café o té. Entonces, clavando mis ojos en los párpados de Úrsula, contesté: "J'aime du lait". Ella levantó los párpados y me mostró sus ojos desnudos; tenían el asombro de un presentimiento. Yo sentía la voluptuosidad de haber empleado el verbo amar para hablarle de la leche. Ella se limitó a decir: "Il n'y a pas de lait". Pero insistí señalando una valija y haciendo señas para que la abriera. Ella tenía la torpeza de un gran animal amaestrado. Sacó un tarro de leche desecada y lo daba vueltas entre sus manos para mirar todas las vacas pintadas alrededor. ... Úrsula se quedaba allí, con su gran barriga, esperando (125).

La relación con Úrsula va a consistir en conectarla con la vaca, familiarizarla con la leche, hacer que su gordura y su calidad vacuna constituyan el vínculo del placer. Ese cuerpo que había sido descripto como los alrededores de un pueblo que a ella no le importa, es el productor de una cadena de voluptuosidades para un protagonista arrastrado hacia la leche, sus olores, la calma del movimiento pesado. El relato no nos dice si después de hacer el amor Úrsula ha comprendido su cuerpo y ha tomado posesión de él por el placer. Por el contrario, su relación con la vaca se vuelve concreta, al punto de sobresaltar al narrador que, un día, tirado en la paja con los ojos cerrados, se despierta para ver que tiene delante suyo una vaca. La visión, en vez de darle placer, lo asusta y trata de exorcizarla gritando el nombre de Úrsula. El final del cuento es feliz: Úrsula llega y se lleva a la vaca, riéndose; las líneas finales dicen: "Las dos iban sacudiendo sus cuerpos hacia un portoncito del fondo; yo las miré hasta que una salió y la otra cerró el portón" (133).

Úrsula ha comprobado varias cosas con este final: su capacidad para generar un juego, la posibilidad de sobresaltar por medio de la presentación súbita de aquello que en el placer sólo existe como una insinuación, y el protagonista, como el Horacio de "Las Hortensias" permanece en un juego que lo mantiene escindido. La vaca es el *afuera* radical y, por eso, le resulta insoportable al protagonista. Chiste cruel, testimonio de control para Úrsula, y, a la vez, humillación de quien, enfrentado a su deseo, sólo conoce el sobresalto.

En la obra de Felisberto recorremos el tenso camino entre aquello que parece desearse auténticamente y el rechazo de su concreción. Los amantes que beben la leche relamiéndose en "Úrsula" deben pasar por la prueba de la vaca real, incorporar el *afuera* de su placer, sucumbiendo así a la crueldad de la dominación.

El protagonista de "Úrsula" mira a Úrsula desde la vaca y a sí mismo desde su deseo de leche. En *La aventura de un fotógrafo en La Plata*[5] de Adolfo Bioy Casares el enmarque de una cámara nos brindará unas reflexiones finales sobre los juegos que, interpuestos, cifran la distancia entre los amantes.

Desde *La invención de Morel*, donde la busca del contacto con Faustine está destinada a la repetición de una máquina de proyección de imágenes, hasta sus obras más recientes, Bioy Casares se ha dedicado a cifrar el peculiar alejamiento que hace del amor una relación asimétrica. En *La aventura de un fotógrafo en La Plata* un fotógrafo cuyo trabajo lo lleva a la ciudad argentina de La Plata se ve asediado por una galería de mujeres y, a pesar de la relativa incomodidad para el contacto físico, tiene relaciones con varias. La incomodidad surge de la posición de la dueña de la pensión en cuanto a las visitas femeninas:

---

[5] Adolfo Bioy Casares, *La aventura de un fotógrafo en La Plata* (Buenos Aires: Emecé, 1985).

>—¿Por qué iba a amargarme?
>—Por la entrada prohibida a las mujeres. ¿Te digo lo que pienso? Para gente como vos y yo es una ventaja. La mujer cargosa que nunca falta, no te molesta. Uno entra en la pensión y está a salvo. Afuera disponemos de la organización Mascardi.
>No quedó otro remedio que preguntar qué era eso. Mascardi explicó que él conocía a unos estudiantes que tenían un departamento. En La Plata, en los departamentos de estudiantes vivían hasta cinco o seis. Como regla general, una vez por semana, los visitaba una mujer.
>... Mirándolo inexpresivamente Almanza comentó: —La verdad que te has vuelto mujeriego (29).

Almanza, el fotógrafo, reacciona con falta de entusiasmo tanto con respecto al fulgor de posibles placeres sexuales como ante el resguardo que le ofrece la pensión, en parte porque acaba de dar sangre a un padre de familia en un episodio con visos de vampirismo y manipulación.

Las mujeres se le ofrecen a Almanza tanto en imagen, para ser fotografiadas, como en inmediatez de contacto sexual. Carmen, la desagradable dueña de la pensión, también lo espía y desea. El fotógrafo no comparte la intensidad de la ambición del contacto corporal; sus relaciones son concebidas a través del lente de la cámara:

>Pensó que Julia, en su llanto, no hacía muecas y que le gustaría fotografiar esa cara tan linda, empapada en lágrimas. Le dijo que era muy linda. Julia contestó:
>—Entonces besáme (109).

Julia le pide que la bese; la dueña de la pensión lo besa después de que él la retrata pensando que el resultado de su fotografía será horrible. Tanto la mujer bella que produce una buena foto (Julia) como la de la fea con papada y pliegues debajo de los ojos (la dueña de la pensión, 125) quieren pasar de la fotografía a los besos. Almanza transcurre por estas invitaciones con el distanciamiento de un turista. La cámara es una suerte de escudo que lo separa de su acaecer y lo convierte en un agente de representación, a salvo de los excesos emotivos de las mujeres, retratándolas *desde afuera*.

La aventura de Almanza termina con la sugerencia de un peligro apenas fundado y una escena que, pese a su valor de clisé sentimental, sólo está ahí para marcar la distancia que rige la relación entre los personajes. Julia, con quien ha vivido un romance, se va sin que se hayan dicho nada que les permita atesorar, conservar, lo ocurrido entre ambos:

>Anunciaron la salida para Balcarce, Tandil y Azul.
>—Mejor que subas.
>Obedeció. Golpeando el vidrio, porque no conseguía abrir la ventanilla, empezó a

gritarle:
—Quería decirte ...
Julia se tapaba la cara, para que no la viera llorar y le decía algo, que no oyó (223).

El lector, también como una cámara, percibe esta escena con ecos de la película *Casablanca* y de tantas otras separaciones, relaciones fallidas, encuadrada, filtrada la carga afectiva para dar lugar a una corriente humorística. Separados por el vidrio, arrastrando en esa barrera las numerosas referencias a ventanas, cristales, caleidoscopios, vitrales, los personajes se refractan y muestran como verdadera esa separación, esas palabras no escuchadas, el silencio que finalmente define la cháchara que los ha unido. Cada uno de ellos con otra historia de esta historia, las mujeres pidiendo el beso al fotógrafo que lo da pero piensa en el encuadre; cada uno ajeno y, sin embargo, atado fervientemente al otro en confirmación de la distancia que no franquearán.

Ascos y placeres entretejidos en las ficciones que transcurren en estas reflexiones, una vaca, cuerpos desnudos, mujeres y hombres que tratan de estrecharse y mostrarse a través de sus acoplamientos y separaciones ... El optimismo de lo caleidoscópico en la sexualidad, de lo plural, la celebración de la libertad, han cedido el lugar a un entrever de la distancia radical que rige estos contactos y estas maniobras de autenticidad. La lógica de estas representaciones nos refiere a cuerpos cuyas realidades y placeres resultan sobrecogedoramente fantásticos y solitarios.

Homosexual Desire in Goytisolo's *Señas de identidad*

PAUL JULIAN SMITH

The Homosexual Question

Critics have often written on the theme of sexuality in Goytisolo, but have rarely raised the question of homosexual desire in its specificity.[1] My aim in this article is to raise that question without either reducing homosexuality to a stable "theme" or "content" or isolating it from those other questions (of gender and "race") by which it is constantly inflected. I shall not be concerned with the relation between the empirical author and the fiction he has produced; nor shall I attempt an "allegorical" reading. This is because both the author function and the appeal to a "latent" meaning deep within the text are often complicit with medicalizing views of homosexuality as the hidden secret which must constantly be brought to the surface, repeatedly exposed to the light of examination.

I treat homosexual desire, then, not as literary theme or psychological trait, but as question, and one posed within language and history. As question, homosexuality constitutes a challenge in a number of spheres: the subjective (the construc-

---

[1] I shall refer to the Barcelona, 1976 edition of *Señas de identidad* (1966). For homosexuality in Goytisolo, mostly with reference to anality, see Abigail Lee Six, *Juan Goytisolo: The Case for Chaos* (New Haven and London: Yale University Press, 1990), 47-8, 114. One critic who assumes that Goytisolo wishes to remain faithful to a homosexual "identity" (albeit an identity displaced into mysticism) is Linda Gould Levine: "El papel paradójico de Sida en *Las virtudes del pájaro solitario*", in *Escritos sobre Juan Goytisolo: II Seminario Internacional sobre la obra de Juan Goytisolo* (Almería: Instituto de Estudios Almerienses, 1990), 225-36 (233). I would argue that Goytisolo offers a critique of "identity" in all its forms. Bradley S. Epps is one of the very few Hispanists familiar with recent gay theory; see "The Violence of the Letter: Oppression and Resistance in Three Texts by Juan Goytisolo", unpublished PhD dissertation (Harvard University, 1990); "The Ecstasy of Disease: Goytisolo, AIDS, and Hispanism", unpublished paper read at the "Questions of Homosexuality" conference, IRS, London, June 1991.

tion of identity); the literary (the conventions of realism); and the sociopolitical (the institutions of the dominant order). My thesis is that homosexual desire creates the possibility of an integrated critique of these three levels as they appear in Goytisolo's fiction: respectively, in his polemic against the literary character; his advocacy of formal experiment; and his proposition of strategies for resisting power.

In this article I take my understanding of homosexual desire mainly from the work of Guy Hocquenghem and from critiques of his work by Jeffrey Weeks and Gilles Deleuze.[2] Weeks's excellent preface to Hocquenghem's major work (the only one to be translated into English) is a good introduction to the field. Paraphrasing Hocquenghem, Weeks claims that homosexual identification serves as a "challange to the bourgeois ideology of familial and reproductive sexuality and male dominance" (9) and suggests that the aim of a theoretically informed lesbian and gay studies would be to analyse "how the 'homosexual' as a social being is constructed in a capitalist society" (10). Weeks makes out three stages in Hocquenghem's argument: first, the analysis of paranoid hostility to homosexuality; second, the relation of that hostility to the Oedipal family and reproductive sexuality; third, the attempt to resist familial sexuality through anti-capitalist and anti-Oedipal struggles. For Hocquenghem, such a programme requires the rejection of the implicitly transhistorical model of the Oedipus found in Freud and Lacan and a re-examination of the role of psychoanalysis within history of the kind carried out by Deleuze and Guattari (16-17). However, unlike Anglo-American anti-psychiatry of the same period, Deleuze and Guattari (and Hocquenghem) are anti-humanist: rather than seeking the liberation of the self from sexual represssion, they suggest we abandon the very concept of "self" and replace it by "desiring machines". The fundamental premise is as follows: confronted by a loss of shared social meaning (or "code"), capitalism reinvents the family (and consequently the self) as the locus of social control. As Weeks puts it:

> As society becomes more "civilized" (capitalist), the level of code in the desiring machines decreases; society struggles against the progressive loss of shared

---

[2] I cite the following texts: *Homosexual Desire* (1972) (London: Allison and Busby, 1978), Introduction by Jeffrey Weeks; *L'Après-mai des faunes; volutions* (Paris: B. Grasset, 1974), Introduction by Gilles Deleuze; *La Dérive homosexuelle* (Paris: J.-P. Delarge, 1977); *La Beauté du métis: réflexions d'un franco-phobe* (Paris: Ramsay, 1979). Hocquenghem was a founder member of the French gay liberation movement (FHAR) and a regular columnist for *Le Gai Pied*. Although Goytisolo was resident in Paris during this period and was aware of Hocquenghem's role as an activist, he did not meet him (private conversation with author).

meaning as it would be destroyed by total decoding (schizophrenia). The family is therefore constituted as an artificially "re-territorialized" unity where social control has been relocated and in which forms of social organization can be reproduced. ... Thus the privatized "individual" that psycholanalysis studies within the Oedipal family unit is an artificial construct, whose social function is to trap and control the disorder that haunts social life under capitalism (18).

The important term here is "territorialization";[3] that is, the investment of libidinal energy within fixed parameters.

This radical attack on the coherence of the "molar" (or unified) self suggests that the naïveties of a certain "homosexual history" (which speculates as to whether a person was "really" gay or not) are no longer possible. Rather we should examine the "conditions of emergence" of definitions of the homosexual, the ways in which "the principal ideological means of thinking about homosexuality ... are intimately, though not mechanically, connected with the advance of Western capitalism" (21). As an example of "perverse reterritorialization", homosexuality is manufactured in a double movement: first, through the creation of a scapegoated minority; second, through "the transformation of repressed homosexual elements of desire into the desire [by 'heterosexuals'] to repress ['homosexuals']". Sublimated homosexuality is thus the basis of the paranoia and panic about homosexuality "which pervades social behaviour" (22).

This paranoid society is dominated by the phallus. And, as an antidote to the hierarchic mode of phallic competition, Hocquenghem proposes a re-evaluation of the anal function. As Weeks points out, Hocquenghem is not to be taken literally at this point: there was no evidence even in the sixties that anal intercourse played a unique or exclusive role in sex between men (24). Rather, Hocquenghem is attempting to "suggest the symbolic consequences of the dominance of the phallus" (25) by proposing a new kind of social organization. The recovery of anal desire (hitherto dismissed or sublimated) would pose a challenge to the division between public and private on which society is based: to lose control of the anus is to risk the loss of individual identity because that control stakes out the boundary between self and other (child and faeces, inside and outside).[4] Hocquenghem's

---

[3] Compare Severo Sarduy, "La desterritorialización", in *Juan Goytisolo*, edited by Gonzalo Sobejano (Madrid: Editorial Fundamentos, 1975).

[4] In spite of superficial appearances, Hocquenghem does not, naïvely, take the anal as a necessarily subversive space; nor does he collapse homosexuality into anality and vice versa. For anal intercourse in D. H. Lawrence as the "perverse" reinscription of heterosexuality in alterity, see Jonathan Dollimore, *Sexual Dissidence: Augustine to Wilde, Freud to Foucault* (Oxford and New York: Clarendon Press and Oxford University Press, 1991), 274-5.

suggestion that the anus be "grouped" (that is admitted to communal representation) is thus not, or not merely, a rationalization of a certain gay sexual activity (polymorphous "scattering") (26); it is also a rejection of homosexuality as an individual "problem" in favour of homosexuality as a communal relation.[5] The ontological definition is replaced by a libidinal position.

Weeks is not uncritical of Hocquenghem's project. He raises three specific questions which, he claims, cannot be accounted for by Hocquenghem's *Homosexual Desire*. First, if anti-homosexual paranoia is a product of capitalism, how can we explain the fact that attitudes have indeed changed in the twentieth century and taboos have not remained fixed? Second, if reterritorialization is a global phenomenon, why is it that certain people become "manufactured" as "homosexuals" and others do not? Third, if the anal is to be promoted an the antidote to phallic supremacy, what significance does this have for lesbian desire (23)? As we shall see later, these three questions (of historical change, subject position, and gender difference) may also be asked with profit of Goytisolo. But Weeks also raises a more general point, which is even more urgent in Goytisolo's case:

> In rejecting the myth of the "normal" and in emphasizing the need for conscious struggle against it, Hocquenghem, like Deleuze and Guattari, is in danger of creating a new myth: the revolutionary potential of the marginal, a myth which ignores the real problems of power in modern capitalism (27).

By aestheticizing marginal subjects (Arabs, "homosexuals") Goytisolo also risks setting up a reverse hierarchy which distracts attention from the power structures which effect that original marginalization. I shall suggest myself, however, that just as Hocquenghem and Deleuze avoid utopianism through a painstaking critique

---

[5] I argue that neither Hocquenghem nor Goytisolo accounts for gender difference in their privileging of anality. For a very different reading of anality in the era of AIDS (which shows how receptive anal sex is gendered as "feminine" in heterosexist fantasy), see Leo Bersani, "Is the Rectum a Grave?" *October* 43 (1987), 197-222. The plurality and laminality of the anal in Hocquenghem might be seen as anticipating later feminist psychoanalytic accounts of the woman's body. See the title essay of Luce Irigaray's *Ce Sexe qui n'en est pas un* (Paris: Minuit, 1977), 23-32; and my *The Body Hispanic* (Oxford and New York: Clarendon Press and Oxford University Press, 1989), 20-1, for an account of this text. But note also Margaret Whitford's warning on Irigaray's supposed "celebration" of femininity: "When Irigaray describes the female imaginary in *This Sex* as plural, non-identical, multiple ... this is not a recommendation that relationships between women in the real world should be of [this] kind." *Luce Irigaray: Philosophy in the Feminine* (London and New York: Routledge, 1991), 81.

of Marx and Freud,[6] so Goytisolo avoids romantic idealism through a far-reaching analysis of Eurocentrism and reproductive sexuality.

Señas de identidad: *Reproducing the Oedipus*

Señas de identidad juxtaposes a narrative in the present of Álvaro Mendiola's return to Spain from Paris with a narrative in the past of his experiences at home and abroad. Goytisolo presents a sequence of scenes in a broadly naturalistic mode of Álvaro's bourgeois childhood in the Civil War; of his post-war education in Barcelona; of his friend Antonio's internal exile in the south of Spain; and finally of Álvaro's experience of the immigrant community in Paris and his affair with fellow exile Dolores. Translated into English as *Signs of Identity*, the French *Pièces d'Identité* suggests more subtly both bureaucracy and fragmentation: the disrupted exposition of the novel will confirm that the "identifying marks" of the title at once constitute and alienate a sense of self.

In the first chapter Álvaro returns to the family home, the "mythical" setting of his childhood (12, 14). In the photo album, with its images of successive generations (including a slave-owning Cuban great-grandfather), Álvaro seeks the "lost key" to his youth (16). However, the family is a "degenerate race", which is fading away (17-19). The various aunts and uncles have died childless and the family tree is now "sterile" (49). Álvaro remembers a scene emblematic of this gulf between the generations, when his senile grandmother failed to recognize him. In spite of his search for soulmates amongst his ancestors, Álvaro's life will be one of rupture and dispossesion (54-5).

From the very beginning, then, *Señas* re-enacts the Oedipal drama. It stages a return to the protagonist's origin and to the scene of his father's death (108); and it sets his quest for identity in the context of that origin and that death. The narrator frequently comes back to images of dissolution and dispersal: just as the father rots in a common grave, so memory of the past is lost for ever (110). However, far from welcoming this dissolution as one might have expected, the rebellious Álvaro is nostalgic for the integration of experience and identity: after so many years of exile, the "lost unity" of self and nation presents him from achieving a

---

[6] In his generally positive account of Hocquenghem's co-option of psychoanalysis for homosexual politics (*Dissidence* 206-9), Dollimore argues that, in spite of the joyful anarchy of his anti-humanism, Hocquenghem still appeals to a disguised essentialism of desire (212). Dollimore is, however, unfamiliar with Hocquenghem's French texts on activist politics and "race".

"reconstitution" or "synthesis" of his personal history (159).⁷ The quest for the father, killed by Republicans in the War, will be fruitless: Álvaro is "unable to know" his father (154). And this interruption of the generative process is experienced as loss, not liberation.

The residual nostalgia for reproduction (of the family and of its history) is supplemented by a compulsory heterosexuality which legitimates casual misogyny and homophobia. In his sentimental education Álvaro's conquests of women are inseparable from his social and political progress: thus his casual initiation into heterosexual intercourse with a Barcelona prostitute (78) mirrors his introduction to the mysterious geography of the Catalan capital. Much later, Álvaro's encounter with Europe is compared to his deepening love for Dolores (317), who comes to embody his past in exile (336). There is thus little reciprocity in heterosexual relations as depicted within the novel: the woman is generally the vehicle through whom man explores his territory and in whom he invests his experience. A free spirit, Dolores is initially presented as the woman who longs to swim naked and pick up men in the street (49). And when they first meet, Álvaro is captivated by her short, masculine hair and "ambiguous" appearance (325). But Dolores is only too willing to sleep with Álvaro's friend Antonio if he so wishes; and in the present day narrative serves mainly to freshen Álvaro's glass and nag him to stop drinking (135). Álvaro satirizes his fellow exiles for the way in which their attitude to France is determined by the treatment they receive at the hands of French women: at first they are fascinated by Gallic language and culture; but after the first disappointment their "manhood" seeks solace with a more conciliatory Spanish spouse (251). Ironically, however, Álvaro's relationship with Dolores is not so very different in kind and if he does not express the brutality and contempt for women that his friend Antonio shows for prostitutes (208, 222), Álvaro's use of women is also acquisitive and instrumental. He has indeed "penetrated Dolores with his desire" (181).

In the Oedipal fantasy of (male) return to origin, women also have a role to play: through cunnilingus Álvaro seeks to return to the womb which he wishes he had never left (120, 158). If Álvaro seeks to preserve the (male) past of political action from oblivion, here he also aspires to a (female) space of atemporality, outside phallic competition. As the representative of a displaced post-war "generation" (155) Álvaro can neither shoulder the masculine burden of paternity

---

⁷ For a Lyotardian reading of history in the trilogy, see Abigail Lee Six, "Breaking Rules, Making History: A Postmodern Reading of Historiography in Juan Goytisolo's Fiction", in *History and Post-War Writing* (Amsterdam: Rodopi, 1990), 33-60; for a Bakhtinian reading, see Ariel del Barrio, *Dialogismo y novela: el principio dialógico en las novelas de Juan Goytisolo* (Guayaquil: Ediciones Documentas, 1990).

nor trust to the feminine function of reproduction: the only women in the novel who bear children are those whose anonymous biographies form the material for a documentary that Álvaro never completes (382). Amongst the new "freedoms" of Spain in the sixties is the "freedom to procreate absurd children" (231). Filiation is re-established only in a grotesque form.

But if (physical) reproduction is disrupted or ridiculed in *Señas*, Goytisolo continues to reproduce misogynistic and homophobic images in the novel. Thus a dissolute college friend of Álvaro remarks that the only interesting people in Barcelona are "whores and queers"; and Álvaro himself pours scorn on "frigid" women (75, 145). Amongst the male friends who help Álvaro in his project of self-discovery is Paco, affectionately called "maricón" by the others (235), as are at least three other characters in twenty pages (279, 286, 298). Here Goytisolo is satirizing youthful exiles in Paris, whose lack of success with Parisiennes makes them eager to insult prospective rivals. But it is not enough to say that such language was (and is) part of everyday (heterosexual) speech. For the narrator himself is the vehicle for a more insidious homophobia: thus amongst prisoners held by police in Barcelona is a callow youth ("jovencito") recognized by a rouged and buttonholed queen; one drunken evening in Paris, Álvaro finds himself in a "curious" literary salon full of pale "jovencitos" with gazelle-like eyes; and men in a Venetian bar are said to have dyed hair and sport "little gold chains" ("cadenitas") (264, 265, 360). The repetition of the dismissive diminutive ending is significant here for it reinforces stereotypes of homosexuality as criminal, effeminate, and effete. More importantly, however, homosexuality appears to be ubiquitous, even as it is exiled from the central space of the narrative, attributed to secondary and marginal characters. As Hocquenghem says (*Desire* 59), there is clearly a desiring relation between disciplinary forces and the homosexual subjects they pursue: the policeman mimes anal penetration behind the *jovencito*'s back. The will to knowledge of government authorities, expressed in the police files cited at length in Chapter Four, extends deep into the sexual arena. But homosexuality is also presented as one of the factors which disrupt reproduction and the smooth succession of generations: the scandal faced by even the best families include "a queer heir" and juvenile leftist agitators (286-7). Here homosexuality and political resistance are juxtaposed but not related to each other: Goytisolo chooses not to make the connection.

Elsewhere, however, there is a clear connection between political repression and sublimated homosexual desire. This is concretized in the leitmotif of the (male) hand placed on the (male) shoulder. Thus Álvaro's fascist uncle Eulogio of the "brilliant black eyes" lays his hand on his young nephew's shoulder; the Falangist doctor does the same to leftist militant Antonio, just as (chillingly) the torturer had done in prison (134, 203, 170). The twists and turns of Goytisolo's homoeroticism here correspond to Hocquenghem's account of "anti-homosexual paranoia". For Hocquenghem, the problem is not homosexual desire, but fear of homosexuality. Through an unholy alliance of clinical and criminal institutions, capitalist society has manufactured homosexuals as a category marginal to society, yet central to society's disciplinary practices (35-7). It follows that homosexuality is inseparable from those dominant forces which have called it into being: as Hocquenghem puts it, "the very mode of existence [of homosexual desire] calls into question again and again the certainty of its existence" (39).

Rejecting Freud's definition of homosexuality as "persecutory mania", Hocquenghem shifts attention to the (heterosexual) paranoia that seeks to persecute. In such libidinally charged sites as the law courts, the "presence of desire in the social machine" is revealed in a nakedly direct manner (42, 47, 58). The sublimation of homosexuality effected by the legal and medical establishments is thus "the basis for the functioning of the great social machines". It masks the triumph of the molar self (monolithic, inflexible, homogeneous) over the molecular subject (multiple, mobile, heterogeneous).

Moreover, this external repression is internalized by means of Oedipal triangulation. Having discovered that the libido is the basis of affective life, Freud abandons his original belief that it was autonomous and polymorphous, and confines the libido within the boundaries of the "privatized family" (59, 63). Homosexuality can then be safely defined as lack (the hatred of women) and desire as production replaced by sexuality as reproduction. The (newly privatized) homosexual is said to be narcissistic: "by making his [sic] anaclitic choice on a narcissistic basis the homosexual is ... deprived of an object" (66). Although it is defined in negative terms (loss, absence), this homosexuality becomes curiously substantial, indeed determining, for the subject: "homosexuality is no longer a relation of desire but an ontological standpoint" (74). From a relative position it becomes an essential identity.

We have seen that *Señas* bears out Hocquenghem's first rule of anti-homosexual paranoia: that the legal system exists to discipline and punish perverse subjects rendered both marginal and ubiquitous by those same authorities. The punishment of scapegoats such as the *jovencito* prevents the generalized and sublimated homosexuality of male institutions (of prisons and political parties) from coming to light. However, elsewhere in the novel Goytisolo also reconfirms the second stage of Hocquenghem's argument: the existence of a privatized, internalized homosexuality fostered by psychoanalysis, which is not a criminal but an ontological category. In the first chapter the child Álvaro comes across the Andalusian migrant worker Jerónimo on the family estate. Jerónimo is said to have black eyebrows and a copper-coloured face (42, 44). Álvaro spends (apparently chaste) nights with him in the barn, even though he knows him to have a gun. When

Jerónimo disappears he is revealed to have been a resistance figher; and his loss, we are told, prefigures the suffering Dolores will later cause the adult Álvaro (48). This childhood episode goes unmentioned for some three hundred pages, only to return unexpectedly in the midst of Álvaro's account of his affair with Dolores. Álvaro confesses that there are things of which he cannot speak, "holes" in his biography (338). He goes on to recount a scene in which he picks up an Arab in a Parisian street:

> Una escena familiar te ronda la memoria: estás en el París industrioso del canal Saint Martin y un sol invernal, rezagado, brilla sobre las aguas.
> Paseas despacio. El árabe ha abandonado la contemplación del panorama de las grúas y suelta a andar a su vez, cauto y receloso, con las manos hundidas en los bolsillos. A una veintena de metros de él puedes observar a tus anchas sus botas de goma, los pantalones de burdo azul machón, la zamarra de cuero con las solapas forradas de piel, el pasamontañas de lana ceñido a la cabeza. Su presencia discreta gobierna la calle. Al llegar a los jardincillos desnudos del square tuerce en dirección al bulevar, aguarda sin volverse el semáforo verde, atraviesa la calzada y, tal como has previsto tú, continúa su marcha hacia La Chapelle bajo el techo del aéreo. Le imitas.
> ... El metro pasa zumbando encima de nosotros y su sacudida estremece brutalmente el suelo. Sustraído de pronto al tiempo y al espacio recuerdas que un día, en un hotelucho cercano, hiciste el amor (¿con quién?) aprisa y corriendo (era tarde, tenías una cita en la France Presse) y tu eyaculación había coincidido exactamente con el temblor provocado por el tránsito de los vagones. (¿Consecuencia lógica del ruido o casualidad pura?) Desde entonces, piensas con nostalgia, no has vuelto a probar jamás.
> .... (Como necesario horizonte para ti, el rostro de Jerónimo, de las sucesivas reencarnaciones de Jerónimo en algún rostro delicado e imperioso, soñador y violento había velado en filigrana los altibajos de tu pasión por Dolores con la fuerza magnética y brusca con que te fulminara la primera vez. Cuando os separásteis se fue sin darte su dirección ni pedirte la tuya. Tenía dos mujeres, seis hijos y nunca supiste como se llamaba.) (339-40)

The scene is "familiar" (it has happened often) and the partner is lent a definite article ("*the* Arab", suggesting a number of nameless others). The narrator lingers fetishistically on the pick-up's clothing. And in the midst of this encounter he is taken back by involuntary memory to a previous occasion, in which the moment of orgasm and the rumbling of a Metro train fortuitously coincide. The present sexual act is not described, is subject to an ellipse. Rather it is explained (parenthetically) as the compulsive repetition of a primal experience, the passion for Jerónimo. Homosexual desire is thus interwoven with the varied course of Álvaro's heterosexual relation with Dolores: it is caught up in the delicate tracery ("filigrana") of the libidinal text.

Here, then, homosexuality is presented in Oedipal form as a compulsion to repeat the past, an internalization of the external, an individual "case history". But it is also (and more positively) presented as a multiple, anonymous relation of desire, which is ignorant of origins and identity, and exists only in an eternal present. This new homosexual desire is directed not to the inside (the same of personal identity) but to the outside (the other man from the south: Andalusia or North Africa).

This eroticization of the other male (of the male as other) will be much developed in the later novels. But what is specific to *Señas* is the problematic status of a bisexual protagonist in a work which offers itself as an allegorical history of the nation. We have seen that Goytisolo relies heavily on heterosexual (indeed heterosexist) narrative structures: women serve as the medium through which male desire achieves transcendence and sublimated homosexuality dare not be acknowledged. But Álvaro's official *Bildungsroman*, in which he appropriates a named woman and a clearly defined north European territory, is interrupted and thus subverted by an unofficial and fragmentary narrative of anonymous homosexual encounters, which permits no development in time or space. This second narrative (which resists allegorization, which speaks only of itself), undermines the totalizing claims of the first. Exiled from history, from the orderly succession of generations, homosexual desire cannot be assimilated to the narrative of national identity. Álvaro's intermittent acknowledgement of his "instinctive" search for love amongst Arabs and blacks (366) betrays the uncomfortable fact that "alongside ... conscious political investments there is a system of unconscious libidinal investments ... [that is] repressed" (*Desire* 122). Although Goytisolo does not make the point himself, Álvaro's alienation from the working class and from traditional class-based politics suggests that the latter "do not tolerate the interference of the private ... in the sphere of official relations between the classes" (123). Once more, homosexual desire is a disruptive anomaly. Moreover, the implication that sexual object choice is arbitrary and impersonal (Goytisolo compares it here to magnetism and lightning) is incompatible with the naturalist idea of a literary character whose plausibility must depend on integration and consistency. In the traditional form to which Goytisolo clings here, a bisexual hero is simply too idiosyncratic to be representative of the national destiny, too anomalous to "typify" his generation. Indeed, he tends to call into question the legitimacy of the term "generation" as a way of approaching history.

Ironically, however, there is indeed a connection (unstressed by the narrator) between homosexual activity and political struggle. There are in the novel a number of scenes where resistance to power takes forms as multiple, fortuitous, and acephalous as Hocquenghem's "pick-up machine" (116). For example, charcoal makers spontaneously rebel against the pre-war *cacique*; and Álvaro's fellow students stage a post-war demonstration in the streets of Barcelona in which participants are mobile, multiple, and anonymous (136, 245). Both these rebellions are doomed to failure. But (like the scene with the Arab) they point the way forward to new structures of politics and desire. If *Señas* tends, still, to reconfirm the belief in a (lost) plenitude of experience to which the individual seeks renewed access, it also suggests, in spite of itself, the possibility of bypassing the Oedipus and hence the very idea of individual (sexual) identity.

Back to the Suture: Patriarchal Discourse and
Susana Thénon's *Ova completa*

BERNARD McGUIRK

> ... the resistance to deconstruction is exactly the
> same as that resistance which is opposed to women's
> studies ... there is always something sexual at stake
> in the resistance to deconstruction.
> Jacques Derrida[1]

In what follows, I shall eventually speak of the poetry of Susana Thénon and, in particular, of her 1987 collection *Ova completa*.[2] In the process, I wish to highlight the recourse of contemporary women's writing to established patterns of patriarchal discourse. It has become commonplace, in the wake of the writings of Luce Irigaray, to trace the passage from mimeticism to mimicry in the undermining (or overwriting) of male canons. Yet the primary *caveat* is worth re-emphasizing: there can be no essentialism. When speaking of gender, therefore, or of sexual difference in the merely biological sense, I do not wish to import any genetic distinctions into my discussion of writing. I shall take it as read, as well as written, that the literatures under discussion are constructions. Which takes me from the physical to the metaphysical ... but not so fast, since such a move itself may, and will, be shown to be a classically masculist trope in discursive practice. There are many possible intervening stages on the way and, in this instance, I shall dwell on the modes whereby a "machista" Argentinian literary

---

[1] Jacques Derrida, "Women in the Beehive: A Seminar with Jacques Derrida", *subjects/objects* 2 (1984), 12. Cited by Elaine Showalter in "Shooting the Rapids: Feminist Criticism in the Mainstream", *Sexual Difference. Oxford Literary Review*, 8, 1-2 (1986), 220.
[2] This paper is dedicated to Susana Reisz who directed my attention to Thénon's engagement with the theoretical issues I am addressing. She and Charles Feiling, to whom I am also indebted, clarified many of the Argentinisms to which I could otherwise have had no access. For a subtle, Bakhtinian, reading of *Ova completa*, see Susana Reisz, "Poesía y polifonía. De la voz poética a las voces del discurso poético en *Ova completa* de Susana Thénon", *Filología* 23 (Buenos Aires, 1988), 177-94.

culture is subsumed into Susan Thénon's poetry (it takes two to tango) so that the male/ female positions are relocatable ever within the strategies of social d(omin)ance. The elaborate footwork, the side-steps, of her poems perform to the beat of her title/text *Ova completa*, itself an echo (parody) of masculine "completeness". Thus, *obra* will be uncovered by Thénon, re-read, re-written; "la obra" will function not as "l'oeuvre" but as "leurre", the work (or lure) of *his* (and now *her*) pomps and vanities.[3]

"The Devil dances in an empty pocket", or so the fifteenth-century adage would have us believe.[4] Yet, in a footnote to her collection's title, Susana Thénon would make us wonder if male pockets are ever empty:

> * OVA: sustantivo plural neutro latino. Literalmente: huevos
> COMPLETA: participio pasivo plural neutro latino en concordancia con huevos. Literalmente: colmados. Variantes posibles: rellenos, repletos, rebosantes, henchidos.[5]

From the outset, then, it should be clear that Thénon's strategy is disruptive and playful, respecting neither strict etymologies nor restrictive plenitudes. In her rendering, the balls are burst or, in echo of Lacan, the eggs are smashed to reveal and to remould "l'homme" as "l'hommelette". Her use of language and languages —Spanish, English, Latin, French or Espinglés— draws on classical and popular cultural and *kitsch*. Riotously, she places her eggs not in one basket but rather in a punnet, a net of puns which at once enmeshes and undoes traditional poetic discourse.

A metaphysics of presence will not tolerate the blank space. Thus, while my example of the devil's dancing in an empty pocket might be said to invert a traditional ethic's insertion of God into the void, it is nonetheless a tell-tale (tail?) pointer to that construction of originary male presence which underlies all Western discourse. How, though, has such a metaphysics operated in lyric poetry? When a poet writes, when a reader reads, what devilish constructions are thrust into textuality?[6]

---

[3] Pomps: "any 'shows' held to be under the patronage of the devil; finally (from 17th c.) tacitly transferred to those of 'the world', and associated with its 'vanities'", *The Compact Edition of the Oxford English Dictionary* (Oxford: Oxford University Press, 1979), 2235.
[4] D. C. Browning, *Everyman's Dictionary of Quotations and Proverbs* (London: Dent, 1962), 501, 9004.
[5] Susana Thénon, "Ova completa", in *Ova completa*, (Buenos Aires: Sudamericana, 1987), 32. All further references to this work will be given in parentheses after the quotation.
[6] "Western philosophy ... has yearned for the sign which will give meaning to all others —'the transcendental signifier'— ... A great number of candidates for this role —God, the Idea, the World Spirit, the Self, substance, matter and so on— have thrust themselves forward from time to time". Terry Eagleton, *Literary Theory: An Introduction* (Oxford: Blackwell, 1983), 131.

In seeking to illustrate the manner in which literary-metaphysical constructions have tended to perform to a predominantly male beat or rhythm, an oft-aired debate of the last two decades, I have opted for a very recent and particularly perceptive analysis of the issue by Susan Winnett. In her 1990 essay "Coming Unstrung: Women, Men, Narrative and Principles of Pleasure",[7] Winnett outlines a model for narrative fiction which is, however, pertinent to lyric poetry. She opens in strikingly subversive fashion:

> I would like to begin with the proposition that female orgasm is unnecessary ... Women's pleasure can take place outside or independent of, the male sexual economy whose pulsations determine the dominant culture, its repressions, its taboos, and its narratives, as well as the "human sciences" developed to explain them (505).

Winnett's enquiry into the explanatory paradigms, though not specifically pitched at the functioning of the erotic in the lyric, raises "the issue of the difference between women's and men's reading pleasures" (505). For my purposes, Susana Thénon's poetry "works on the difference",[8] to the extent that it performs "a woman's encounter with the text" analogously to Winnett's principal claim:

> ... [in] a possible erotics of reading, we find a woman's encounter with the text determined by a broad range of options for pleasure that have nothing to do (or can choose to have nothing to do) with [male] notions of representability ... (507).

The question, then, is two-fold, concerning not merely the age-old problem of woman's representation by man but, inseparably, her finding a reading position outside, beyond, different from, masculist universalizing. The opening poem of *Ova completa* addresses the issue head on, picking up and reworking the cliché-fragments of a street-vendor's cry into a dialogic which unsettles both a standard image of woman and a reader's capacity to accept it:

> ¿por qué grita esa mujer?
> ¿por qué grita?
> ¿por qué grita esa mujer?
> *andá a saber*

---

[7] Susan Winnett, "Coming Unstrung: Women, Men, Narrative, and Principles of Pleasure", *PMLA* 105, 3 (May 1990), 505-518. All further references to this article will be given in parentheses after the quotation.
[8] An echo of Hélène Cixous, "Entretien avec Françoise van Rossum-Guyon", *Revue des Science Humaines* (1977), 480.

> esa mujer ¿por qué grita?
> *andá a saber*
> *mirá que flores bonitas*
> ¿por qué grita?
> *jacintos   margaritas*
> ¿por qué?
> ¿por qué qué?
> ¿por qué grita esa mujer?
>
> ¿y esa mujer?
> ¿y esa mujer?
> *vaya a saber*
> *estará loca esa mujer*
> *mirá   mirá los espejitos*
> ¿será por su corcel?
> andá a saber
>
> *¿y dónde oíste*
> *la palabra corcel?*
> es un secreto   esa mujer
> ¿por qué grita?
> *mirá las margaritas*
> la mujer
>
> *espejitos*
> *pajaritas*
> *que no cantan*
> ¿por qué grita?
> *que no vuelan*
> ¿por qué grita?
> *que no estorban*
>
> la mujer
> y esa mujer
> ¿y estaba loca esa mujer?
>
> ya no grita
>
> (¿te acordás de esa mujer?)
>   (7-8)

The chosen framework of coy popular wisdom contained in rhetorical questioning allows Thénon's interventions to operate palimpsestically, providing a commentary on the very convention which is being mimicked. The key-words are simply repeated over and over again, as in many a song tradition: "grita" (x10), "mujer" (x13), and "por qué" (x12). Yet within and from the patterns of repetition, there emerges an answer not to the question originally posed but rather to the bracketed (marginalized) question of the final line. The absence of an answer to "¿por qué grita esa mujer?" is, in fact, a stock-feature broached overtly as such, in the opening sequence, by "*andá a saber*". Since no direct reason can be given or expected, a series of speculations will ensue. The first eight instances of "mujer" are accompanied by "esa", reifying the object of the reader's attention as a yelling, flower- and cheap jewel-adorned creature whose presumed hysteria ("*¿estará loca?*") might be explained in the most traditional of Hollywood styles—¿será por su corcel? Now "*andá a saber*" might be said to operate as a throwaway "but of course!" ("Don't *all* women pine for Prince Charming on a dashing white steed?") A corrective intervention undermines such an assumption, however, in the form of the question:

> *¿y dónde oíste*
> *la palabra corcel?*
> es un secreto   esa mujer

The "exotic" location of the word *corcel* is highlighted and questioned but, ultimately, emerges out of a conspiracy —"un secreto". The gap between "secreto" and "esa mujer" is resonant, the blank space, I would suggest, inhabited by a shadow, the shadow of narrator, or focalizer, or vocalist, or reader-of-the-popular-tradition ... or man. Preferring the silent place of concealment, it is nonetheless this voice which opts to shift attention to "esa mujer", the deemed "proper" object of contemplation, the "normal" enshrinement of whim, of fantasy, of emotion. But another voice, another reader, is about to twist the genre to different ends. "Esa" is suddenly replaced by "la", breaking through the "chuchería" trinketry of "margaritas", "espejitos", "pajaritas", breaking free from trivial diminutives, the unproductive nature of which is stressed in "no vuelan", "no cantan", "no estorban". "La mujer" emerges, then, as an alternative to the reified image of "esa mujer", is juxtaposed with it, leading to the pressingly relevant question, no longer hypothetical ("¿estará?") but real: "¿y estaba loca esa mujer?" The madness is displaced from woman to reader of woman, from false attribution to falsifying attributor. Consequently, the poem ends with a further twist to the tale: "ya no grita" removes hysteria; ("¿te acordás de esa mujer?") adds a sting to the tail. Did she ever exist, and if so, do you even remember her? The bracketed question is, of course, directed to and targeted at the putative male-reader who by now doesn't care; and at a newly alerted female (or non-traditional male) reader who may never be able to hear "esa ..." again.

This first poem by Thénon effectively operates the strategy of questioning the "gendering" of readership noted by Winnett, pursuing "a possible erotics" in a way which picks up Susan Sontag's "sixties" plea for an erotics in preference to a hermeneutics of reading. And the replacement of *analysis*, textual and psychotherapeutic, is one of the devices constantly exploited by Thénon:

> el struss
> uno de los grandes males
> que afectan a la womanidad
> antes se llamaba stress
> y antes strass
> o Strauss
> es como un vals trastabillado
> por la mujer sin sombra
> no hay drama
> está borracha
> borracha la puerca
>
> el struss   (39)

In Thénon's poetry, song and dance figure and, usually, disfigure. The treatment of waltz, in this poem, is a striking case. The organizing centre of the text is the line "o Strauss", a surrogate figure, Father-of-the-Waltz, in whose Shadow, the steps of a supposedly "erotic" dance are performed. But the pattern is spoilt, tripped up, "trastabillado". And who is at fault but "la mujer"? The *faux pas*, however, is turned to startling effect, triggering a series of dislocations of the interdictory original lawgiver so that the path to Strauss is paved with good inventions, a *stress*ful, *strass*ful, *struss*ful, process. When turned inside out, the rigid partnership of woman/man dance/dominance is revealed as but the floor-show of public role-playing. The private reality is stark: "uno de los grandes males / que afectan a la womanidad". The stress of "la mujer sin sombra" derives from any attempt to step out of the shadow, into independence. The male hermeneutic demands analysis. The shadowy figure of man will always presume to dance with the woman seeking to break free; for without him, or his shadow, there can be no drama, no excitement. To think other is to enter the realm of condemnation: "está borracha / borracha la puerca". "Has she hit the bottle? ... the slut!"

"El struss", a nonsense, a no-sense word, gains context and meaning only in the absence of hermeneutic, in the absence of man, of me ... and my shadow. The erotics of this poem involve dance and play, dance as play, as un-dance, un-done. In "Choreographies", an interview-dance with Christie McDonald, Jacques Derrida responds to her question: "how would you describe woman's place?"

This step only constitutes a step on the condition that it challenge a certain idea of the *locus* [*lieu*] and the place [*place*] (the entire history of the West and of its metaphysics) and that it dance otherwise. ... The most innocent of dances would thwart the *assignation à résidence*, escape those residences under surveillance; the dance changes place and above all changes women's movements, and of some women in particular, has actually brought with it the chance for a certain risky turbulence in the assigning of places. ... Is one then going to start all over again making maps, topographies, etc.? distributing sexual identity cards?
The most serious part of the difficulty is the necessity to bring the dance and its tempo into tune with the "revolution". The lack of place for [*l'atopie*] or the madness of the dance ... can also compromise the political chances of feminism and serve as an alibi for deserting organized, patient, laborious "feminist" struggles ... an incessant, daily negotiation —individual or not— sometimes microscopic, sometimes punctuated by a poker-like gamble; always deprived of insurance, whether it be in private life or within institutions. Each man and each woman must commit his or her own singularity, the untranslatable factor of his or her life and death.[9]

For once —rare occurrence— a Derrida text demands little or no commentary, explicitly and politically pointing up the disruptive power —and responsibilities— of choreographies. The disruption of place, however, is indistinguishable from the disruption of language, as the Thénon poem has just shown. The "place" of analysis, be it dance-floor, psychoanalyst's couch or literary text, must be subjected to stress if the neurosis is to be shifted from the analysand and the analyst construed as partnership, as sphere of action rather than static cure.

A Thénon text "works on the difference" between the psychic —or psychoanalytic— structures of time and the "institutional" space in which men and women are often invited to commit or "play out" their supposedly "translatable" (indeed curable-through-talk) *singularity*:

    MURGATORIO

        olé olé
        olé olá
        yo soy el nieto
        de mi papá

        olé olé
        olé olá

---

[9] Jacques Derrida and Christie V. McDonald, "Choreographies", Interview, *Diacritics* 12 (Baltimore: The Johns Hopkins Press, 1982), 66-76, 68-9.

voy al piscólogo
a investigar

por qué por qué
pour quoi pour quoi
la vie en rose
no es pour moi

tal vez tal vez
quizá quizá
esto hay que verlo en
profundidad

molta lettura
molta poesia
molta cultura
molta pazzia

Nevsky Stogorny
Drugoi Igrushky
Gogol Andreiev
Chejov Tiburshky

y cuando supe
mis perspectivas
ya me encontraba
en la intensiva

hombre de ciencia
hombre de mundo
oh gran maestro
oh viejo inmundo

todo supiste
todo pudiste
más ahora viste
que esto no es chiste

olé olé
olé olá
nadie con   testa en
el más
a

cá   (73-4)

Song and dance come together, again, to perform Thénon's re-siting of that provisional theological space *par excellence*, Purgatory. "Murga", an informal carnival group which chants often obscene songs to such popular rhythms as the Uruguayan *candombe* of the text "under analysis", serves here to undermine the inherited psychological "Grand" narrative. The "olé olé, olé olá" mockery of respectable "abolengo", the broaching of the taboo-topic of incest, echoes the problematic "locura" of the opening poem. Here, however, the voice is consistently masculine, "el nieto de mi papá", who resorts to investigating, to deep analysis, in pursuit of a happiness more locatable in a Piaf popular song than in a reality. The axial quartets of the poem play with foreign-sounding, "hi-falutin" culture and authorities —though hinging on "molta pazzia", or folly. In light of this revelation, of the persona's true "perspectivas" or prospects, comes the lapse into intensive care. The great Freudian sh(ad)ow is dethroned, debunked, turned upside down in carnival-fashion as "oh viejo inmundo". All-knowing, all-powerful, in theory; unable, not present, to answer this query ... "What do I do, *not* about my past, but my here and now?" "El más a   cá", protracted present *space*, regardless of time, of history, of lineage, is forever the unanswerable question, the confounding disruption, not a "purgatorio" with the promise of eventual release into the Divine (and all-resolving) Presence ... merely another obscene, "murga-torio".

For both male and female voices, Thénon's strategy undoes metaphysical constructs of time, institutional con-tricks of psychology, and gender-based confidence. In so doing, it exemplifies Julia Kristeva's claim:

> A psychoanalyst would call this "obsessional time", recognizing in the mastery of time the true structure of the slave. The hysteric (either male or female) who suffers from reminiscences would, rather, recognize his or her self in the anterior temporal modalities: cyclical or monumental ... The reader will undoubtedly have been struck by a fluctuation in the term of reference: mother, woman, hysteric ... I think that the apparent coherence which the term "woman" assumes in contemporary ideology ... has the negative effect of effacing the differences among the diverse functions or structures which operate beneath this word ... [T]he real *fundamental difference* between the two sexes: a difference that feminism has had the enormous merit of rendering painful [is] productive of surprises and of symbolic life in a civilization which, outside the stock exchange and wars, is bored to death.[10]

If "woman" is reduced to any one, given, space —other than that of the consulting room— it is often to that of her literal sex, the genital place/ space which is at once rendered sacred and dissected:

---

[10] Julia Kristeva, "Women's Time", *Signs. Journal of Women in Culture and Society* 7, 11 (University of Chicago, 1981), 18. All references to this essay will be given in parentheses after the quotation.

LA DISECCIÓN

cosa casi sagrada
es una cosa casi sagrada
una cosa casi
casi sagrada
tan casi sagrada es esta cosa
que llama poderosamente la atención
la casi absoluta ceguera de la gente
para tener en cuenta que a fin de cuentas
es casi innecesario ver para creer en cosa tan casi
tan consecuentemente casi
sagrada
y es que además este elemento o cosa
ha sangrado
o casi
y podemos apreciarlo por la sombra de lo casi sangrado
sobre el suelo sobre el suelo sobre el mismísimo suelo
y retomando la demostración
tenemos esta cosa
una cosa bah el montón
de cosa casi medio sagrada
y además sangrada y por ende
y en ciernes casi *ad nauseam*
y en otro orden de cosas esta cosa
se resiste con casi todos sus botones
a ser casi descubierta
analizada remolida destripada
en sus causales últimos internos
mejor dicho casi internos porque la cosa en sí
no se deshoja fácilmente
sino capa tras capa
como los alcauciles
los inviernos
y el tiempo ah el tiempo ese factor
disyuntivo que casi aquí se agota
y por lo tanto nos impide
llegar al gran por qué
y al supercómo de esta cosa
casi sagrada
tam tam casi sagrada
tan casi casi
casi tan sagrada   (15-6)

What is being probed in "La Disección" is a space both literal and metaphorical, an attempt to penetrate that Platonic *chora* which, to echo Kristeva, was the "*unnameable matrix which defied metaphysics*" (16). Unnameability is the key to the poem's organization, for the literal "subject" of the text is never divulged, always hidden — too sacred to be uttered— as if it were equivalent to the Tetragrammaton, the ineffable four-letter holy name of YHWH/God. The interplay of "cosa"/"casi" undoes the plenitude of the object's being; its "sacred" nature, therefore is constructed from the outside, from that "attentive" readership whose principal insight is its "powerful" and "almost absolute" blindness ("ceguera"). So obsessed by an economy of "cuenta"/ "cuentas" that calculation comes to replace vision ("es casi innecesario ver para creer") in the construction of what begins to appear not so much Godhead as maidenhead. The slippage from "sagrada" to "sangrado" proves to be the hinge of blasphemy as a masculist theological trajectory is mimicked and mocked. For what is left of guilt (*mea culpa, mea culpa, mea maxima culpa*) but a bathetic echo of "cielo"-"suelo ...", "suelo ...", "mismísimo suelo"? For what bled on the Cross, read what bleeds at the crux; for four-letter "unnameability" hear (but do not read) not *Dios* but *coño*. You doubters, you Thomases who would not believe without putting your hand into the sacred wound are invited to listen, and to see, again ("retomando la demostración"). Hear the "mound" or "mount" ("una cosa bah el montón"); see the opening and flowering ("en ciernes") *ad nauseam*; listen to the resistance of buttons ("en otro orden de cosas") — resistance to the order of man? Recall, indeed, *Spéculum, de l'autre* ... but not of Irigaray's "autre femme"; rather of "l'autre/homme".

The fate of *la cosa* ... "a ser casi descubierta / analizada remolida / destripada / en sus causales últimos internos" is a re-write of Luce Irigaray's analysis of gynaecology, in the hollowed concave mirror of which the enquiring male often fails to see "other" than his intruding self:

> porque la cosa en sí
> no se deshoja fácilmente
> sino capa tras capa
> como los alcauciles

"Alcauciles", artichokes, are stripped layer by layer to reveal a soft and juicy centre; but, in Argentinian slang, "alcaucil" also means a buffoon, a silly man. Long ago did Barthes warn readers to eschew the apricot of interpretation lest at the lapidary kernel they should break their teeth.[11] Thénon, in turn, replaces Barthes' many-layered onion with a less tearful, though equally multi-layered, dissolving, pun.

---

[11] *Literary Style: A Symposium*, edited by Seymour Chatman (Oxford: Oxford University Press, 1977), 10.

Now what is "el tiempo ah el tiempo" doing at the end, the "resolution", of this poem? Could Thénon be mocking so overtly the post-penetration metaphysic of a masculist model? Perhaps *not* post-penetration; and even if so, penetration is not the be-all-and-end-all. For Time is called "ese factor disyuntivo", the possibility of breaking away, certainly, but never an answer of universal proportions "al gran por qué". The "supercómo de esta cosa" will remain but provisionally sacred ("casi sagrada") as the poem ends amidst the ceremonial drum-beats of vestal virginity — or non-virginity— who knows?

> tam tam casi sagrada
> tan casi casi
> casi tan sagrada

> As for time, female subjectivity would seem to provide a specific measure that essentially means *repetition* and eternity from among the multiple modalities of time known through the history of civilizations ... there are cycles, gestation, the eternal recurrence of a biological rhythm which conforms to that of nature and imposes a temporality whose stereotyping may shock, but whose regularity and unison with what is experienced as extrasubjective time, cosmic time, occasion vertiginous visions and unnameable jouissance (16).

This further commentary, coincidentally applicable to "La Disección", is not mine but that of Julia Kristeva.

If, as I have attempted to show, Thénon's poetry performs counter to the restoration of any one, originary, Edenic *place* via a temporal trajectory which stresses disjunction rather than the conjunctions of a "historically" linear time, hers is a poetry, too, which revels in the fragmentation of Babel. In language, otherness and dispersion, far from producing nostalgia or anguish, are exploited and celebrated. Thénon's play is both on and with ..., is both pun and fun, pleasurable steps within the choreography of difference.[12]

---

[12] In a recent article, Linda R. Boone writes engagingly of a direct parody of a Neruda love-poem, "Barcarola", namely, Arsenio Cué's "Si tú te llamaras Babel y no Beba Martínez", in Cabrera Infante's *Tres tristes tigres*: "In order to satisfy Arsenio's requirements for the perfect woman, Beba must become precisely what she is not: Babel, fluent in witty language of literary wordplay ...". Unlike Thénon's poetry, however, Arsenio's language, for Boone, "is identified as an *anti-language* ... aimed not toward communication but sheer playfulness". I would add that, in Cabrera Infante's ingenious *mise en abyme*, the construction of an idealized transformation of Beba into Babel, yet another projection of male readership, is suggestively *culbuté* by being inserted in the (Anglo-Portuguese) banality of Arsenio Cué's name. See Linda R. Boone, "'Si tú te llamaras Babel ...': Love Poetry, Parody and Irony in *Tres tristes tigres*", *Siglo XX/20th Century* 8, 1-2 (University of Colorado, 1990-91), 33, 35.

AND SO ARE YOU

hay sacarina
la bandada de albatros
o yo qué sé
digo de albatros
dólares
*de albatros*dólares
nunca vi un pájaro pishar eso no quiere decir nada
los canadienses pishan aunque vos no los veas
y los peces
los peces pishan mar
vos sos poeta ¿no?
o Sappho made in Shitland
poetisa
¿no ves que es mujer?
vamos mujer
si no puedes tú con Dios hablar
¿para qué preguntarle si yo alguna vez?
te lo digo personalmente
en efecto
alguna que otra vez te he dejado de adorar
pero el inglés es más práctico
te ingeniás en todas partes
verbigracia en las pudendas
do it   don't
y aunque pronuncies mal
igual te entienden
do it   don't
o te expresás por señas
vieras cómo te arreglás
cómo aprendés a *do it*
cómo *don't* te acostumbrás
cómo hacés *do* lo que querés
it cómo
don't   (13-14)

Dialogics operate strongly in the title "And So Are You", anticipating the question "vos sos poeta ¿no?" The poet attempting self-definition depends heavily on the reader/interlocutor ... and vice-versa. The saccharine-sweet legacy of the post-Baudelairean image of a *poète par définition* ("prince des nuées ... exilé sur le sol"), is at once evoked and derided by Thénon's "de albatros/o yo qué sé". Intrusively, "dólares" thrusts writing forward as profession rather than as confession; "Confiteor de l'artiste", for

Thénon, involves an economy of art, "*albatros*dólares", a rejection of *l'art pour l'art* purity, illustrated by the four-line bi-lingual play on "pishar". The grossness of tactic renders "for the birds" too facile a definition of poet:

> vos sos poeta ¿no?
> o Sappho made in Shitland
> poetisa,
> ¿no ves que es mujer?

The interplay of "pish" and "shit" besmirches the ready-made label ineptly attached to the "poetisa"-inheritor of Sappho. Poet-ess thus becomes the unacceptable term; rejected as forcefully as was the reified "esa mujer" and, again, in a pastiche of popular art, subverting a famous bolero:

> Mujer
> si puedes tú con Dios hablar
> pregúntale si yo alguna vez
> te he dejado de adorar.[13]

The "undoing" of the inherited bolero-perception of woman —a creature who needs to corroborate male declarations of love by reference to masculine Authority *par excellence*, the Great-Man-in-the-Sky— says simply: "Who needs all that? *I'm* telling you 'en efecto', here and now, watch this space, hear this voice. And while we're at it, I *have* on occasion stopped loving you!" The sudden shift sideways, to the apparently lateral thought, in English of the "*do it   don't*" play, is subtly relevant. For woman as capricious creature of whim, of "now I love you, now I don't", is not only portrayable in the saccharine poetry of the bolero line, where her yes/no is dressed up. *Un*dressed, too, she may playfully change her mind —"*verbigracia en las pudendas*" (eloquent sextuality?); and across language-barriers, regardless of pronunciation, even by sign-language. The final lines of the poem are a bonanza of vertiginous word-play, of pun as fun: "arreglás" - "get by"; "have your period"; "get made up"; and so on. All is a chaotic learning process of "aprendés", "acustumbrás", "do", "don't", "it", "como", "lo que querés" ... desire, what you will, or will not (have done to you) ... "*don't*".

One of the "things" done to poets, even "woman" poets, is to be anthologized. This particular version of having a label hung round the neck is hilariously broached by Thénon:

---

[13] Alberto Domínguez, "Perfidia".

LA ANTOLOGÍA

¿tú eres
la gran poietisa
Susana Etcétera?
mucho gusto
me llamo Petrona Smith-Jones
soy profesora adjunta
de la Universidad de Paughkeepsie
que queda un poquipsi al sur de Vancouver
y estoy en Argentina becada
por la Putifar Comissión
para hacer una antología
de escritoras en vías de desarrollo
desarrolladas y también menopáusicas
aunque es cosa sabida que sea como fuere
todas las que escribieron y escribirán en Argentina
ya pertenecen a la generación del 60
incluso las que están en guardería
e inclusísimamente las que están en geriátrico

pero lo que me importa profundamente
de tu poesía y alrededores
es esa profesión —aaah ¿cómo se dice?—
profusión de íconos e índices
¿tú qué opinas del ícono?

¿lo usan todas las mujeres
o es también cosa del machismo?

porque tú sabes que en realidad
lo que a mí me interesa
es no sólo que escriban
sino que sean feministas
y si es posible alcohólicas
y si es posible anoréxicas
y si es posible violadas
y si es posible lesbianas
y si es posible muy desdichadas

es una antología democrática
pero por favor no me traigas
ni sanas ni independientes   (69-70)

Again, the resistance to fixed identity refuses the tired process of "naming" of the academic interview. What emerges instead is a Rabelaisian feast of perceptions and misperceptions; of cultural difference and condescension (working both ways); of institutions and subversions which, of a sudden, switches from Petrona Smith-Jones and her Putifar Comission to that no less restrictive missionary band, the radical feminist ghetto-mongers. I take for granted that further commentary on this poem would be superfluous, save to point out the heightened awareness in Thénon's text of the dangerous power which any and all institutions design for "íconos e índices", instruments which are humorously and healthily eroticized as fetish-gadgets of both men and women. In short, "la antología" is always a choice; but a choice which merely parades as "democrática". Politically, what system can tolerate [personas] "sanas e independientes"?

Completeness, or closed system, is anathema to the disruptive workings of *Ova completa*. In Thénon's open system, words are abused, in reversal of language-systems' traditional strategies of power:

OVA COMPLETA*

Filosofía significa "violación de un ser viviente".
Viene del griego *filoso*, "que corta mucho",
y *fía*, 3ª. persona del verbo *fiar*, que quiere decir
"confiar" y también "dar sin cobrar *ad referendum*"
Ejercen esta actividad los llamados *friends*
o "Cofradía de los Sonrientes"
los fiadores —desde luego—,
los que de veras tienen la manija y los que creen tenerla
en la descomunal mezquita de Oj-Alá.

Una vez consumada la filosofía
se hacen presentes por orden de aparición:

la taquería el comisario el juez de la causa
el forense el abogado de oficio el reportero gráfico
el secreto del sumario Max Scheler una familia vecina
un psiquiatra dos guardias

Ya adentro, hay:

1 que perdió entrambas gambas 1 sacerdote
1 indiferente 1 sádico 1 calcomaníaco de Racing
1 (UN) ejemplar del Erasmo Ilustrado para Niños

BACK TO THE SUTURE: PATRIARCHAL DISCOURSE ...   179

> Ya más
> ya bien adentro:
>
> el recuerdo de una frase famosa el olvido de esa
> frase famosa al que sigue el olvido de todo lo
> famoso y lo que no lo es salvo tu culo
>
> Filosofía significa "violación de un ser viviente"
>
> cuando tu pena es condonada 26 años después
> retomás su ejercicio o te lo ejercen
>
> * OVA: sustantivo plural neutro latino. Literalmente: huevos
>   COMPLETA: participio pasivo plural neutro latino en concordancia con
>   huevos. Literalmente: colmados. Variantes posibles: rellenos, repletos,
>   rebosantes, henchidos.   (31-2)

To read the discourse of love, after Thénon, tends to render the passage from Eros to the erection of an all-embracing world-view a preposterous enterprise. Much the same can be said for her puncturing of the inflated ideologies which she detects all around and throughout history, in her own "Latin" culture but, equally, in a Greco-Roman legacy of thought-policing. A "filoso" cutting-edge is employed to dissect and dismember many a body or confraternity ("Cofradía") of (Make-)Believers, fake believers, unmasked (pre-Rushdie) in "la descomunal mezquita de Oj-Alá". Not accidentally, the axis of change from debunking "Grand Theory" to mocking petty institutionality is the line, "Una vez consumada la filosofía". Consummation, the summit of masculist self-regard, is promptly followed by a post-coital parade of male bodies: "taquería", "comisario", "juez", "forense", "abogado", "reportero gráfico" and so on. In arch-surrealist fashion, a comically incongruous list divulges "entrambas gambas"—where else? who else?—"el sacerdote"; alongside the bored, the sadistic, the football-transfer collector ... the further in you go, the closer the inspection, the more urgent the need to remember (or to forget) "una frase famosa", the nearer you get to ... the contemplation of your own (infamous) ass.

The total effect of all this verbiage is to (un)cover a stark primal scene of intellectuality construed as incarceration and torture:

> Filosofía significa "violación de un ser viviente".

Enigmatically, the poem ends. Twenty-six years of punishment, daily exercise sinisterly other than the compulsive repetition of routine: the passage from "su" to "te" throws the switch from the exercise of incarcerating philosophy to the philosophy of exercising torture, the clear implication of "o te lo ejercen" —which brings this discussion of Thénon's poetry to a near-contemporary confrontation with politics:

>PUNTO FONAL (TANGO CON VECTOR CRÍTICO)
>
>"la picana en el ropero
>todavía está colgada
>nadie en ella amputa nada
>ni hace sus voltios vibrar"
>
>¡*ESO* ES DECLAMACIÓN!   (47)

Alfonsín's first law, a guillotine to prevent military personnel "acting under orders" from having to face due legal processes, was designated PUNTO FINAL. The instruments of torture, then, and the memories of torturers, are to be hidden away, in the Argentinian psyche, as easily as the sadly dormant guitar of the popular tango:

>la guitarra en el ropero
>todavía está colgada
>nadie en ella canta nada
>ni hace sus cuerdas vibrar.

The play "final"/"fonal" occurs at the intersection of politics and art, of direct ideological reference and the intertextual echo of tango. While I have argued throughout this treatment of Thénon's poetry that her word games disrupt masculist metaphysics, narrow erotics and linear temporality, I would end by stressing her own heightened awareness of the danger inherent in a writing, or a reading, which is too dependent on the ludics of language. It is my recent experience that feminist critical practice is often politically the most subversive. But Thénon is ever prepared to subvert her own practice as exemplified in *Ova completa*.

>ROUND 15
>
>ah sí
>fácil
>*word games*
>tampón de voces tales
>mimpide
>tra
>gar

> más fácil que no hacer
> o hacer nada
> como el tío de dios
>
> como el tío de dios
> que no hizo nada
>
> volar delalf abeto
> me ahogo   (75)

The spontaneous, arguably facile, way *word games* stifle the personal voice which, even in the most extreme heteroglossia, will struggle to re-affirm its presence, threatens to render Susana Thénon as open as Jacques Derrida to accusations of self-indulgent *jouissance*. Yet in "Round 15", she goes down ("me ahogo") struggling. Her attempts to unpick the seams, to break free of the constraints, to come out of the closet of language, "volar delalf abeto", have been exemplified by her own poetic practice in an undeniably feminist *Ova completa*. Yet my argument has been, all along, that the text creates a new kind of reader. So you must be the judges of whether Thénon's enterprise has been "más fácil que no hacer / o hacer nada" ... in fact you must decide, too, on what she "gags".

La vanguardia a partir de sus exclusiones

GEORGE YÚDICE

La suplementación de la historia literaria

Con el paso del tiempo, cada vez más se indagan las exclusiones a partir de las cuales se pudo creer en algún momento que las vanguardias latinoamericanas eran un mero eco de las europeas. Tras de enfatizar el cosmopolitismo de la temprana vanguardia latinoamericana, que favorecía la asimilación de los primeros libros de Huidobro, Borges y Girondo al cubismo, al expresionismo o al dadaísmo, se prestó mayor atención a lo que los distinguía de sus congéneres europeos. A saber, *el complejo de excentricidad o perifericidad* de Huidobro que no sólo lo lleva a codearse con los poetas y artistas europeos más destacados y a luchar con ellos por el reconocimiento, sino que se inscribe en la estructura misma de su poesía.[1] En el caso de Borges se ha señalado que su marginalidad como sudamericano le hace posible tomar una actitud irreverente si no subversiva hacia "los temas europeos".[2] A partir de la modernización transformadora de Buenos Aires de las primeras décadas del siglo, el *flâneur* Girondo, el "ojo-poeta" al decir de Beatriz Sarlo, va despojando la percepción del espacio nacional de toda dimensión filosófica o simbólica, desconstruyendo así todo valor moral, en especial la religión y el erotismo, y proyectando su Buenos Aires poetizado como epítome de la modernidad.[3]

---

[1] Ana Pizarro, *Vicente Huidobro, un poeta ambivalente* (Concepción, Chile: Imprenta Universitaria de Concepción, 1971).
[2] Sylvia Molloy cita de "El escritor argentino y la tradición": "creo que los argentinos, los sudamericanos en general, estamos en una situación análoga [a la de los judíos y los irlandeses]; podemos manejar los temas europeos, manejarlos sin supersticiones, con una irreverencia que puede tener, y ya tiene, consecuencias afortunadas." (Jorge Luis Borges, *Discusión* [Buenos Aires: Emecé, 1957], 161), citado en *Las letras de Borges* (Buenos Aires: Sudamericana, 1979), 61.
[3] Beatriz Sarlo, *Una modernidad periférica: Buenos Aires 1920 y 1930* (Buenos Aires: Nueva Visión, 1988), 62-67.

Junto a esta comprobación de que lo nacional no ha sido excluido de las vanguardias, se han ensayado otros tipos de "nativización". Por ejemplo, se ha mostrado que no todos los vanguardismos fueron practicados por las élites cosmopolitas sino que también hubo versiones comprometidas que se "incorporan ... a la crítica del sistema social e incluso a las luchas por el socialismo".[4] Esta crítica incluía no sólo una perspectiva socialista sino también la de sectores de la burguesía que en los países andinos o en Nicaragua, por ejemplo, procuraron articular las tradiciones indígenas al proyecto de renovación cultural.[5] Nelson Osorio examina las distintas formas que toma esta crítica social: dependiendo de su particular contexto puede ser antirracista, antiburguesa y antiimperialista. Es decir, a partir del particular proyecto contrahegemónico de que se trate, estas vanguardias articulan contenidos mundonovistas basados en la identidad racial y social a programas por la renovación de la cultura nacional. Así pues, Osorio muestra que las particularidades que en un principio quedaban excluidas del vanguardismo en realidad eran constituyentes de su contexto más amplio.

Claro está, todas las particularidades menos la identidad sexual. No es de extrañar que Osorio no mencione a ninguna escritora en su examen de la vanguardia, pues con la excepción de la noruego-argentina Norah Lange y la peruana Magda Portal, ni se concebía hasta recién que debiera considerarse este aspecto en el examen de esta literatura de ruptura. Sencillamente la crítica literaria suponía que la mujer poco tenía que ver con la ruptura, de ahí que se construyera una historia literaria en la cual las escritoras de esta época eran relegadas a una categoría —el postmodernismo (de las primeras décadas de este siglo)— fundada en criterios que dan relieve a la experiencia íntima y privada. Por ejemplo, la *Historia crítica de la literatura hispanoamericana* de Orlando Gómez-Gil caracteriza el postmodernismo así:

> Los llamados poetas postmodernistas nunca se consideraron un movimiento literario formalmente organizado como el romanticismo o el propio modernismo ... Por ese motivo es muy difícil la clasificación de estos poetas, ya que trataron de desarrollar sus propios estilos y tema, en una época de transición en los gustos literarios y estéticos ... Lo esteticista deja de ser el centro poético: lo es ahora la

---

[4] Nelson Osorio, "Para una caracterización histórica del vanguardismo literario hispanoamericano," *Revista Iberoamericana*, 114-115 (enero-junio 1981), 231.
[5] Para los países andinos ver David Wise, "Vanguardismo a 3800 metros: El caso del *Boletín Titikaka* (Puno, 1926-1930)", *Revista de Crítica Literaria Latinoamericana*, 20: 89-100; Wilfredo Kapsoli, "Prospecto del grupo 'Los zurdos' de Arequipa," *Revista de Crítica Literaria Latinoamericana*, 20: 101-111; para la vanguardia nicaragüense, ver George Yúdice, "Rethinking the Theory of the Avant-Garde from the Periphery", inédito.

intimidad del poeta, la realidad que lo rodea. Todos los postmodernistas se caracterizan por el subjetivismo, la emoción refrenada, la sobriedad en la expresión, aunque su actitud es también de renovación y modernidad.[6]

Luego de establecer cuatro subcategorías del postmodernismo, ofrece su definición de la "poesía femenina" que es la primera subcategoría:

> La poesía hispanoamericana siempre ha contado con magníficas representantes femeninos, pero durante el postmodernismo escribe el grupo de mujeres más amplio e importante de nuestra historia literaria. Estas poetisas cantan el amor, el yo íntimo y todos los sentimientos de la mujer, con amplitud y efectiva libertad.[7]

Cabe añadir que la caracterización de cada una de estas "poetisas" desmiente la atribución de "emoción refrenada" y "sobriedad" al postmodernismo: Gabriela Mistral expresa un "intenso lirismo", Delmira Agustini canta un "erotismo descarnado", la "exaltación erótica", Alfonsina Storni manifiesta una "rebeldía a someterse a un mundo materialista y dominado por el hombre", Juana de Ibarbourou "expresa el amor lleno de ardores de la juventud". Otro comentario que vale la pena mencionar —anticipándome a lo que diré luego— es el elogio de Ibarbourou por su "vida de mujer sana, felizmente lograda en el hogar y la compañía del esposo y los niños" en contraste con lo que hemos de suponer es la vida menos sana o no sana de las otras escritoras.

Ahora bien, las investigaciones llevadas a cabo en la última década por Jean Franco, Marta Morello-Frosch, Elizabeth Garrels, Gwen Kirkpatrick, Francine Masiello, Mary Louise Pratt, Eliana Rivero, Beatriz Sarlo, Doris Sommer y otras estudiosas muestran que las escritoras aludidas, así como las dos que a veces son incluidas en la vanguardia, no sólo no se quedaron en el intimismo sino que militaron en varias causas sociales, militancia que implicaba un lugar destacado en las polémicas llevadas a cabo en la esfera pública que, precisamente por estas fechas, tuvo que abrirse a las perspectivas femeninas y feministas. Así pues, habría que añadir este activismo a la renovación social y literaria que Osorio describe en la conclusión de su ensayo:

> Desde la perspectiva que proponemos, las tendencias de la vanguardia en Hispanoamérica deben ser *comprendidas* dentro de un proceso más amplio de renovación que se generaliza a partir del término de la Primera Guerra Mundial

---

[6] Orlando Gómez-Gil, *Historia crítica de la literatura hispanoamericana* (Nueva York: Holt, Rinehart & Winston, 1968), 479.
[7] *Ibid.*, 480.

en el continente. El Vanguardismo pasa a ser entendido así como un aspecto de la renovación postmodernista. Pero este mismo proceso de renovación que comprende el Vanguardismo, debe a su vez ser *comprendido* dentro de un proceso de cuestionamiento crítico más general, que se relaciona tanto con la crisis por la que se atraviesa en ese momento como con el ascenso de nuevos sectores sociales que buscan incorporarse críticamente a la vida económica, política y cultural del continente.[8]

La vanguardia, ¿ignora a las escritoras?

En primer lugar, la vanguardia no "ignora" la renovación que mujeres como Alfonsina Storni, Gabriela Mistral y Magda Portal estaban llevando a cabo. Lejos de ignorarla, la atacaban. Por ejemplo, habiendo él mismo celebrado su ciudad natal en *Fervor de Buenos Aires* (1923) y ostentado, según propia confesión, su orgullo patrio en *Luna de enfrente* (1925), Borges se siente irritado por el aburrimiento expresado acerca de ese mismo contexto patrio en la poesía de Storni:

> De la Storni y de otras personas que han metrificado su tedio de vivir en esta ciudá de calles derechas, sólo diré que el aburrimiento es quizá la única emoción impoética ... y que es también, la que con preferencia ensalzan sus plumas. Son rubenistas vergonzantes, miedosos.[9]

Puede verse en este comentario la tentativa de controlar la valoración estética. Más precisa todavía en este respecto es la opinión de González Lanuza, quien atribuye a Storni una "impureza estética" derivada de su identificación como mujer.

> Mujer inteligente y fuerte, no logró realizarse como poeta por no haber sabido superarse a sí misma. En sus mejores poemas aparece con regularidad fatal un elemento de impureza estética, un residuo inorgánico no asimilado, un prosaísmo que se enquista y resta vitalidad a sus versos. ... Su sexo constituía una traba. Aun teniendo genio, las dificultades hubieran sido inmensas.... Aceptó el reto, y ése fue su mayor mérito y su irreparable error. Su mérito como mujer que supo tomarse los derechos que se le negaban; su error como poeta, porque la poesía no

---

[8] *Ibid.*, 254.
[9] Jorge Luis Borges, "Prólogo (III)," *Índice de la nueva poesía americana*, editado por Alberto Hidalgo *et al.* (Buenos Aires: Sociedad de Publicaciones el Inca, 1926), 15, citado por Gwendolyn Kirkpatrick, "The Journalism of Alfonsina Storni: A New Approach to Women's History in Argentina", en "Seminar on Feminism and Culture in Latin America", *Women, Culture, and Politics in Latin America* (Berkeley: University of California Press, 1990), 107.

puede servir para nada ajeno a sus propios fines. Menos aun puede servir de válvula de escape para resentimientos personales; y en cada poema de la primera época de Alfonsina alienta, apenas reprimido, el resentimiento contra el hombre y la obsesión del eterno masculino.[10]

Contrario a lo que afirma González Lanuza, el problema aquí no es la sujeción insuperable de Storni a su identidad sexual, sino el que se vea esto como impedimento poético, especialmente si se abandona el criterio estético de la autonomía, es que la poesía no sirva sino sus propios fines. Pero, como veremos, en el caso de los hombres que han hecho poesía a partir de su particular dilema sexual, la crítica no ha considerado necesario abandonar el criterio autonomista para apreciar su poeticidad. Comparemos dos casos: un poema de Storni y otro de Neruda.

El dilema de Storni, a partir del cual expresó su frustración y su hostilidad para con los hombres, lo ha explicado ella misma:

> Soy superior al término medio de los hombres que me rodean, y físicamente, como mujer, soy su esclava, su molde, su arcilla. No puedo amarlo libremente: hay demasiado orgullo en mí para someterme. Me faltan medios físicos para someterlo. El dolor de mi drama es en mí superior al deseo de cantar.[11]

No veo yo impedimento aquí, pues las contradicciones que llevan a la imposibilidad del éxito en el amor son milenarias en la poesía. Basta pensar en Catulo. Esta imposibilidad se poetiza en "El engaño":

> Soy tuya, Dios lo sabe por qué, ya que comprendo que habrás de abandonarme, fríamente, mañana, y que, bajo el encanto de mis ojos, te gana otro encanto el deseo, pero no me defiendo.
>
> Espero que esto un día cualquiera se concluya pues intuyo al instante lo que piensas o quieres; con voz indiferente te hablo de otras mujeres y hasta ensayo el elogio de alguna que fue tuya.
>
> Pero tú sabes menos que yo y algo orgulloso de que te pertenezca en tu juego engañoso persistes con un aire de actor de papel dueño.

---

[10] Eduardo González Lanuza, "Ubicación de Alfonsina", *Sur* 7 (noviembre de 1938), 55-56, citado en Kirkpatrick, 108.
[11] Citado en Gómez-Gil, 484.

> Yo te miro callada con mi dulce sonrisa y cuando te entusiasmas, pienso: no te des prisa no eres tú el que me engaña; quien me engaña es mi sueño.[12]

En la superficie, el poema expresa el resentimiento que la hablante siente por el hombre que la ha de abandonar conforme a su deseo, que se desplaza de una mujer en otra. Ella reconoce la ubicuidad del deseo masculino —en otro poema dice "Y el hombre, en las mujeres, busca un poco de fiesta"[13]— pero sabe que necesita ese deseo del otro para proyectarse su propio sueño. Se trata, pues, de dos soñadores, enajenados cada uno en la ilusión de que se hacen el amor. La hablante, al menos, entiende que el hombre espera que ella se acomode al deseo de él. Cada cual sueña su engaño en el contacto ilusorio del otro; él engañándose a sí mismo a través del engaño a ella, de que la desea; ella engañándolo a él —mostrándole la "dulce sonrisa"— para poder engañarse a sí misma. Entendido así el poema podría ser una respuesta a los *20 poemas de amor y una canción desesperada* de Neruda, en que el hablante domina —hace callar— a la mujer precisamente para alejarla, pues detrás del pretexto de ella, es él mismo quien desea confirmarse.

> Me gustas cuando callas porque estás como ausente,
> y me oyes desde lejos, y mi voz no te toca.
> Parece que los ojos se te hubieran volado
> y parece que un beso te cerrara la boca.
>
> Como todas las cosas están llenas de mi alma,
> emerges de las cosas, llena del alma mía.
> Mariposa de sueño, te pareces a mi alma,
> y te pareces a la palabra melancolía.
>
> Me gustas cuanda callas y estás como distante.
> Y estás como quejándote, mariposa en arrullo.
> Y me oyes desde lejos, y mi voz no te alcanza:
> Déjame que me calle con el silencio tuyo.
>
> Déjame que te hable también con tu silencio
> claro como una lámpara, simple como un anillo.
> Eres como la noche, callada y constelada.
> Tu silencio es de estrella, tan lejano y sencillo.

---

[12] Alfonsina Storni, *Ocre* (Buenos Aires: Agencia de Librerías y Publicaciones, 1925), 49.
[13] *Ibid.*, 253.

> Me gustas cuando callas porque estás como ausente.
> Distante y dolorosa como si hubieras muerto.
> Una palabra entonces, una sonrisa bastan.
> Y estoy alegre, alegre de que no sea cierto.[14]

El poema de Storni también podría ser respuesta al verso final del poema "XVII" de Neruda —"¿Quién eres tú, quién eres?"[15] pregunta ante cual ella se declararía ser el sueño que él cree aprisionar con su "música para que así nazca su propia alma":

> En la red de mi música estás presa, amor mío,
> y mis redes de música son anchas como el cielo.
> Mi alma nace a la orilla de tus ojos de luto.
> En tus ojos de luto comienza el país del sueño.[16]

Así pues, la interpretación que hace Jaime Concha del poema "XV" parece tener también validez para el de Storni:

> En realidad, lo que unifica estas tres variedades de la amada (la "mujer interior" o imagen subjetiva; la "enamorada juvenil" u objeto de un recuerdo; la "mujer poseída" si bien irrealizada) es el vínculo concreto del Deseo. La subjetividad se define en esta poesía por su más primario conato de autoconciencia, la búsqueda anhelosa de algo de lo cual se depende pero cuya posesión es mortal para esa misma búsqueda.[17]

Ahora bien, me parece importante que Storni caracterice el engaño del hombre como deseo y el de ella como sueño. El psicoanálisis define el deseo del hombre como la remisión a la escisión entre la necesidad y la demanda, excluyendo así cualquier relación con un objeto, por una parte, y, por otra, imponiéndose sin tener en cuenta el lenguaje o el inconsciente del otro.[18] Ello explicaría que la amada interpelada sea una fantasía o una máscara que funciona como la pantalla en que se proyecta la constante indagación de la ausencia. De ahí que el poeta diga

---

[14] Pablo Neruda, "XV", *20 poemas de amor y una canción desesperada* (Buenos Aires: Losada, 1944), 73-74.
[15] Pablo Neruda, "XVII", *ibid.*, 83.
[16] "XV", *ibid.*, 78.
[17] Jaime Concha, "Sexo y pobreza. Ensayo sobre la poesía de Pablo Neruda", *Revista Iberoamericana*, 82-83 (enero-junio de 1973), 144.
[18] J. Laplanche y J.-B. Pontalis, *The Language of Psycho-Analysis* (Nueva York: Norton, 1973), 483.

"Me gustas cuando callas porque estás como ausente", reconociendo a la vez en la "alegría de que no sea cierto" el que "Una palabra entonces, una sonrisa bastan", pues nada basta y el sujeto tendrá que continuar esta "pelea contra [sí] mismo", que Concha interpreta como la constitución de la subjetividad,[19] y que no es sino la entrada no en la materia sino en la negación de la mujer, ausencia que deviene el soporte del lugar simbólico del sujeto masculino.[20] Acaso la mejor escenificación de este deseo masculino se encuentra en *La invención de Morel* de Bioy Casares, donde el protagonista logra descubrir los mecanismos del orden simbólico que rige en la isla precisamente a partir de su enamoramiento con Faustine, a quien puede ver pero que no existe sino como efecto del deseo, proceso mediador entre él y el discurso del otro, de Morel.[21]

El orden imaginario: ¿resistencia o acomodación de la mujer al orden patriarcal?

Por contraste al deseo del poeta, el "sueño" del poema de Storni es otra manera de caracterizar el orden imaginario, orden presimbólico que se cifra en la "naturaleza" de la mujer, como dice en el poema "Traición":

> Corazón que me vienes de mujer:
> Hay algo superior al propio ser
> En las mujeres: su naturaleza.[22]

La relación entre el orden imaginario y la naturaleza —hipóstasis del cuerpo femenino— se puede ver más claramente en la novelística de María Luisa Bombal, escritora que algunas comentadoras han tildado de vanguardista feminista.[23] *La última niebla* es la historia de una mujer que se casa con un hombre que, como en

---

[19] *Ibid.*, 149.

[20] Jacqueline Rose, "Introduction-II", in *Jacques Lacan and the École freudienne. Feminine Sexuality*, editado por Juliet Mitchell and Jacqueline Rose (Nueva York: Norton, 1983), 50.

[21] Adolfo Bioy Casares, *La invención de Morel* (Buenos Aires: Emecé, 1953).

[22] *Ocre*, 266.

[23] Francine Masiello, "Texto, ley, transgresión: especulación sobre la novela (feminista) de vanguardia", *Revista Iberoamericana*, 132-133 (julio-diciembre de 1985), 807-22, y "Woman, State, and Family in Latin American Literature of the 1920s", en "Seminar on Feminism and Culture in Latin America" (ver nota 9), 27-47. Creo que podría defenderse la tensión entre Bombal y los vanguardistas pero caracterizarla como "vanguardista" para ponerla en el mismo rango de los escritores consagrados por la historia literaria me parece que implica una aceptación problemática de los criterios vanguardistas de canonización.

el poema de Storni, busca a otra, a "la mujer" (que según Lacan "no existe"), en su cuerpo:

> Mi cuerpo y mis besos no pudieron hacerlo temblar, pero lo hicieron, como antes, pensar en otro cuerpo y en otros labios. Como hace años, lo volví a ver tratando furiosamente de acariciar y desear mi carne y encontrando siempre el recuerdo de la muerta entre él y yo.[24]

Se ve en este pasaje el reconocimiento de que el deseo masculino se instala en el lugar de la representación que proporciona la mujer pero que no habita, desplazándose necesariamente del objeto de su necesidad y del otro al que demanda reconocimiento. Y si bien el cuerpo de la protagonista no es sino el simulacro al que se liga su deseo, al menos proporciona un lugar preciso. En contraste, el deseo de la protagonista, que acaso sería mejor caracterizar como ensueño, no ocupa un lugar preciso, sino que se disemina en el ambiente como la niebla que le proporciona el título a la novela:

> La niebla se estrecha, cada día más, contra la casa. Ya hizo desaparecer las araucarias cuyas ramas golpeaban la balaustrada de la terraza. Anoche soñé que, por entre las rendijas de las puertas y ventanas, se infiltraba lentamente en la casa, en mi cuarto, y esfumaba el color de las paredes, los contornos de los muebles, y se entrelazaba a mis cabellos, y se me adhería al cuerpo y lo deshacía todo, todo ... Sólo, en medio del desastre, quedaba intacto el rostro de Regina, con su mirada de fuego y sus labios llenos de secretos.[25]

La referencia que hace la protagonista a Regina se debe a que a partir de observarla con su amante, "que la envuelve en deseo cada uno de sus pasos", se desencadena su propia sueño fantástico, primero en su explayamiento en la naturaleza:

> Me acomete una extraña languidez. Cierro los ojos y me abandono contra un árbol. ¡Oh, echar los brazos alrededor de un cuerpo ardiente y rodar con él, enlazada, por una pendiente sin fin ...! Me siento desfallecer y en vano sacudo la cabeza para disipar el sopor que se apodera de mí.
> Entonces me quito las ropas, todas, hasta que mi carne se tiñe del mismo resplandor que flota entre los árboles. Y así, desnuda y dorada, me sumerjo en el estanque.

---

[24] María Luisa Bombal, *La última niebla* (Buenos Aires: Andina, 1970), 75.
[25] *Ibid.*, 51-52.

No me sabía tan blanca y tan hermosa. El agua alarga mis formas, que toman proporciones irreales. Nunca me atreví antes a mirar mis senos; ahora los miro. Pequeños y redondos, parecen diminutas corolas suspendidas sobre el agua.
    Me voy enterrando hasta la rodilla en un espesa arna de terciopelo. Tibias corrientes me acarician y penetran. Como con brazos de seda, las plantas acuáticas me enlazan el torso con sus largas raíces. Me besa la nuca y sube hasta mi frente el aliento fresco del agua.[26]

Cabe señalar aquí la semejanza entre este ensueño erótico y el que expresa Storni en "Un cementerio que mira al mar".[27] En ambos textos el erotismo se cifra en la interpenetración con el agua, resultando en la dispersión del cuerpo en partes que flotan en la superificie:

> Y en un lenguaje que ninguno entiende
> Gritáis: —Venid, olas del mar, rodando,
> Venid de golpe y envolvednos como
> Nos envolvieron, de pasión movidos,
> Brazos amantes. Estrujadnos, olas,
> Movednos de este lecho donde estamos
> Horizontales, viendo como pasan
> Los mundos por el cielo, noche a noche ...
>
> [...]
>
> Y algunas desprendidas cabelleras.
> Rubias acaso, como el sol que baje
> Curioso a veros, islas delicadas
> Formarán sobre el mar y acaso atraigan
> A los pequeños pájaros y viajeros.

El carácter paradójico de la felicidad que experimenta la protagonista de Bombal se hace patente cuando dice: "Vivo agobiada por la felicidad".[28] El sentimentalismo que se expresa en este texto se vincula, no obstante, a una experiencia casi sublime; su amante, como el Esposo de los poetas místicos, es "más que un amor, es mi razón de ser, mi ayer, mi hoy, mi mañana".[29] Es su propio ensueño, que puja contra los límites de ella y del otro, que le da forma al tipo de

---

[26] *Ibid.*, 47-48.
[27] Alfonsina Storni, *Languidez* (Buenos Aires, 1920), 224-25.
[28] *Ibid.*, 71.
[29] *Ibid.*, 89.

sublime que se proyecta aquí. El cuerpo de la protagonista se funde con su contorno y con la naturaleza, casi como si su cuerpo y sus proyecciones se convirtieran en el lenguaje de su deseo. Desde una perspectiva franco-feminista —pienso en Montrelay e Irigaray— este tipo de proyección del cuerpo se entiende como una manera de retirarse del dominio del hombre, de su función fálica. Es como si Bombal creara una sensualidad para lograr un sublime ilegítimo, fuera del alcance de lo fálico, del poder.

> Puesto que es el orden del lenguaje que estructura la sexualidad en torno del término masculino, o que el privilegio de ese término revela que la sexualidad se construye dentro del lenguaje, este hecho hace considerar simultáneamente la relación de la mujer a ese lenguaje y a esa sexualidad ... El objetivo es retirar a la mujer del dominio del término fálico y del lenguaje a la misma vez. Ello significa que la feminidad es asignada a un punto de origen previo a la marca de la diferencia simbólica y de la ley. Esta relación privilegiada de la mujer a ese origen le da acceso a una forma arcaica de expresividad fuera del circuito del intercambio lingüístico.[30]

En *La útima niebla*, el amante de la protagonista está, de hecho, fuera del circuito lingüístico; cuando el marido le pregunta si recuerda la voz del amante, ella no puede, pues nunca la ha oído.[31] Más bien, el amante es parte de la niebla y de los otros elementos acuosos que permean su mundo. En un momento dado ella dice que "su carne huele a fruta, a vegetal",[32] pues como en la escena citada antes, su cuerpo se fusiona eróticamente con todo lo que vive del agua. Su cuerpo se explaya en la naturaleza, así como "todo a [su] alrededor estaba saturado de [su] sentimiento".[33] El amante, pues, es la proyección de su sexualidad femenina y no una función fálica. Esta interpenetración con la naturaleza concuerda con la idea de que el punto de origen de la expresividad arcaica que está fuera del circuito lingüístico es el cuerpo femenino o materno. Ello implica, además, un rechazo de la escisión —contra el término fálico y también contra la pérdida de origen implícita en la teoría lacaniana— "que proporciona a la mujer el acceso a una esfera diferente del lenguaje, en la que las palabras y las cosas no están diferenciadas, y la realidad del cuerpo materno amenaza o suspende el acceso de la mujer a la prohibición y la ley",[34] encarnada por el esposo en el caso de *La última niebla*.

---

[30] Rose, 53-54.
[31] *Ibid.*, 82.
[32] *Ibid.*, 59.
[33] *Ibid.*, 87
[34] *Ibid.*, 55.

Asimismo ha interpretado Amado Alonso esta novela en su ensayo de introducción a la edición de la Editorial Andina:

> es una emoción radical, nacida de los impulsos primarios de la mujer, sentidos oscura y tempestuosamente y sublimados por el ansia de absoluto. Una pasión morosa que llena a una mujer como la linfa al junco, y que, sin embargo, no está dirigida todavía diferenciadamente... hacia ningún hombre, ni donjuanescamente hacia el hombre genérico, o hacia el individuo insaciablemente renovado; pues, en verdad, esta emoción no está de ningún modo dirigida, sino que es como una agua estancada cada vez más envenenada con sus propios fermentos... Emoción que se alimenta y se devora a sí misma.[35]

Esta extrema sensualidad y "chillonería" sentimentalista (palabra que usó Borges para caracterizar la poesía de Storni), frisa en lo cursi; al menos así lo entiende la protagonista misma. Nunca oye la voz de su amante pero sí oye las voces de los hombres que le hacen burla:

> Ayer una voz lejana respondía a la mía: "¡Amooor!" Me detuve, pero aguzando el oído, percibí un rumor confuso de risas ahogadas. Muerta de vergüenza caí en la cuenta de que los leñadores parodiaban así mi llamado.[36]

Este pasaje parece comprobar la idea de que el sentimentalismo y la sensualidad a todo dar de la protagonista y de la novela —como también de la poesía de las escritoras tildadas de postmodernistas— están en oposición con una perspectiva masculina y, por ende, con la escritura masculina. Debe recordarse que la vanguardia, así como el sublime kantiano, está marcada genéricamente —en el sentido sexual— por una misoginia muy específica. (Debe aclararse que uso aquí el término género —*gender*— siguiendo su acepción en el feminismo norteamericano para referirse a la construcción social de la identidad sexual.) La imaginación, asignada por Kant a una capacidad femenina —es decir, "débil"— no es acosada totalmente contra su voluntad sino que es la víctima voluntaria que consiente a y hasta participa en su propia violación:

> Así pues, el goce del sublime natural es sólo *negativo* (mientras el goce en el sublime bello es *positivo*): ello quiere decir que se trata de un sentimiento de la imaginación que por acto propio se despoja de su propia libertad al recibir una determinación final de acuerda a una ley que no sea la de su empleo empírico. De esta manera logra una extensión y un poder mayor que el que sacrifica. Pero el

---

[35] Amado Alonso, "Aparición de una novelista", en *La última niebla*, 29-30.
[36] *Ibid.*, 72.

fundamenteo de esto se desconoce y en su lugar *siente* el sacrificio de la privación, y de su causa, a la cual está sujeta.³⁷

La imaginación es, pues, la víctima de fuerzas superiores ya que recibe las órdenes de su sacrificio de una ley que no es propia y también es el agente de su auto-mutilación: cede su actividad no dirigida de percepción y se priva de libertad por acto propio. La imaginación puede compartir una partícula del poder de la razón, si no su placer, sólo al identificarse con su opresor y así consentir a su propia subordinación. Es de esta manera que logra "una extensión y un poder mayor del que sacrifica" y se le permite participar, al menos hasta cierto punto, en la captación mental de su propia vocación suprasensible. La única actividad por la que no puede ser castigada es, pues, su auto-victimización, y sólo se le permite tener acceso al momento sublime bajo la condición de que se convierta en su propio chivo expiatorio.

En los textos de Storni como en el de Bombal las protagonistas son las víctimas de su propia imaginación o "engaño". Si, como he sugerido, la imaginación se comporta como —y está en la posición tradicionalmente requerida de la— mujer, entonces el sublime kantiano nos narra el relato de una opresión internalizada, una de las estrategias principales por medio de las cuales el patriarcado se reproduce. Por añadidura describe una misoginia específicamente femenina, pues lo que narra son las condiciones bajo las cuales la mujer aprende a hacerse a sí misma y a otras lo que la sociedad les ha hecho. Como a menudo es el caso en las escenas de violencia dirigida a la mujer, lo que se dramatiza aquí es el consentimiento, el cual, particularmente en el contexto de la misoginia, nos hace comprender, en conformidad con el sublime kantiano, que toda proclama de que la imaginación es subversiva tiene que hacerse fuera del orden de lo simbólico. La protagonista reconoce esto al final de *La última niebla* cuando accede al *status quo* del mundo de su esposo:

> Lo sigo para llevar a cabo una infinidad de pequeños menesteres; para cumplir con una infinidad de frivolidades amenas; para llorar por costumbre y sonreír por deber. Lo sigo para vivir correctamente, para morir correctamente, algún día.³⁸

Sublime y masculinidad: el control del discurso

Asimismo, al final de su encuentro con la razón, la imaginación consiente a su propio sacrificio. Pero ¿en qué consiste este consentimiento si su única

---

³⁷ Immanuel Kant, *The Critique of Judgement*, traducido por James Creed Meredith (Oxford: Clarendon Press, 1952), 120.
³⁸ *Ibid.*, 103.

posibilidad de elección es acceder? ¿Si su única opción es aceptar el juicio de su cursilería? Pero esta es una *impasse* aparente, pues se puede reivindicar lo rechazado o subordinado por la ley masculina que emite el juicio. Se trata de una lucha por la valoración de la cultura ya no definida necesariamente según el modelo del sublime vanguardista. Quedan pocos que crean a pies juntillas en la universalidad del juicio estético. La condición postmoderna en que vivimos nos sugiere que no hay ningún metarrelato (*grand récit*) o discurso privilegiado que determine el valor. Y con el ocaso de estos grandiosos relatos también han perdido legitimidad los corifeos del "nuevo hombre" que ha de instaurar el discurso vanguardista. Si en la gloria de la vanguardia se podía considerar cursi la escritura de Storni o de Bombal, hoy día las frases sagradas de un Octavio Paz, pongamos por ejemplo, pueden hacer sonreír, por ingenuas, en algunos sectores: "La poesía es conocimiento, salvación, poder, abandono"; "La poesía pone en tela de juicio los fundamentos de la metafísica y pone en su lugar el lenguaje mismo como terreno de autoconocimiento"; "El hombre es un ser que se ha creado a sí mismo al crear un lenguaje". Y conste que cuando Paz dice "hombre" se está refiriendo al género masculino, pues el lenguaje de que se trata, de que está hecho el poema redentor es un "lenguaje erguido",[39] tan erecto como el falo que sustenta el orden simbólico. De ahí que la mujer para Paz, como la mujer para Neruda o Huidobro o Vallejo o Girondo, existe sólo como el medio a través del cual el hombre se sale de sí mismo y vuelve a la confirmación de su ser. Y la mujer, claro está, queda al margen de esa confirmación:

> Ante la Aparición [de la ausente, como en Neruda], porque se trata de una verdadera aparición, dudamos entre avanzar y retroceder. El carácter contradictorio de nuestras emociones nos paraliza. Ese cuerpo, esos ojos, esa voz nos hacen daño y al mismo tiempo nos hechizan. Nunca habíamos visto ese rostro y ya se confunde con nuestro pasado más remoto. Es la extrañeza total y la vuelta a algo que no admite más calificativo que el de entrañable. Tocar ese cuerpo es perderse en lo desconocido; pero, asimismo, es alcanzar tierra firme. Nada más ajeno y nada más nuestro. El amor nos suspende, nos arranca de nosotros mismos y nos arroja a lo extraño por excelencia: otro cuerpo, otros ojos, otro ser. Y sólo en ese cuerpo que no es el nuestro y en esa vida irremediablemente ajena, podemos ser nosotros mismos....
> Las semejanzas entre el amor y la experiencia de lo sagrado son algo más que coincidencias... La comunión, para citar un ejemplo muy socorrido, opera como un cambio en la naturaleza del creyente. El manjar sagrado nos trasmuta. Y ese ser "otros" no es sino un recobrar nuestra naturaleza o condición original. "La

---

[39] Octavio Paz, *Los hijos del limo* (México: Fondo de Cultura Económica, 1956), 35.

mujer —decía Novalis— es el alimento corporal más elevado." Gracias al canibalismo erótico el hombre cambia, esto es, regresa a su estado anterior. La idea del regreso —presente en todos los actos religiosos, en todos los mitos y aun en las utopías— es la fuerza de gravedad del amor. La mujer nos exalta, nos hace salir de nosotros y, simultáneamente, nos hace volver. Caer: volver a ser. Hambre de vida: hambre de muerte. Salto de la energía, disparo, expansión del ser: pereza, inercia cósmica, caer en el sinfín.[40]

Dice Paz que lo sagrado trasciende la sexualidad; en esa palabra —trascender— lo dice todo, pues, no sólo se legitima como experiencia valiosa la que confirme el orden simbólico: donde estuvo Dios —lugar de lo sagrado— ahora está el Otro, que a su vez, es simulado en el acto amoroso por la mujer y en el acto poético por la imagen lingüística que se basta a sí misma. Ambas sacan al hombre de sí y lo devuelven. Paz describe el fenómeno como una liberación, y así se seguirá haciendo hasta que el Boom de la novela y de la crítica literaria latinoamericana, esa otra vanguardia, como señaló Rodríguez Monegal, se agoten y su concepción de liberación deje de tener significado alguno. Pues, desde una perspectiva postmoderna (la de hoy día) no hay nada más ridículo que esta concepción. Y eso no porque la noción de liberación sea absurda sino por la manera en que el orden simbólico en que se inscribe y contiene requiere que ciertos otros hagan el papel de medium para la trascendencia de los que definen el valor cultural.

Al fin de cuentas, la marginalidad de la escritura de mujeres y de la temática sensual y sentimental es cuestión de legitimación en la esfera pública. Con tal de que un solo discurso domine, el valor se medirá en términos de fuerza, de violencia, de erguidez. Pero ésta es ya una vieja historia que la diversidad de esferas públicas hoy día está re-escribiendo sin tener que acudir al sagrado, al eros o a la poesía que la vanguardia dotó de supremos poderes. Como ha observado Terry Eagleton en *The Ideology of the Aesthetic*, la estética ha funcionado a lo largo de la modernidad como un sustituto [*surrogate*] del poder, efectuando exclusiones de los y las que no tenían las propiedades para intervenir y ser reconocidos en la esfera pública.

---

[40] *Ibid.*, 135-36.

Staging the Pre-scription of Gender:
Manuel Puig's *La traición de Rita Hayworth*

SHARON MAGNARELLI

If we understand engenderment as a process by which the individual and/or society seeks, discovers (or creates), and subsequently marks difference(s) (that is, assures their visibility), then there can be little doubt that engenderment not only parallels the production of discourse but in fact is informed by it.[1] At the same time, the discourse of gender is subject to constant affirmation or correction by the various patriarchal institutions —Church, State, family— which have determined and codified parameters of appropriate speech and action for each gender, arbitrary though those parameters may be deemed. In volume one of *The History of Sexuality*, Michel Foucault has convincingly argued that discourse and its production are forms of codifying and controlling sexuality.[2] He also notes that much of the proliferation of discourse regarding sexuality originated in the confession, precisely the discursive mode upon which Church, State, and family have relied for their "knowledge" about sexuality. Surely, much of what Foucault posits about sexuality can be applied to gender, to the extent that the latter informs sexuality and vice versa —prescribed codes provide different socially acceptable outlets for one's sexual impulses, depending upon one's gender.[3] I would like to carry Foucault's theories one step further and

---

[1] Both depend upon establishing and inscribing difference. If we label something X, by implication we separate and differentiate it from not-X. Similarly, much of our perception of gender is marked by negativity; to be manly is to prove oneself *not* feminine. For example, see Chapter Five of my *The Lost Rib* (Lewisburg, PA: Bucknell University Press, 1985).
[2] Michel Foucault, *The History of Sexuality*, Vol. 1, trans. Robert Hurley (New York: Vintage, 1980). Similarly, Carroll Smith-Rosenberg has posited that gender like class constitutes a conceptual system, an organizing principle, that imposes a fictive order on social and economic development. "They constitute codes of behavior by which people are expected to structure their lives." "Writing History: Language, Class and Gender", *Feminist Studies/Critical Studies*, edited by Teresa de Lauretis (Bloomington: Indiana University Press, 1986), 33.
[3] I in no way intend to conflate gender and sexuality, but as Jill Dolan has noted, "sexuality, in Western Culture, is as rigidly constructed and prescribed as gender ... Expressions of

suggest, first, that gender is intricately related to the question of theatricality,[4] and second, that confession (already an inherently theatrical gesture) is one, among many, of the forms of discourse used to discern, articulate, and inscribe gender, and then, in a metalepsis, a reversal of tropes, cause and effect, first to confirm it and subsequently to prescribe or to decree it, in a process of circular imitation and self reflection.[5]

To aid us in our inquiry, let us define confession in terms that focus on the theatrical gesture of that narrative act. First, confession is predicated on an audience. One implicitly confesses to another, an implied audience, even though that other (interlocutor/spectator) may be mere mental chimera. Second, when I confess, I tell about myself and convert myself into a persona for my confessor/audience. In the theatre of confession one presents a theatrical self to be viewed by the others as one re-enacts dual (generally contradictory) positions: a linguistic subject/object, a temporal now/then, and a moral good/bad. But, to confess is to position one of those personae center stage and implicitly displace the other (potential) subject positions as one supplants the "bad" with the "good," the then with the now. In this respect, the theatre of confession is predicated on the tacit recognition of multiple subject positions (morally conflated and polarized as good and bad), but these positions are presumed to be sequential (either/or, now/then) rather than concurrent (and/also). Third, the act of confession is motivated by a sense of guilt which implies that a law has been broken, that the individual has not complied with the prescribed standards and that (s)he is conscious of this breach. Thus, the confession will simultaneously stage, re-present,

---

sexuality further illustrate the operation of gender codes and constructs". Jill Dolan, *The Feminist Spectator as Critic* (Ann Arbor: University of Michigan Press, 1988), 63. Quoted in Gayle Austin, *Feminist Theories for Dramatic Criticism* (Ann Arbor: University of Michigan Press, 1990), 14.

I intentionally use the term "prescribe" in all its meanings and connotations: "to lay down, in writing or otherwise, as a rule or a course to be followed; appoint, ordain or enjoin ... to designate or order for use, as a remedy or treatment" (*The American College Dictionary* [New York: Random, 1964]). Etymologically, the term evokes the notion of writing before, temporally and perhaps also spatially.

[4] I use the term theatricality in the sense defined by Barbara Freedman: "What do we mean when we say that someone or something is theatrical? What we mean is that such a person is aware that she is seen, reflects that awareness, and so deflects our look". Barbara Freedman, *Staging the Gaze: Postmodernism, Psychoanalysis and Shakespearean Comedy* (Ithaca, NY: Cornell University Press, 1991), 1. I am indebted throughout this study to insights on theatre and the gaze gained from my reading of Freedman's provocative analysis and readings of Shakespeare in *Staging the Gaze*.

[5] In reference to the Puig novel, Kerr has noted the "circular model of imitation, through which the origins of desire are impossible to locate". Lucille Kerr, *Suspended Fictions: Reading Novels by Manuel Puig* (Urbana: University of Illinois Press, 1987), 30.

the transgression even as it closes up around it, effacing it and its effects. And, it stages the attempt to eclipse (make invisible as it were) the "old" (and by implication "bad") subject position in order to secure a new (visible) mask, persona, which does in fact comply with prescribed standards. One must be *seen* by one's audience (regardless of how fictitious it may be) as one's new persona, as converted —that is, in a single, stable subject position of "goodness".

In this regard, the confessional mode is posited on the notions of reward and power. If the theatrical discourse fulfills its implicit goal so that one is *viewed* as a "new", "good" persona, one will be rewarded with catharsis, condonation, and/or suitable compensation. Ostensibly, these rewards can be proffered and validated only by an audience (interlocutor/spectator) who is more powerful than the narrator/actor.[6] Nonetheless, the relationships of power in this theatrical arena are far more complex than we may have imagined, for in his/her bid for "proper" recognition the narrator has the power to position and displace not only the self but also the other, the interlocutor/ spectator. The narrator focuses the gaze of the audience on that which the narrator chooses, in a gesture which recalls the cinematographic camera as it focuses and to large degree dominates the eye of the spectator. Thus, the narrator simultaneously acknowledges the superiority of the interlocutor/spectator while subverting that superiority and imposing her/his own view (visual frame) and control.

With that theoretical framework, I propose to examine the relationship between gender and the theatre/narration of confession by analyzing two pseudo confessions in Manuel Puig's *La traición de Rita Hayworth*. Published in 1968, the novel proffers numerous modes of written and spoken discourse. One of its principal objectives, no doubt, is to dramatize the effects of popular culture, particularly movies, but also books and all forms of popular discourse, on personal (and in turn social) development.[7] But, particularly, I believe, Puig is interested in the effects of these media on gender development, the degree to which gender is the product of and in turn produces popular discourses, the degree to which each is prescribed by the other. Specifically, I propose a reading of the novel as a *mise en scène* of the theatre of confession and the misrecognition on which traditional prescriptions of gender are predicated and staged.

---

[6] Foucault, *op. cit.*, has noted that confession is a "ritual of discourse", and the interlocutor is "the authority who requires the confession, prescribes and appreciates it, and intervenes in order to judge, punish, forgive, console, and reconcile" (61-62). Surely both Toto and Berto expect the same from their interlocutors, imaginary though they may be.

[7] In "Woman as Dramatized Reader: *María* and *La traición de Rita Hayworth*", *Hispanófila* 94 (1988), 79-88, I have shown how the literature of Romanticism influences one of the female narrators, Paquita. All references will be to the 1971 edition of the novel (Barcelona: Seix Barral).

And, by implication, I suggest that although the cinema is one of the main leitmotivs of the text and although Puig has unquestionably employed a number of cinematographic techniques,[8] the text paradoxically challenges those techniques and their imposition of "right spectatorship".[9]

Barbara Freedman employs the term "right spectatorship" in reference to the "controlling patriarchal perspective" or point of view with which one is implicitly led to identify (2). "Right spectatorship" then might be understood as the visual arts' (theatre's and cinema's) analogy of the "immasculation" which Judith Fetterley defines as the process by which women are taught to identify with the male point of view in fiction and to accept it as normal,[10] and, we might add, natural. I would expand the definitions of these two critics by noting that males as well as females are subject to "right spectatorship" and immasculation, particularly in regard to the prescription of gender (as the Puig text will demonstrate). More specifically, I propose that Puig links the rigidity and implicit "right spectatorship" of the movie camera's focus with that of "proper" gender role playing while undermining that "right spectatorship" as he employs techniques borrowed from theatre which proffer an alternative to those of cinema and encourage us to reconsider the question of "right spectatorship" in the theatre of gender. Indeed, one of the characteristics which separates theatre from cinema is precisely the former's less rigid and tyrannical control over the spectator's eye. Surely, throughout *La traición* the *hablante básico* (the organizing, editorial persona) demonstrates a paradoxical control/non-control of perspective and the spectator's eye as the reader is proffered any number of visual frames in the various chapters but virtually not told where to look or how to focus for any length of time or definitively. Paradoxically, then, Puig reproduces the gesture of "right spectatorship" as the reader temporarily adopts the perspectives of the various narrators, even as he undermines it by refusing to endorse or authorize any of those possibilities in the totality of the novel.

---

[8] For a more comprehensive view of the novel's themes and the questions of cinematography and polyphony see Lucille Kerr, *op. cit.*; René Alberto Campos, *Espejos: La textura cinemática en "La traición de Rita Hayworth"* (Madrid: Pliegos, 1985); Jorgelina Corbatta, *Mito personal y mitos colectivos en las novelas de Manuel Puig* (Madrid: Orígenes, 1988); and Roberto Echavarren and Enrique Giordano, *Manuel Puig: montaje y alteridad del sujeto* (Santiago, Chile: Monografías del Maitén, 1986).
[9] Freedman also points out, spectatorship is a cultural production, *Staging the Gaze*, 5. Similary, as Kerr has noted, Puig simultaneously appropriates and renounces the various fictions (including movies) he utilizes in his novels, *Suspended Fictions*, x.
[10] Judith Fetterley, *The Resisting Reader: A Feminist Approach to American Fiction* (Bloomington: Indiana University Press, 1981), xx.

This ostensible lack of focus and control is already apparent in the opening lines of the text which center on embroidery in a theatrical and metaphoric visualization of how seemingly irrelevant, peripheral discourse is superimposed on our lives and our perception of our surroundings. Nonetheless, the opening chapter with its "wandering" perspective also dramatizes how "right spectatorship" is imposed via our daily discourse, for it is here, in the "unsigned" discourse, that we learn that Berto is just like a movie star, a fact we first read to mean handsome but later discover (in the last chapter) is also an oblique reference to his position as an actor, role player.[11] Similarly, although the wide array of characters and their various modes of discourse throughout the novel leave readers wondering where to concentrate our look, as Puig's technique effectively precludes the decisive focus of the cinematographic camera, one spectator position (and the one most frequently endorsed by the novel's critics) would be to focus on Mita and Berto, already mentioned a number of times in the opening dialogue, and their son Toto. With this spectator position, we might read the novel, in which each chapter is marked by year, as a chronological "progression" through a series of multifarious views of that family and the society in which they move. This spectator/reader position is challenged, however, when the novel concludes ahistorically with a letter, from Berto, the father, written not at the chronological conclusion of the story line, as the structure (instrument of "right spectatorship") has led us to expect, but rather during the temporal period of the first two segments. I propose to analyze that letter with its anachronism that subverts our confident "right spectatorship" in relation to the stream of consciousness (that is unwritten discourse) of Berto's son, Toto, for both are informed by a confessional mode of narration to the extent that each narrator directs his discourse to another in an attempt to exonerate himself while placing a theatrical persona of himself at center stage, making himself central, visible, and the focus of our and, more significantly, the (m)other's gaze.

Paradoxically, although neither the stream of consciousness nor the letter is overtly presented within the confessional mode, each evinces the characteristics of confession (including its theatricality). More importantly, I suggest that each is based on the character's (mis)recognition that he has not complied with the social code and has committed some transgression.[12] Such a (mis)recognition leads the narrators to assume masks of innocence with which they will attempt to (mis)direct the viewer's/interlocutor's gaze (and, implicitly, their own) as they attempt to impose their own

---

[11] These "nameless" conversations might also be seen as the "phantasmal voices" to which Campos refers: "hemos sido condicionados a representarnos, a ver desde la perspectiva de estas voces fantasmales", *Espejos*, 29.

[12] The notion of misrecognition is, of course, borrowed from Lacan, although as I shall argue, Lacan is himself a victim of his own misrecognition.

brands of "right spectatorship". As we shall see, their respective discourses vary from the theatre of confession principally insofar as their (good and bad) personae prove to be temporally synchronous rather than successive. One mask or subject position does not totally succeed in replacing or eliding the other(s) to produce the desired reflection —the illusion of a single, stable, secure subject position of "goodness". The lesson of both characters/actors and perhaps that of the novel as a whole is that outside the cinema spectatorship is inevitably less controllable.

Neither male character openly acknowledges any wrongdoing on his part, but each indirectly evokes some moral issue. Little Toto is obsessed with the questions of good and bad, lying, and punishment as he repeatedly insists that he does behave himself and that he is a "pescadito bueno" (already a theatrical pose) who should not be punished. Similarly, Berto is preoccupied with forgiveness and behavior (his own and others') as he insists that "nunca le hice mal a nadie" (289) and that his economic situation is not his fault, "yo no tengo la culpa si todo se me pone en contra" (292). Furthermore, he seeks the brother's forgiveness a number of times during the course of the letter although ultimately, in an inverse mirror reflection, it is he who will not forgive the brother. In their eagerness to assure their narratees/spectators that they are not guilty or "bad", each evokes a dual subject position and underlines the fact that each is conscious of having breached some social more. The act of narration thus stages the attempt to locate the malfeasance, understand and justify the narrator's imperfection, and finally vindicate himself as he casts the blame onto an other (the brother in Berto's case, Pocha or Rita Hayworth in Toto's) in his endeavor to have his audience see (and mirror) him as he would be seen (and mirrored). And, I suggest, in both cases, first that the perceived "transgression" is a failure "properly" to assimilate oneself within the prescribed parameters of the codified gender role, and second that proper assimilation of the gender role is misconstrued as a moral issue which leads to the confessional mode.

Revealingly, the two narratives are informed by analogous frames: the siesta hour with its forced solitude and silence, a silence and solitude produced by the absence of the/a female. Yet, that solitude and silence are broken, subversively transgressed via the theatre of confessional discourse which bidirectionally stages the loss of that female presence (both Mita and Berto's mother) while attempting to re-present the absent figure and thereby eliminate or render ineffective the same absence.

For example, in Chapter Three, entitled, "Toto, 1939", we learn that Toto plays alone because his mother, Mita, is working at the pharmacy to help supplement the family income or has been called by the father to spend the siesta with him: "Papá la llamó y mamá tuvo que irse a dormir la siesta" (36). Since he plays by himself, Toto's interlocutor would seem to be only himself. But, as is the case throughout the text and as the final letter will attest, appearances (like "right spectatorship") can be deceiving: Toto's interlocutor often proves to be his absent mother, Mita. There are several direct addresses to her as well as numerous other allusions to a *tú* whose referent is unquestionably she. Thus, his discourse compensates for her absence as it re-presents a mythic rendition of her, his ideal narratee/spectator, whose gaze (and by implication universe) would center on him and whose presence and gaze (re-created via the discourse) are necessary to reflect and confirm the "good" persona he would assume.[13]

At the same time, Toto's free-flowing internal monologue stages his efforts, within the fiction, to comprehend the world that surrounds him and more specifically the language that describes that world as well as the signs that mark gender. Yet his preoccupation with the issue of lying underlines the tenuous relationship between language (or any sign) and its referent. What someone says may not accurately reflect reality. Who should he trust? Who is good? Who is bad? He is not always punished when he is bad and sometimes is when he is good. And, mother's absence is vaguely confused with that punishment. If he is bad, she will not be there, and if he interrupts their siesta in order to see her and be seen by her, father may destroy him ("el día que te ponga la mano encima te deshago", 37). In either case, the result of the (imagined) punishment will be that she will not see him; for her, he will be invisible. And, inversely, if she cannot see him she cannot reflect the "good" persona he would assume. Thus, in the child's mind being "bad" or punished is confusedly associated with the mother's absence or presence and with his own visibility and centrality.[14] Bad little fishies are eaten and no longer seen; bad girls, like Pocha, are (in his wishful thinking) consumed and rendered invisible by the gypsy. The question for the child, not unlike what we will find in Berto's letter, is how to secure the focus of her look on him, how to ensure his own visibility, centrality, and "goodness", so that he will not be punished and disappear from the mirror of her gaze, in a world where access to vision cannot be controlled by the "right spectatorship" the movie camera affords.

Toto's preoccupations and the framework/stage for his discourse are mirrored in the letter Berto writes his brother in 1933, eight months after the birth of Toto. Like Toto's discourse, Berto's letter is composed precisely during the solitude and silence of siesta hour, a solitude, although six years earlier, still occasioned by Mita's absence: "Mita hoy está de turno en el hospital hasta las seis" (290). And, while Berto's audience

---

[13] There can be little doubt that Toto's fascination with "women's movies" is an indication of this same mythic gesture as he substitutes actresses, many times removed from any corporeal referentiality, to fill the void created by the absence of the mother. In his article, "Las 'películas de mujeres' y *La traición de Rita Hayworth*", *Literature and Popular Culture in the Hispanic World*, edited by Rose S. Minc (Gaithersburg, MD: Hispamérica, 1981), 59-67, René Campos analyzes this element of the novel.

[14] As will be apparent to my reader, I disagree with René Campos's reading of the novel as a search for the lost father, the absent phallus (*Espejos*). In order to reach this conclusion, Campos has had to invent an entire prehistory for Toto, a prehistory which is not a part of the literary product and to which the novel never explicitly refers.

may initially appear less imaginary than Toto's, in fact, he is equally an absence and a re-invention, even within the fiction, as evidenced by the epistolary mode. Like Toto, Berto finds himself without that positive reinforcement of the return look; since neither Mita nor his mother are there, he needs the brother to write and acknowledge his existence. Thus, Berto's discourse is not only the fruit of Mita's current absence, but it is also related to the earlier absence of his own mother: "todavía no me puedo resignar a que mamá se nos fue para siempre y no la vamos a ver más" (read, nor will she see us/me) (290). The implication is that because as a child Berto suffered the loss of his mother, he must now write to his brother (a mother and father substitute) and blame him for the series of decisions which led to his current financial predicament, a predicament which in turn has produced Mita's absence —she is working to help support the family. Again, in a direct reflection of the mental frame we saw in Toto's monologue, none of this would have happened, from Berto's perspective at any rate, had his own mother been present to provide for him, to see him and allow him to see himself in the mirror of her gaze as well as to prevent the brother from ignoring him and refusing him the starring role that she presumably would have afforded. Thus, the absence of his mother resulted in a situation that produced its own mirror reflection, Mita's absence, years later, while, not unlike Toto, Berto is also unsure about whom he should have trusted, where the truth lies. Who is good and who is bad? Which reflection (spectator position) is right?

In the letter, Berto recalls his mother's funeral and notes: "yo estaba sentado en un rincón del velorio y te veía a vos que recibías el pésame de la gente que llegaba" (290). Again, like Toto, he finds himself not center stage, not the focus of the spectators' gaze, and resorts to his theatrical confession to centralize himself (make himself visible as it were) as he both positions and displaces not only himself but also the spectators' gaze. Both Toto and Berto want the (m)other's gaze to focus on them and mirror the self (subject position of goodness) they would make their own and unique. Their discourse reveals their fear that the (m)other's gaze might focus elsewhere or might see an/other. In addition, Berto's reference to having been seated in a corner evokes his perception that he was being punished for having been "bad"[15] and leads him to assert his present goodness, masculinity, and centrality with "y ahora que soy un hombre y tengo un hijo". Implied here, of course, is "soy un hombre *porque* tengo un hijo" —now there are two of us to be seen and to occupy center stage, me and my mirror reflection. (But, of course, as we know from the rest of the text, Toto too fails to provide Berto with the mirror reflection he seeks and vice versa.) Thus, throughout the letter we watch Berto's repeated self-visualization as a man who is visible, powerful, and "good" status proven by his having fathered a son and provided

---

[15] Children frequently perceive the death of a parent (like divorce) as "their fault", something that occurs because they were "bad".

for his family, as he attempts to impose on the brother the "right spectatorship" to which he himself has submitted.

Finally, too, Berto's resentment of his brother's success with women (a "success" which echoes his earlier "successful" visible relationship of proximity to their mother and his "goodness") highlights the psycholinguistic links between manliness, visibility, and goodness: "me imagino que ... ya habrás degenerado a la mitad de las madrileñas. Qué distintos somos en eso, Jaime. Yo desde que conocí a Mita me olvidé de que existen las mujeres" (291). Clearly, the problem here is the perceived contrast between Jaime's ability to surround himself with women, make himself central and visible to them (first their mother and then the *madrileñas*), and Berto's incapacity to maintain the presence of even one (first their mother and then Mita) who will see him and make him central. The fact that the rest of the novel negates Berto's assertion here about his lack of interest in other women suggests that this statement is a misdirection of attention and the spectator's gaze, i.e. the imposition of "right spectatorship".[16] It would appear, then, that the projection of moral rectitude and gender (in this case, masculinity and visibility) may necessitate language that masks and (mis)directs more than it reveals, and Puig subtly debunks the potential of narrative or theatre, particularly confessional, for disclosing anything. In its endeavor to reveal, invent, or focus on one subject position, the discourse would cover another. Still, that discursive, visible mask continually threatens to crack and betray itself as it does here, revealing that what we witness (as in theatre) are multiple, simultaneous, concurrent subject positions, personae, rather than the single, stable, unified subject position the character would project for the world, the (m)other, to see —as we shall see, Berto both looks like and ultimately is an actor (multiple, superimposed subject positions).[17] Although Berto repeatedly assures his brother of his moral rectitude as he cinematographically frames and makes visible a single subject position, his language highlights his prevarication ("te juro que no son macanas"), his less visible sense of the precarious nature of the subject position he would project, and degenerates into verbal aggression —"gran crápula"— as it calls into question his professed virtue. In this way, the text discretely exposes masculinity as a mask and underlines the metalepsis that disguises the primary importance of and desire for the female presence.

It is in regard to the issue of female presence/absence and her gaze that the Puig novel departs from Western narrative tradition and proffers the possibility of being

---

[16] In the second segment of the novel, "En casa de Berto, Vallejos 1933", whose action is simultaneous to the writing of Berto's letter, his maids refer to his extramarital affairs and to his sexual advances to them: "Tu patrón se salvó ya más de una vez" (25); "¿De qué se salvó el señor? —De que lo matara un marido cornudo" (26); "Porque somos sirvientas se creen que nos pueden levantar las polleras y hacernos lo que quieran" (22).

[17] In theatre one is always somewhat conscious of the concurrent presence of the character and that of the actor.

read other than as a replay of Freud's version of the Oedipus myth (or psychoanalysis's reading of the same). As Freedman has noted, one of the characteristics that marks postmodernism is a turning away from the Western narratives of mastery (including the Oedipus myth) and the move from narrative to theatre as the observer's stable position is subverted and replaced with a continuous play of partial viewpoints [18] —words that might well describe the Puig novel. What seems to be particularly at stake in *La traición de Rita Hayworth* is modern psychoanalysis's reading of the Oedipus myth (notice I did not say the Oedipus myth but rather psychoanalysis's reading of it) and its concurrent imposition of "right spectatorship" that is, psychoanalysis's fascination with the male, father figure. Departing from Western narrative tradition (or our reading of it), the male characters of the Puig text are obsessed *not* with the much promulgated, albeit absent, father's phallus *à la* Freud and Lacan but rather, very specifically, with the absent mother and, as we shall see, with the food associated with her. In fact, the text might well be read as the ironic mirroring of psychoanalysis's (mis)staging of male visibility and female invisibility. As Luce Irigaray has postulated, due to Freud's, and in turn Lacan's, "reading" or staging of the sight (site) of genitalia, the male is implicitly linked with visibility and the female with invisibility (she has nothing to show, to be seen).[19] Nonetheless, such a perception is predicated on cinematographically controlling the look, the eye, framing the (primal?) "scene" as it were, in such a way as to produce "right spectatorship" so that the focus is on male (external) genitalia rather than on the (m)other, female, or some other part of the body (breasts, for example, where females do have something to show, to be seen, in relation to males). Similarly, what may seem to be, and in fact has been interpreted by some critics as, a preoccupation with the absent father/phallus in the Puig novel proves to be a metalepsis, an inversion and confusion of tropes.[20] To insist that the father or the phallus, rather than the mother, is the object of desire here is to impose a metonymy, refuse to recognize it as such, and then invert it. In this novel at least (but perhaps also in a less visible way in the theories of Freud and Lacan), the preoccupation is clearly with the absent female; the other male is merely the impediment to the actualization of her presence, tangential to her to be sure, but not the veritable object of desire

---

[18] *Staging the Gaze*, 73-74.

[19] Luce Irigaray, *Speculum of the Other Woman*, translated by Gillian C. Gill (Ithaca, NY: Cornell University Press, 1985).

[20] Adrienne Munich has convincingly demonstrated how metalepsis governs the Biblical Genesis where biological time sequences are reversed or collapsed. She attributes the metalepsis to a violent desire to obliterate woman's role in the early childhood years, a role which threatens male domination. Adrienne Munich, "Notorious signs, feminist criticism and literary tradition", *Making a Difference*, edited by Gayle Greene and Coppélia Kahn (New York: Methuen, 1985), 241.

himself. In each case there is the suggestion that although the other male has contributed to the female's absence, her presence would have rendered that other male ineffective as a barrier to the fulfillment of desire, which in the Puig text at least is often food-related.

If we return to Toto's mental meandering in Chapter Three, the focus on the female and food as well as their metonymic relationship to gender and morality will soon become apparent. Like the rest of this novel, in which "right", stable spectatorship is continually undermined, at first glance Toto's internal monologue seems meaningless as he considers the relationship between *muñequitos* and people that share visible similarities with them and yet are not the same. And, Toto connects this paradox of similarity/dissimilarity with the visible manifestations of gender and gender roles. As he notes, "las muñecas con traje de seda y los muñecos con traje de seda también, mami" (31). He is confused, for his father has repeatedly insisted on the visible differences between males and females and has been angered when Toto acts or dresses like a girl, assuring him that this is "bad", and threatening to put him in a skirt if he is not "good". In this manner, Berto imposes "right spectatorship" as he conflates the visible sign of femininity (the skirt) with badness (that is, with a moral issue). How then can male and female figurines wear the same attire? Toto's confusion continues, "y la pechera blanca los hombres igual que la tuya" (31).

Significantly, Toto's preoccupation here reflects one we encounter in a more overt form in Berto's letter. Not only does Mita use the same *pechera* as the male figurines, but in Berto's letter we learn that Mita is the principal financial support in the family, a fact which highlights her links to patriarchal power and authority as traditionally defined. Her ambiguous position, like that of Toto's figurines, suggests that masculine and feminine are not always as neatly differentiated as one might like in spite of the fact that Berto's self doubts (like our binary structures) demand well defined, visible divisions. Even more threatening to Berto's perception of his masculinity, Mita's sister had suggested to her that she not turn her entire salary over to Berto but rather maintain some of the power symbolized by the money. This possibility leads Berto to call the sister "una hija de puta" (292), in a gesture that converts the economic issue into a moral one.[21] The (metonymic) juxtaposition of the topics of Mita's salary and Berto's mother's death underlines the similarity of the two situations: both create economic and moral insecurity in Berto as they make him feel invisible and bad and thus call into question his perceived masculinity. Still, according

---

[21] I have discussed the implication of calling one an *hijo de puta* in Chapter Five of *The Lost Rib*. Ironically, of course, such a derogatory phrase merely boomerangs back and reflects upon him, for Adela and Mita are sisters, born of the same mother. Were the term valid for Adela, it would be equally applicable to Mita, the woman he chose to marry. And, if it is applicable to Mita, what does that make Berto?

to Berto he has managed to re-establish those lines of division along with his own visibility and centrality: "últimamente me ha dado íntegro el sueldo" (292). That is, she will hand him the salary, recognize his superiority, and each member of the family will play the socially codified, visible gender (theatrical) role: he will wear the proverbial (good) pants, and she the (bad) skirt. Which returns us to Toto.

The importance of Toto's deliberations on the *pechera* that Mita and the male figurines share is unquestionably highlighted later in the same chapter when Toto ponders his new vocabulary word, *cogía*. As I have posited elsewhere, his lengthy speculation on this vulgarity evidences his attempt to understand the sex roles —who does or did what to whom.[22] Although it is never quite clear to Toto, he does seem to recognize that it is preferable to be the active (aggressive) partner, for, as in the movie with the fish-eating plant, those who allow this *cogía* to happen to them "no se ven más porque la planta de pelos se los tragó" (42). Again sex and gender are conflated and linked to eating and goodness, for in his mind only bad little fishies are punished (read, eaten). Thus, sex roles (and later gender roles) are linked here to the notion of annihilation and invisibility. Self-preservation, future existence, will depend upon assimilating the proper role, so one does not get eaten and disappear from sight.

This concern with eating and visibility is overt throughout Toto's stream of consciousness as it begins with the question of eating the *muñequitos*, moves through the disappearance of the canary that was eaten by the cat, continues with the school play and the food served there, and finally centers on the movie with the fish-eating plant before it goes on to "rewrite" (re-stage and metonymically re-view) some of the other movies he has seen, eventually recasting the characters and superimposing them on his own life as he determines who is good and who is bad, who will be eaten and disappear from sight. The psycholinguistic links are revealing. First, from the child's perspective, there are two types of *muñequitos*, both of which resemble people, but some you eat and some you do not eat —a polarity perhaps easily linked to gender or sex roles in the child's mind. What he is sure of is that the result of being eaten is disappearance, as in the case of the canary eaten by the cat: "el gato se lo tragó entero y se lo mandó al buche" (32).[23] Revealingly, the segment concludes with Toto's deliberations about being in the clouds, a metaphoric heaven where one goes if one is good. He is concerned about whether or not there might be black birds as big as cats up there, who, by implication, might devour him with their hooked beaks. Obviously, there is no point in spending one's life being good only to end up in a heaven where one still has to worry about being eaten rather than being able to eat at will. Thus, in the child's mind goodness, badness, and punishment become linked to eating.

---

[22] See Chapter Six of *The Lost Rib*.

[23] It is worth noting too that the interdiction which immediately follows this quotation, "¡no lo mires!" suggests the possibility that the cat may well be pregnant.

Similarly, the mother's absence (already associated with punishment) deprives the child of the sweets he likes: at the school play they attended without Mita, Berto refused to give him the sweets he desired. Thus, to the child's mind mother provides food, while father frustrates the desire for food: directly, by not giving him what he wants, either eating it himself or allowing it to be taken away (disappear from sight), or indirectly, by causing the mother's absence. (Let us note that the pattern here mirrors that of Berto's letter: his mother's absence [death] led to economic problems and by implication the lack of food.) And, these vague, tangentially related notions are directly carried over into Toto's attempts to understand this word *cogía*, which he associates with eating, since the "victim", be it the fish, the *muñequito*, the canary, or "la chica que lo hace", always disappears: "porque si una chica lo hace está perdida, está terminada para siempre" (41). Bad little fishies are eaten by the *planta de pelos* or the *planta de cogía* just as the bad girl is eaten by the gypsy and his *pelos*, and the child who is not good is subject to being destroyed ("te deshago"), eliminated, not seen. Because the child takes the metaphor literally (one will disappear, lose one's visibility), to his mind to eat is to make disappear and is associated with power and "goodness" (non-punishment) while to be eaten evokes obliteration and is both "bad" and the result of being bad (punishment), in a metaphoric and metonymic process which directly parallels many of the obscenities which refer to copulation in almost every language. Let us note, however, that at this point Toto still has not yet fully nor consciously associated either gender with either position. For him, at age six, it is more a moral question, a question of good and bad and punishment, than a gender issue and signals his preoccupation with assuring his own visibility and existence. At this point he does not consistently link the male gender with goodness and eating, the female with badness and being eaten (metaleptically, as both the cause and effect of being punished), as Berto will/has, although all the foundations for doing so have surely been laid: Toto does associate grown-up manliness with *pelos* ("pelos en el pecho") and, of course, it is the plant with *pelos* and the gypsy with *pelos* (or synecdochically the *pelos* themselves) which eat and make others (the "bad" ones) disappear. At the same time his lengthy speculation on the *pájaros* and their *picos*, throughout the segment but particularly at its conclusion, might well be read as a parallel linguistic preoccupation with the synecdoche of masculinity since in the slang both terms may refer to the penis.

Similarly, in his letter Berto reaffirms his masculinity precisely through food or food-related metaphors. He refers to eight-month-old Toto as a "bolita de grasa" (287), with eyes that are "dos uvitas", and later brags that Mita is "gorda por la crianza, al fin ahora por el hijo se largó a comer como yo quiero que coma, y está redonda" (288). The continuation of this quotation underlines the tacit goal of his epistolary discourse and brings us back to the question of spectatorship: "Mita está muy miedosa en la cuestión moneda, y si ella hace la digestión tranquila es porque *yo no le dejo ver* la gravedad de la situación" (288, emphasis added). Thus, Berto has been good; he has eaten and provided food for others. In his mind this is confusedly associated with gender; the well-fed mother and son are visible signs of *his* goodness and *his* masculinity. Yet, paradoxically if indeed revealingly, they are also the product of his capacity to cover: she eats because he does not let her see beyond his visible and consciously staged mask of economic wellbeing which, in turn, he "sees" reflected in them (again, the metalepsis of cause and effect). Thus, chronologically he may be more mature than little Toto, but his perception of what constitutes goodness and masculinity differs little from that of the six year old —to be "good" (and manly) is to be able to eat (*tener pelos*).

Doubtlessly, it is the very anachronism of the letter, located as it is at the conclusion of the text, which forces us as readers/spectators to look other than where the instruments of "right spectatorship" might have directed us. As we know from the rest of the text, the theatre we have seen is merely that: Berto has not provided and Toto has not been as good as he pretends. The theatre of confession, perhaps not unlike Hamlet's mirror or the stage, is designed to mirror the mask one would project; nonetheless if the eye cannot be controlled (as it is in the cinema) and wanders to look more closely or with less restraint (as it might in the theatre), other subject positions, which one (or even society) would elide, might be perceived. Thus, the theatre of confession, the desire to ingratiate and vindicate oneself, to "show" oneself "good", to centralize oneself and impose "right spectatorship", is subverted in the Puig text. First, the family's economic situation is not much improved as evidenced by Berto's final aggressive statement that he does not plan to spend a cent on stamps for the brother (an aggression that mirrors and is mirrored by any number of aggressive acts on Toto's part throughout the text). Secondly, whatever economic security has been provided, has been provided by Mita, the mother. Thus, while Berto's missive inverts the historicity of the text, it also proffers an extended metalepsis which inverts and disguises the basic fact that the provider of food is indeed Mita, the mother.

Surely we might posit an analogy between the Puig text and the broader issue of our Western perception and prescription of the masculine gender as the provider. This too may well be the product of a similar, more widely staged and accepted metalepsis that diverts attention (the spectator's eye) from the essential biological fact that the mother (not the father) is the original provider of food. As Karen Horney proposed long ago, Freud's famous penis envy may well be a metalepsis and a discursive mask for breast envy.[24] It may be simply a matter of where science and Western culture (like

---

[24] It is important to recognize, however, that such a metaphor, like that of the phallus, is supplemental and risks being taken too literally, as has so often been done with the image of the phallus. Elaine Showalter's warning against invoking anatomy due to the risk of returning

the cinematographic camera) have chosen to focus the look and what they have elided, left out of the camera's frame. Again, as Irigaray and Freedman have suggested in very different ways, it is all a matter of "right spectatorship", of what our eyes have been taught to see as we have ignored what Kappeler labels "who is holding the mirror [of art or science], for whose benefit, and from what angle".[25] Or we might make an even more radical proposal and suggest that Freud's penis envy, like Lacan's phallic symbol (or psychoanalysis's reading of the same), are predicated on processes of metaphorization that seek (to a large degree successfully) to control and tame otherness (the female) "by proving that everything strange [the (m)other] can ... be made to reflect a part of oneself" (Freedman 163, bracketed material added).[26] At the same time perhaps the gestures and relationships of Lacan and his psychoanalytical father, Freud, are not unlike those of Toto and his father, Berto, as each stages and assures his own visibility (and by implication that of the male in general) to (over)compensate for a sense of lack, a deep-seated fear or suspicion of invisibility, badness, and inadequacy, a sense of lack predicated on trying to "measure up" as it were to a fictive projection: that mask of adequacy, goodness, and superiority produced by the patriarchal "right spectatorship". At the same time that sense of lack may be largely based on an unwillingness or inability to "see", envision one's inherently multiple subject positions, an unwillingness or inability ameliorated by making visible (i.e. focusing on, overemphasizing, bringing into the center of the cinematographic frame) one of one's subject positions while eliding, making invisible the others —the very same gesture on which the theatres of gender and confession are predicated. Codified masculinity, of course, is predicated on the absence of femininity and vice versa, while goodness depends upon the absence of badness— i.e. on a single subject position.

Thus, the letter with its ahistoricity stages the site (and sight) of (mis)recognition —the powerful patriarchal figure is (and perhaps always has been) a sham. Berto not

---

to crude essentialism that oppressed women in the past is well taken. Elaine Showalter, "Feminist Criticism in the Wilderness", *Writing and Sexual Difference*, edited by Elizabeth Abel (Chicago: University of Chicago Press, 1982), 17.

[25] Susanne Kappeler, *The Pornography of Representation* (Minneapolis: University of Minnesota Press, 1986), 2.

[26] Although for Lacan the phallus is the privileged signifier, he insists that it is not to be confused with the penis. Nonetheless, as Jane Gallop validly notes, "as long as the attribute of power is a phallus which refers to and can be confused ... with a penis, this confusion will support a structure in which it seems reasonable that men have power and women do not". Jane Gallop, *The Daughter's Seduction: Feminism and Psychoanalysis* (Ithaca, NY: Cornell University Press, 1982), 97. At the same time, Freud's penis envy, like Lacan's designation of the phallus as the privileged signifier, assures male visibility and centrality while limiting the female to representation only in relation to (in terms of) the male.

only looks like an actor, he is one. In this regard, what is staged here is ultimately the inverse of confession to the extent that confession presents the "bad" persona and then wipes the slate clean, elides (eliminates) that persona via penance and forgiveness to replace it with the "good" persona. Puig's characters, on the other hand, attempt to present (stage) the good personae in an effort to elide the bad and wipe the slate clean, but their endeavors fail. That which they would eclipse peeks through as both characters and readers are forced to face the ineluctability of multiple subject positions (but unsure on which to focus) that will not allow for a neat perception of good and bad as predicated by "right spectatorship". Perhaps the originality of the text rests in the fact that although its polyvision and multiple perspectivism do not privilege (for long) a single eye or perspective (as the cinematographic camera must), it does stage and undermine the game of "right spectatorship" by proposing not just the unreliability of a single privileged eye, but also the (mis)recognition inherent in all perspectives. All the characters as well as (and as a result) the reader/spectator erroneously "see" Berto as a self-confident, powerful patriarchal figure. The subversion of this "vision" is the function of the anachronism of the letter (which some critics have viewed as bad faith on the part of the *hablante básico*). Nonetheless, by forcing us as readers/spectators to rethink what we have "seen" (and, by implication, known) at the conclusion of the novel, Puig forces us to re-consider all we have seen (and, by implication, known) in the world outside the text —including gender roles and single subject positions.

In this manner, Puig dramatizes that our childhood "education" and mythology (including that of the movies and novels, which perhaps more than any other art forms impose "right spectatorship" and presuppose a single subject position), particularly in regard to gender roles, will be with us throughout adulthood, even when the oral voice is converted to a written voice, for that authoritative written voice will inevitably prescribe, literally, figuratively, and etymologically as it frames and centralizes one subject position and elides others.[27] Clearly, Berto's perception of the gender roles essentially reflects and is reflected by that of six-year-old Toto, while it simultaneously prescribes (writes before and dictates) that role for him. The major difference, however, manifests itself in their respective responses to the imposition of this prescribed gender code. Since neither male, Toto nor Berto, perceives himself as completely commensurate and compliant with the socially imposed standards that demand a single, unequivocal, visible subject position mirroring and mirrored by those proffered by the media of "right spectatorship", each experiences the sense of being "bad" and the guilt that generates the pseudo-confessional mode, the search for exoneration, even if only mediated by the self. Paradoxically, however, this theatre

---

[27] Jorge Panesi has noted that the text of the novel begins with voices and moves towards writing. "Manuel Puig: las relaciones peligrosas", *Revista Iberoamericana* 49 (1983), 903.

of confession makes visible, as it were, the very same multiple subject positions it would suppress or conflate. As a result, and in a gesture reminiscent of Freud, Lacan, and modern psychoanalysis, Berto overcompensates for and attempts to disguise his perceived transgression; via his theatrical discourse he assumes the role of masculinist aggressor, he who would eat and devour, as he condemns others to invisibility (devoured). But, this verbal, aggressive mask is always on the verge of betraying him and revealing itself as mask, theatre, for Berto is not "just like" an actor; he is an actor, if indeed one who may not have chosen his role. Toto, on the other hand, withdraws into himself and alternates between the subject position of the aggressor, the devourer, and that of the victim, the devoured (the visible and the invisible, the seer and the seen) as he internalizes more and more the fictitious discourse of movies and popular culture. Narrating to himself, he converts himself into both subject and object of his ever more alienated discourse with its unrealizable gender models —unrealizable because one can only appear to comply with the gender code by pretending to be what one knows one is not (a single, unified subject position), by employing the covering of discourse to distract attention from what one is (multiple subject positions), that is, by staging (mis)recognition. In each case, much of the problem resides in the (mis)perception of masculinity and femininity in their socially codified definitions as mutually exclusive absolutes with no margin for variation or juxtaposition, and in the blindness generated by these same codes, a blindness that may well be reflected in the theories of Freud and Lacan (or their proponents) who insist on eliding the female's significance as primary object of desire and on transferring that desire to the father's phallus as they impose their brand of "right spectatorship," making visible and insisting we "see" the sign of masculinity but marking femininity as "nothing to see" and conflating it with a certain inadequacy or "badness". The ultimate question, both inside and outside the text, is already obliquely posed in the title of the novel, *La traición de Rita Hayworth*. Is she the betrayer or the betrayed? Who has betrayed whom?[28]

---

[28] The title, literally *The Betrayal of Rita Hayworth*, is ambiguous and might be understood in terms of the actress as the betrayer or the betrayed. An earlier version of this essay, "Prescribing Gender: Manuel Puig's *La traición de Rita Hayworth*," was published in *Paunch*, 65-66 (December 1991), 31-52. The essay published here has undergone significant revision.

An Interview with Manuel Puig
Rio de Janeiro, 10th August 1987

PAMELA BACARISSE

PB: It's five years since your last novel was published. Since then you've been involved in the theatre. Does this mean that you're not going to interest yourself in the novel any more?
MP: No. I'm writing a novel now, and I've also abandoned one.
PB: What was the abandoned one about?
MP: It was, for the first time, a fantasy. In fiction, it was my first try at fantasy.
PB: And why did you abandon it?
MP: Because I couldn't find the voice of the narrator. I couldn't believe in the narrator. If I don't believe in the voice I have to drop everything. I tried many voices and none of them worked.
PB: And will you go back to it?
MP: Maybe, but it's a subject more suitable for a film.
PB: Is it in dialogue?
MP: No, not at all. It's all action. Really, it was a great disappointment because seldom have I liked a subject so much.
PB: But you've compensated for that by thinking of another ...
MP: Well, yes. Before the fantasy there was another project though —now I remember— and that was realistic. It was about wartime in Argentina: '41-'42-'43. The activities of the Embassies in Buenos Aires, the tensions between the British and the German Embassies.
PB: And why did you give that one up?
MP: Well ... I sort of disliked the central character. I don't like to condemn anybody, and the way it was going at the end there was a sort of, you know, look of disapproval from my side.
PB: Well, in your novels you seem to avoid coming down on one side or the other.
MP: Yes, I dislike that very much. And that's because I write about people who may make mistakes but always have an alibi. Somehow their environment distorted them.

PB: And you don't feel that the forties in Argentina presented you with people who have that sort of alibi? After all, they'd lived through the thirties in Argentina ...

MP: Yes ... well, I've written about that period before but I lost interest in that particular subject (it was a spy yarn) because I want to sympathize with my characters, to understand them, not to condemn them. I don't enjoy that.

PB: What about the novel you're writing now?

MP: The new one, the one I'm trying to write now if all the other theatrical projects allow me to breathe, takes place in contemporary Rio and everything is seen through old people's eyes: Argentinian old women living here.[1]

PB: In enforced exile or chosen exile?

MP: Enforced ... which is not my case, thank God.

PB: These people have had a past which has hurt them and they're suffering, is that it?

MP: The novel is mainly about the need for affective projection.

PB: It's not a question of nationality, then, or political circumstances, but to do with the psyche, with the upbringing and the attitudes of these women?

MP: Yes, it's mainly about the human need to be "attached".

PB: If it's about old people, you've left your favourite theme of sexuality, have you?

MP: Oh, no, no, no. These old people can see the problems of the young. They discuss them all the time.

PB: Comparing different epochs?

MP: Yes ... and trying to play a part in the story.

PB: Do they condemn the young?

MP: No, no.

PB: Do you condemn the young?

MP: No, I envy them.

PB: I suppose we all do.

MP: Not only because they still have opportunities but because they have been blessed with a better era. Apart from Aids it's so much better.

PB: You say "apart from Aids": isn't Aids a big enough factor to inhibit all the new freedom?

MP: I have this big hope that a vaccine will be ready tomorrow.

PB: It's not impossible, I suppose.

MP: At least they now understand how the virus operates.

PB: If you remove the Aids factor, then, you approve of what its critics have called the new permissiveness?

---

[1] This is *Cae la noche tropical* (Barcelona: Seix Barral, 1988).

MP: Oh, yes. I hope ... I think it's the beginning of a new world.
PB: Do you think people will be happier?
MP: Yes, certainly. For me sexual oppression is the school of all the other oppressions.
PB: And the whole equilibrium of the individual will be affected by liberalization?
MP: Totally, totally.
PB: In what way would this make things easier? Wouldn't it make life less stable?
MP: No ... if the accent is on *affection* rather than sex I think people will see things more clearly. The whole misunderstanding starts when one gives sex a moral meaning. I believe that sex is just an activity of the vegetative life, like eating and sleeping. As important as those two but —just like them— devoid of any moral meaning.
PB: But "moral meaning" has been attached to sexual activity for thousand of years. How do you eliminate it?
MP: It will happen in time.
PB: But who's going to make it happen?
MP: It's happening already. The young are changing things so quickly.
PB: You don't believe that this New Morality that's being talked about exists?
MP: That's a logical backlash. But they say that the one who invented this especially damaging concept of sexual transcendence was the patriarch.
PB: But women have accepted it, and accepted it gladly, for so long ...
MP: Not gladly. I think, you know, that it was an awful misunderstanding: taking cultural concepts as orders from nature. And they say that the patriarch invented that in order to make a distinction between the saintly woman at home and the prostitute in the street. Once they could be told apart he could control them.
PB: It's a question of power, then.
MP: What for me has transcendence, has importance, is affection.
PB: On a practical level, how do you envisage a relationship in the future? If people fall in love, they won't be sexually faithful to each other, will they? Only emotionally?
MP: Yes, that's right.
PB: And what about the family?
MP: I don't think we can imagine what a world without sexual repression would be like. I think it would be more real and marriages would be based on affection
...
PB: So you still envisage the existence of marriage in this utopian society?
MP: Well, yes ... I've seen friendships last a lifetime and I see marriage as a friendship.
PB: What about homosexual "marriage"? Would that be a possibility too?
MP: Well, you see, I said that sex has no moral transcendence. By that I mean that sex is morally banal. So identity cannot be derived from sexual activity.

PB: But it *is* derived from sexual activity ...
MP: Yes, but this will stop. It *has* to stop ... Homosexuality doesn't exist in nature and heterosexuality doesn't either. The concepts as they are now are just figments of the reactionary mind.
PB: It's a semantic problem, then? The words have connotations that they shouldn't have? Because, obviously relations between people of the same sex do exist.
MP: Yes, they are technically possible.
PB: What doesn't exist is any truth behind our moral climate?
MP: That's right.
PB: How do you see the future of the couple?
MP: I see it as assured because problems of sexual fidelity will stop being problems. I don't think sexual fidelity is healthy. I think at a certain point a couple needs some sort of variation in order to revitalize them.
PB: But you think that affective fidelity is possible?
MP: Yes.
PB: So you're a romantic, basically?
MP: Oh, sure. I think that emphasis on sex has impoverished the other side and I dislike certain Freudian interpretations of the matter —when some of Freud's followers claim that all energy is sexual. I disagree. What happens is that we're all so sexually unsatisfied because of a repressive society that the sexual yearning is always there: it hasn't been taken care of. But once that ...
PB: But wouldn't there be complete anarchy if free rein were given to sexual energies?
MP: No ... no. I don't think so. There would be much more tolerance because people would be less uptight, less nervous.
PB: Don't you think that Foucault's ideas are more realistic? When he says that although the utopian ideal of being totally free sounds very good, the centuries of repression are going to be virtually impossible to eradicate? There's always going to be a focus of power somewhere, isn't there? Probably within the sexual relationship.
MP: There's one thing that Foucault may have overlooked, and that is that we cannot really imagine a sexually satisfied human being.
PB: Is that because it's an impossibility?
MP: No, no, no. I think that the need for power and the evils of power are directly derived from sexual dissatisfaction, sexual frustration, and that a major change will take place in the human psyche when that is finally taken care of. We take care of our sleep and our nourishment but we have chosen not to take care of the third great need.
PB: You think that the third great need has been misrepresented by defining sexual love as the desire for self-gratification and other forms of love as the desire for

the benefit of the other person? You don't think that a sexually satisfied person might be comparable to someone who, say, eats all the time, and who wouldn't be all that appealing?
MP: He would be someone who eats enough to feel well.
PB: You don't think that man is so evil that once he is satisfied he will want to take things to extremes ... like *La Grande bouffe*. Do you remember that film?
MP: Of course. As I said, it's impossible to imagine, but I prefer to be optimistic. It's the one chance that humanity has to be given.
PB: It's the one thing that's never been tried ...
MP: Exactly.
PB: I was going to end by asking you whether you were an optimist or not. I always claim that you're not, but you are, are you?
MP: I am, because I've seen so many changes in my lifetime. I remember women in the forties and early fifties saying with a straight face: "I can't respect a man ...," or "I can't desire a man ... unless I fear him a little".
PB: Molina says that, more or less, in *El beso de la mujer araña*.
MP: Yes, because I've heard it said by women who were not especially sick in the mind.
PB: You don't think there's anything constitutional in this at all? It's just conditioning?
MP: It is. Because it takes for granted that the man has a grudge; he's evil because he's dissatisfied with something. You don't fear a beast that has eaten. You only fear a hungry lion. You feel afraid and derive pleasure from someone's anger, but that man is angry because he's been mistreated, because he's not getting what he wants ...
PB: A lot of women have learned new roles, but how do you teach the men who don't accept that women should be anything but subservient?
MP: I think now that many men have understood that they were not too well served either ...
PB: Many? This may have happened in certain places but it doesn't happen very often in Latin countries.
MP: It's changing.
PB: Even here in Brazil? And in Spain?
MP: It is. Amazingly so. It's unbelievable.
PB: You don't think that those who have enjoyed power for so long are going to be loath to relinquish it?
MP: No, because men have felt that their role wasn't that gratifying either. Power is a cross too.
PB: You often make that point in your work, don't you? The burden of masculinity both on a social and a sexual level. Nobody is happy with *machismo*.

MP: No. Everybody is uncomfortable.
PB: So in your liberal society any balance of power within relationships would come about naturally, would it?
MP: I hope so. You see, I think this misunderstanding of sexual transcendence is so blatant. How nobody sees it I don't know.
PB: Possibly because it suits people not to see it. In the past the subservient woman enjoyed a certain stability, at least financially.
MP: I have a theory about that.
PB: Good.
MP: You know, *El beso de la mujer araña* was going to be a different novel. The main character was going to be a woman at first. At the centre of the novel I wanted someone who would defend the role of the submissive woman, but as I always do in my work, I used models from real life. And I couldn't find one. In Buenos Aires in '72 I couldn't find anyone without doubts. And so I looked and looked, and only the Molinas of this world ...
PB: Those who emulate the most extreme female subservience?
MP: Yes, because they cannot actually *experience* marriage to a domineering male, so they stay in their dreams. After the novel, you know ... after listening to Molina for two years in my room in New York and Mexico (I started the book in New York on 1st January 1974, then went on with it in Mexico), I thought I'd discovered one reason why things have stayed the same for so long. Though I agreed totally with feminist claims I saw that they were only talking about the *disadvantages* of the role.
PB: And there must be some advantages?
MP: What kept that thing going were adventures of the imagination. Women were born hearing this nonsense that men are superior. I've even heard it said, almost up to the sixties, that the cortex of men is richer. Women heard this and they had to believe it. It wasn't a question of liking it. It sounded as if nature had been unfair, but that's how it was. Nature had decided. So these women were unlucky. And the moment came for them to look for that superior man, the man who would justify any sacrifice. And generally they didn't find him; they had to content themselves with imagining.
PB: And Molina, of course, is condemned by circumstances never to find him.
MP: That's right. Of course.
PB: This is just taking the situation one step further, then? For him it's *entirely* fantasy.
MP: Yes.
PB: Do you think that women no longer feel that way and that their lives have improved?

MP: Yes, because everything is so much more realistic. A dialogue has been established with men.
PB: But Manuel, you'd be the first person, surely, to admit that facing up to pedestrian reality is *not* life-enhancing, and that fantasy and the imagination are very important. What do women do when they realize that men are not superior, that Prince Charming is not going to come along?
MP: There's a possibility of great enjoyment with an equal ...
PB: You promise?

www.ingramcontent.com/pod-product-compliance
Lightning Source LLC
Chambersburg PA
CBHW071409300426
44114CB00016B/2238